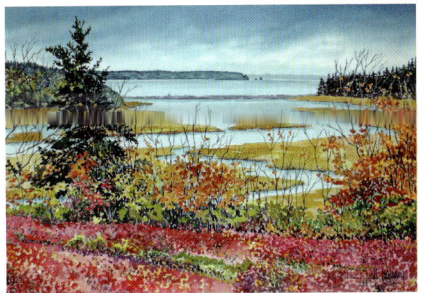

THE PAINTED PROVINCE

Joy Snihur Wyatt Laking

Nova Scotia Through an Artist's Eyes

POTTERSFIELD PRESS

Lawrencetown Beach, Nova Scotia, Canada

Copyright © Joy Snihur Wyatt Laking 2020

All rights reserved. No part of this publication may be reproduced or used or stored in any form or by any means — graphic, electronic or mechanical, including photocopying — or by any information storage or retrieval system without the prior written permission of the publisher. Any requests for photocopying, recording, taping or information storage and retrieval systems shall be directed in writing to the publisher or to Access Copyright, The Canadian Copyright Licensing Agency (www.AccessCopyright.ca). This also applies to classroom use.

Library and Archives Canada Cataloguing in Publication

Title: The painted province : Nova Scotia through an artist's eyes / Joy Snihur Wyatt Laking.
Other titles: Nova Scotia through an artist's eyes
Names: Laking, Joy Snihur Wyatt, artist, writer of added text.
Identifiers: Canadiana (print) 20200278479 | Canadiana (ebook) 20200278959 | ISBN 9781989725252 (softcover) | ISBN 9781989725269 (EPUB)
Subjects: LCSH: Laking, Joy Snihur Wyatt. | LCSH: Nova Scotia—In art. | LCSH: Landscapes in art.
Classification: LCC ND249.L339 A4 2020 | DDC 759.11—dc23

Front cover credit: Joy Snihur Wyatt Laking

Cover design: Gail LeBlanc

Pottersfield Press gratefully acknowledges the financial support of the Government of Canada for our publishing activities. We also acknowledge the support of the Canada Council for the Arts and the Province of Nova Scotia which has assisted us to develop and promote our creative industries for the benefit of all Nova Scotians.

Pottersfield Press
248 Leslie Road
East Lawrencetown, Nova Scotia, Canada, B2Z 1T4
Website: www.PottersfieldPress.com
To order, phone 1-800-NIMBUS9 (1-800-646-2879) www.nimbus.ns.ca
Printed in Canada
Pottersfield Press is committed to preserving the environment and the appropriate harvesting of trees and has printed this book on Forest Stewardship Council® certified paper.

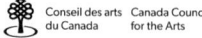 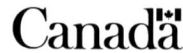 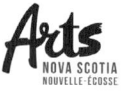 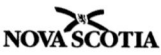

DEDICATION

I would like to express my appreciation to Julia Swan, my editor from Pottersfield Press, Gail LeBlanc, my designer, and to Lesley Choyce for taking the chance on me and for publishing *The Painted Province*.

This book is dedicated to everyone who helped me to do the paintings: the lady from the Taco Truck who gave me a free taco, the people of Gabarus who all seemed to offer me food, and the many people who have offered me accommodation. Some of you have become friends, but many of you are unsung heroes and I am grateful to you all. I am also dedicating this book to all of my friends and family who continually encourage and inspire me and who sometimes accompany me on wild adventures. Particular thanks to three friends: Shawna Macivor, Krista Wells, and Carol McNutt, who all volunteered their time to help me make this book the best it could be. I also dedicate this book to my family: my children, Kelsey, Danica, and Yolande, and to my husband, Jim Wyatt, for his ongoing encouragement and help and the fact that he actually enjoys the challenge of living with a creative person.

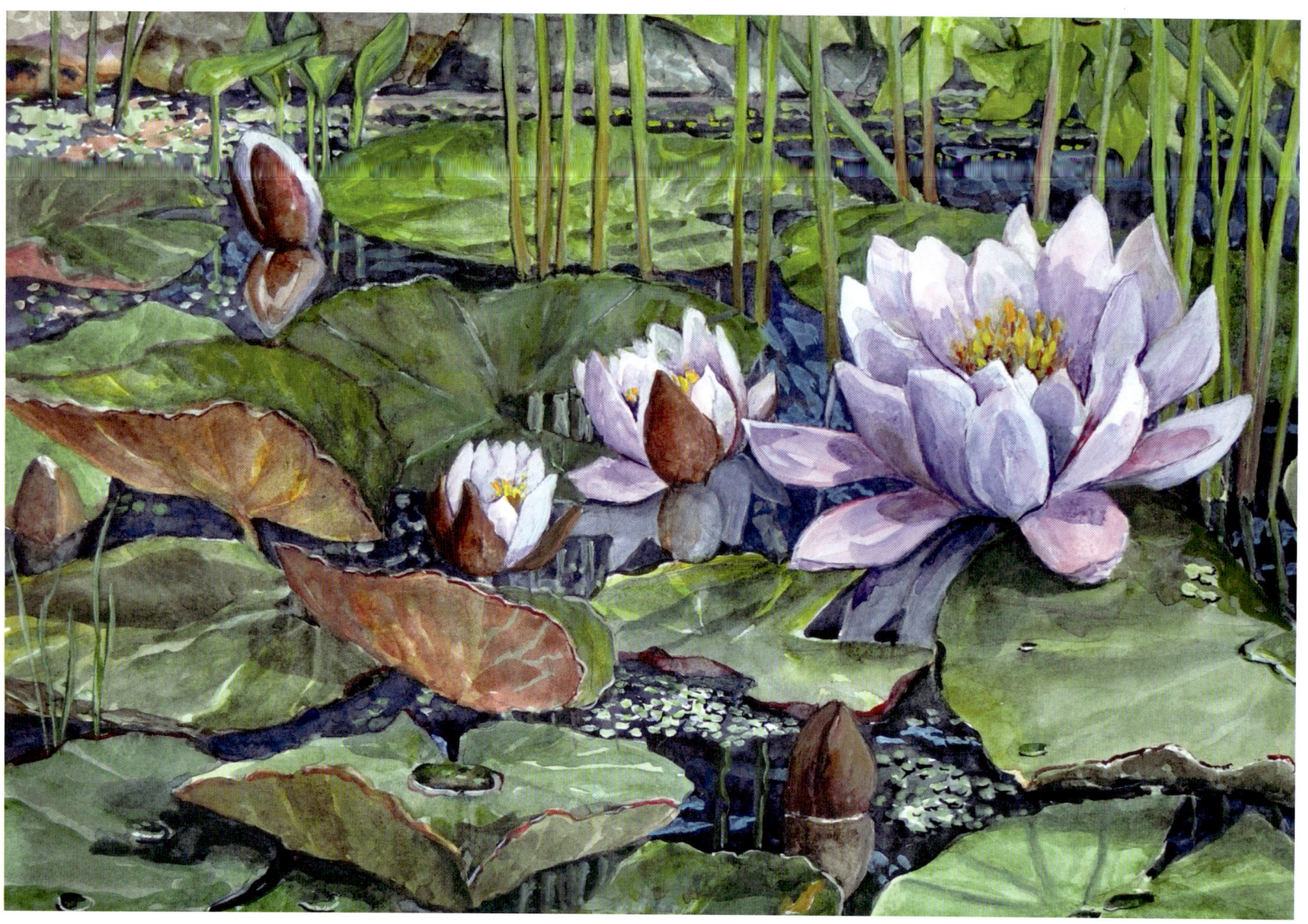

INTRODUCTION

WHEN I MOVED TO NOVA SCOTIA FROM Ontario almost five decades ago, the ocean, the people, the old villages, the pace of life, and the natural beauty captured my heart. For many years, I felt most at home with the rocks and water of the wild Atlantic, since it was most like my childhood scenery of Georgian Bay on Lake Huron. Gradually, the beauty of the Bay of Fundy with its huge tides, its muddy pink water, vast mud flats, and pastoral salt marshes wormed its way into my soul. I feel like an old tree that has put down roots. I have developed a deep love for Nova Scotia and I still have many places to discover.

I usually paint within an hour of my home in Portaupique (between Great Village and Bass River) in Colchester County. One of the first decisions I had to make for this book was whether to spell Portaupique the way it was spelled on old churches and schools or Portapique the way the government of Nova Scotia spells it.

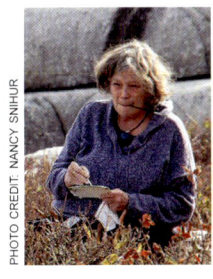

PHOTO CREDIT: NANCY SNIHUR

In honour of the Acadian settlers, I have chosen to spell it the way it was historically spelled. This book features lots of areas close to my home. Every year I also paint in unfamiliar places so I can return home and see my area from a new perspective. Each year, I make several one- or two-week painting trips within Nova Scotia and every winter I paint for a month or two in an unfamiliar country.

In addition to painting in new surroundings, I also reinvigorate my creative life by trying unfamiliar media, such as oils instead of watercolours, as well as trying unfamiliar materials, new papers, new approaches. I also try entirely new art forms, such as hooking, dyeing, felting, and pit-firing our local clay. In this book, I have slipped in a few of these divergent experiments with the paintings.

All of this joyous exploration helps me appreciate and capture Nova Scotia's beauty with "fresh" eyes.

I love to write in many formats: plays, stories, books, and word pictures. For the text of *The Painted Province*, there are three themes. One is "Word Pictures." These little offerings are my attempt to capture the beauty of a place in words rather than in paint. The second theme is "Let me tell you a story." My Grandpa Henderson was a master storyteller and I have had a huge appreciation for stories ever since. The purpose of the stories, all of them true, is just to make you smile. My third theme is "Creative Process." The creative process is fragile, quirky, very special, and usually underappreciated. Creativity does require nurturing and understanding. I hope that those of you who are learning to paint or are interested in exploring your own creativity might gain some insight or ideas.

When making paintings for this book, I started out by trying to cover most of the province. A few of the paintings suffered from the "having to be painted syndrome." Artists do not like to be told what to paint. The joy seemed to be missing in some of these paintings. In the end, I decided to include only paintings that I particularly love. I hope you will enjoy seeing some of our province through my eyes and that you will notice your own scenic "beauty" wherever and whenever you are out and about.

(www.joylakinggallery.com)

LIST OF AREAS FOR THE PAINTED PROVINCE

1. Portaupique 12
2. Bass River 14
3. Economy 16
4. Five Islands 18
5. Parrsboro 20
6. Areas around Parrsboro 22
7. Diligent River, Spencer's Island 24
8. Advocate, Cape D'Or 26
9. Amherst, North Port, Pugwash, Malagash 28
10. Tatamagouche, Brule 30
11. River John, Pictou 32
12. Arisaig, Balllantynes Cove 34
13. Port Hawkesbury 36
14. Port Hood, Inverness, Egypt Falls 38
15. Margaree, Margaree Harbour, Whale Cove, Dunvegan ... 40
16. Four Mile Beach, Meat Cove, White Point 42
17. Neil's Harbour, Ingonish 44
18. Whitney Pier, Gabarus 46
19. Grand Greve, L'Ardoise, Little Harbour 48
20. Canso, Fisherman's Cove, The Shanties 50
21. Port Bickerton 52
22. Sherbrooke Village, West Jeddore, West Chezzetcook, Martinique Beach 54
23. Lawrencetown (Eastern Shore) 56
24. Halifax Regional Municipality, Grand Lake 58
25. Herring Cove, Chebucto Head 60
26. Prospect 62
27. Indian Harbour, Peggy's Cove 64
28. Head of St. Margaret's Bay, Chester, Mahone Bay, Mader's Cove 66
29. Lunenburg 68
30. Blue Rocks 70
31. Stonehurst West, Front Centre, Gaff Point, Bayport, Mason's Beach 72
32. Bridgewater, Carter's Beach, Port Medway, Summerville, South West Port Mouton 74
33. Port Joli, Kejimkujik National Seaside Adjunct 76
34. Shelburne, Green Cove, Barrington Passage, Yarmouth 78
35. Cape Saint Mary's, Meteghan, Comeauville 80
36. Bear River, Annapolis Royal, Sandy Cove, Port Royal 82
37. Harbourville, Hall's Harbour, Wolfville, Kentville 84
38. Burntcoat Head, Truro, Shortt's Lake 86
39. Great Village 88
40. Highland Village, Portaupique Mountain 90
41. Painting Internationally (Bolivia, Ghana, France, Sri Lanka, India, Portugal) 92

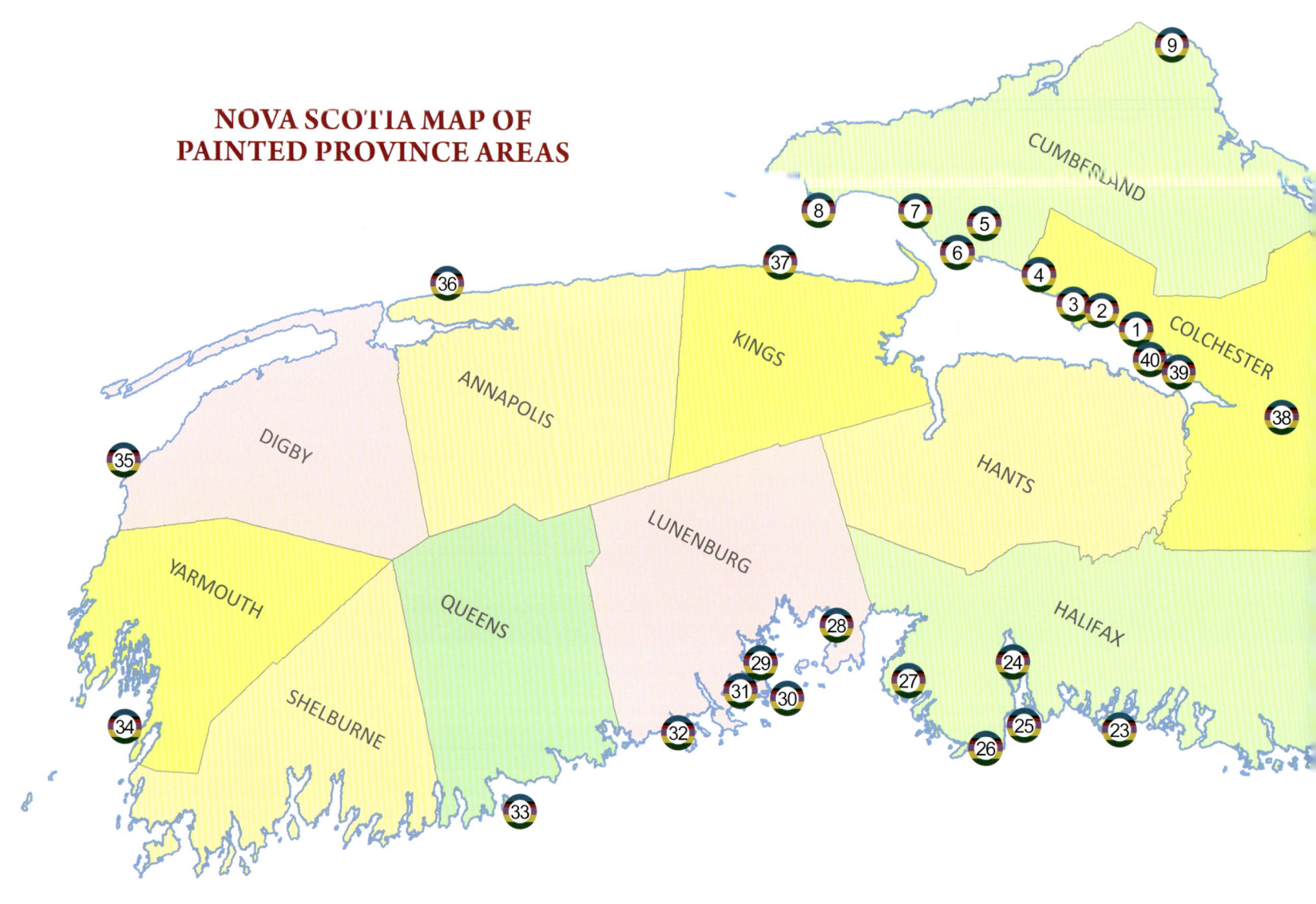

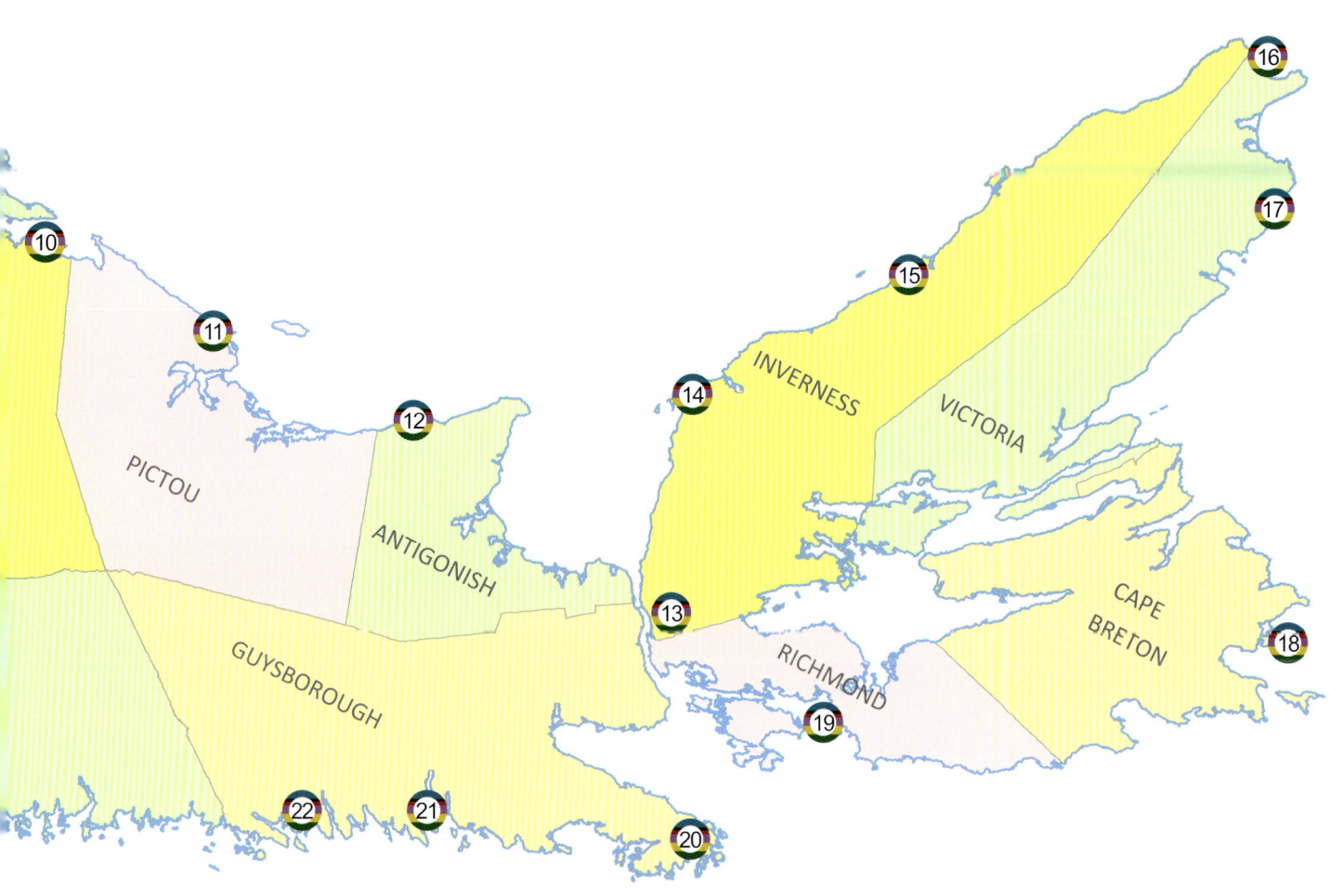

Map courtesy of Geographic Information Services, Nova Scotia Geomatics Centre – Amherst

GPS COORDINATES

In each of the forty areas in this book, I included the GPS coordinates for one painting. If it sounds intriguing, you might keep this book in your glovebox and find some of the spots where I sat and painted.

If you are out for a drive with children, you can ask them how many differences they can spot between the painting and what you are seeing. This exercise helps everyone really look. When you really look, you often find unexpected beauty.

There is a "The Painted Province, Nova Scotia" Group Facebook page. If you take a photo of a spot that is in the book, please post it. I have only painted hundreds of the many thousands of places of beauty in Nova Scotia. If you have a favourite spot that isn't in the book, please take a photo of it and tell us the GPS coordinates. It could prompt us all to visit and enjoy the beauty. As well, artists, including me, might be inspired to go and paint it.

Where GPS is showing with an image, the first number is latitude and the second number is longitude.

THE PAINTED PROVINCE

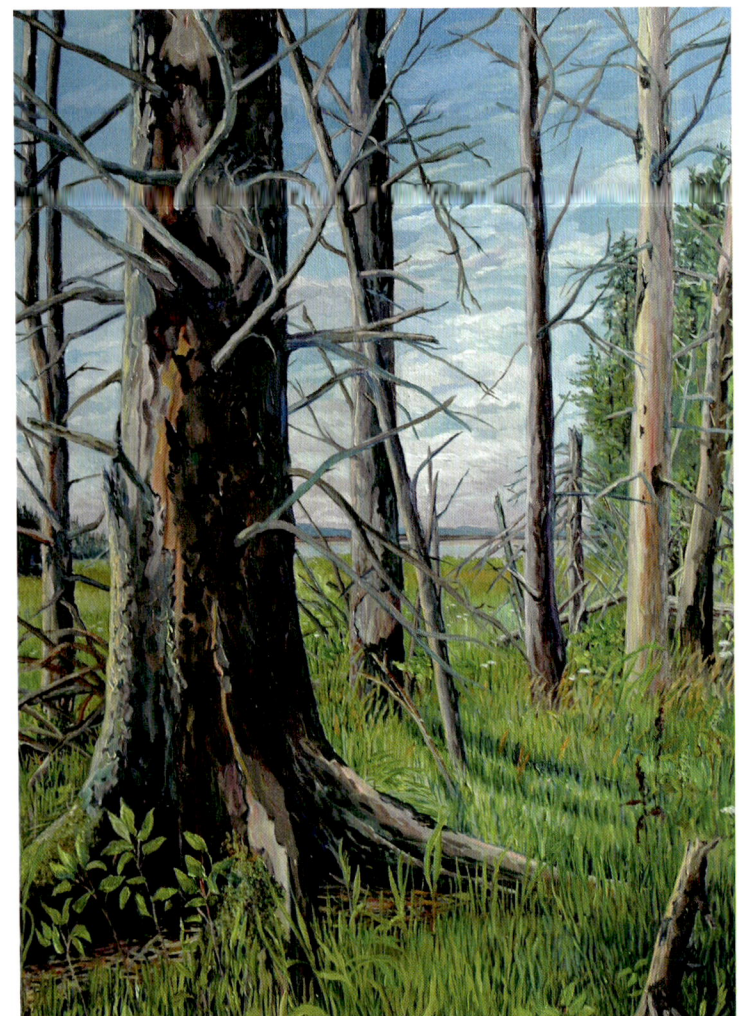

Trees at the Marsh 45.4034 -63.7144

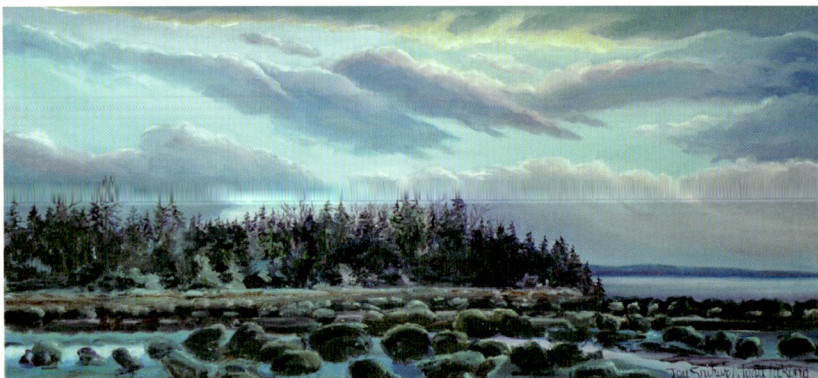

Portaupique Marsh

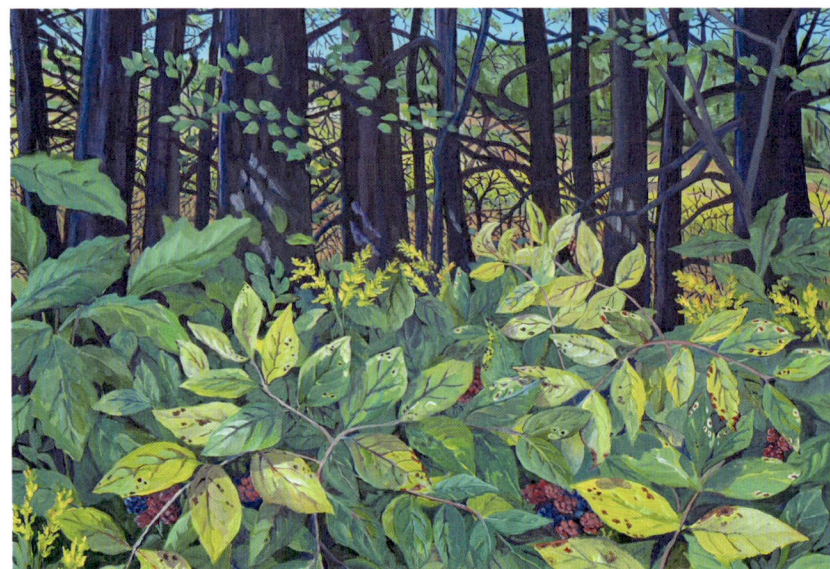

Autumn Trees and Leaves

It is early spring and I wake up to this view out our bedroom window. I start a tiny watercolour sketch. The forsythia is glowing yellow. The marsh is dry and ochre. Naked pointy limbs of deciduous trees catch the early sun and cast long, low shadows. It is so beautiful I cover the carpet with plastic, set up my easel, and start a large oil painting right in the bedroom. The scene remains much the same for the two mornings of under-painting. Then, almost overnight, everything starts changing. The trees and bushes are cloaked in new green. Blossoms burst out on the serviceberry, chokecherry, hawthorn, highbush cranberry. The fragrance of lilac wafts through the air. The forest floor is sprinkled with nodding trilliums, violets, false lily of the valley, and starflowers. Patches of strawberry and blueberry blossoms promise a delicious treat to come.

I have missed my morning walks with Jim and our old dog Marsh because I am painting. One morning, as they walk across my view, they startle a grouse with her new family. The grouse madly rounds up her chicks and I decide to slip Jim and Marsh into my painting.

At this point, I have to make a choice: will I capture my original vision of "the hint of spring to come" or change the vision to "the glory of spring arrived"? I decide to amalgamate the vision to include the luminous yellow forsythia as well as the glorious billows of soft pink apple blossoms.

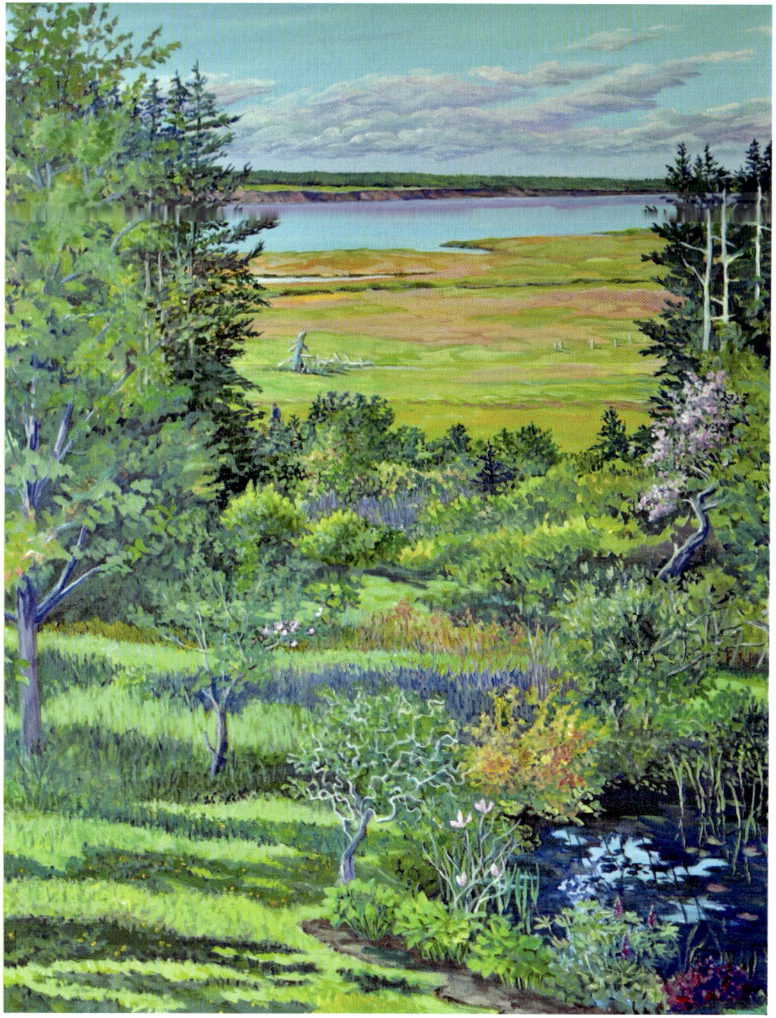

Spring out our Bedroom Window

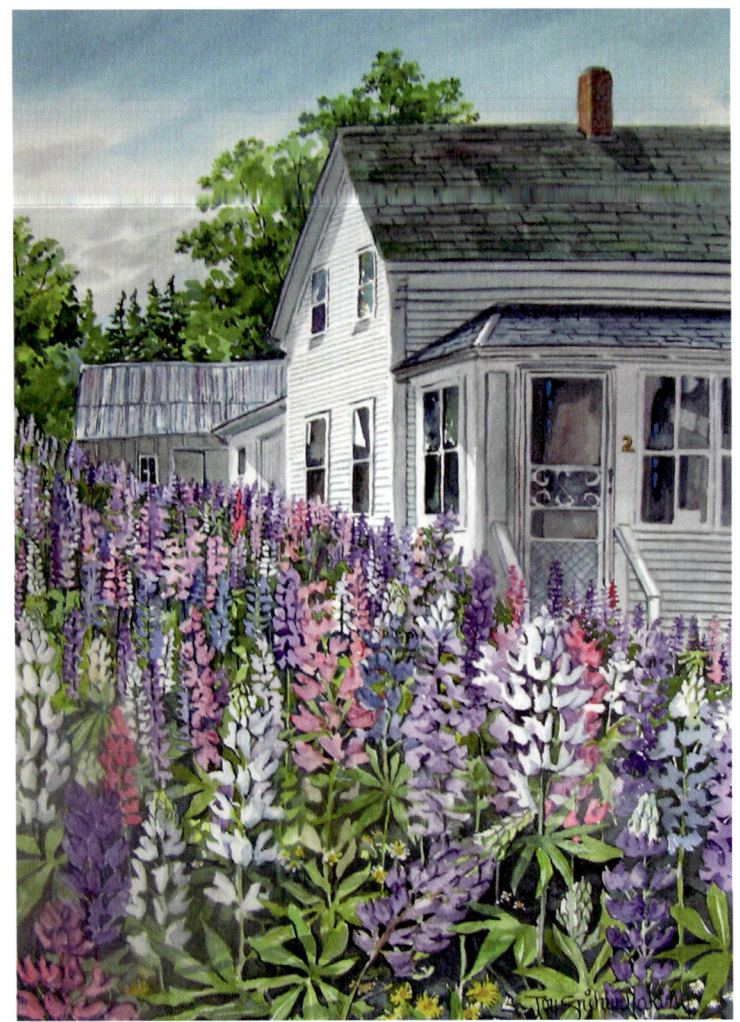

Lester's Lupins 45.4996 -63.8077

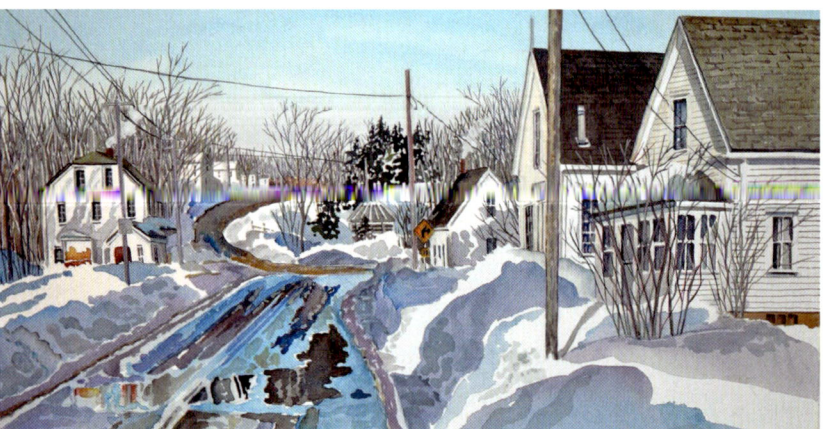

Bass River Flat

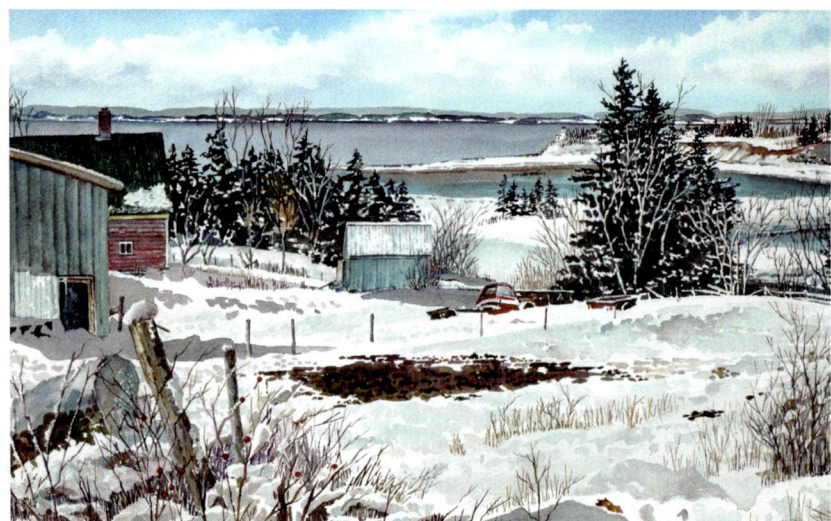

King's Rest

2

Weekdays, the Dominion Chair Factory blew its whistle at 8, 12, 1, and 5. I loved this old factory. It intrigued me that this place defined the village. In its hundred-plus years of operation, it burnt to the ground several times. The first three times, everyone pitched in to rebuild it. The chair factory had its own wood land up at Castlereigh and the wood for the chairs was harvested with horses, then sluiced down the mountain in the river to be milled, kiln-dried, and made into chairs. Power for the plant and the steam generator came from burning the bark and scrap wood. All of the machines were belt-driven from one big central shaft. Bass River Chairs were sold all over North America and many are still in use today.

At that time, I didn't own a camera. I would stand in the snow and draw the factory or go inside and perch next to a chair maker to draw the machines and the process.

Before moving to Bass River, I had been doing a series of paintings of large round figures. I called this my potato series as the figures were like large friendly vegetables, colourless and bland. One day when I went into the company store, Joyce, the clerk, offered the man in front of me a Dominion Chair calendar with a colourfully but scantily dressed woman on it. When it was my turn she offered me a calendar with kittens or mountains. "No," I said, "I want the naked lady." This was the inspiration for my version of the Dominion Chair calendar.

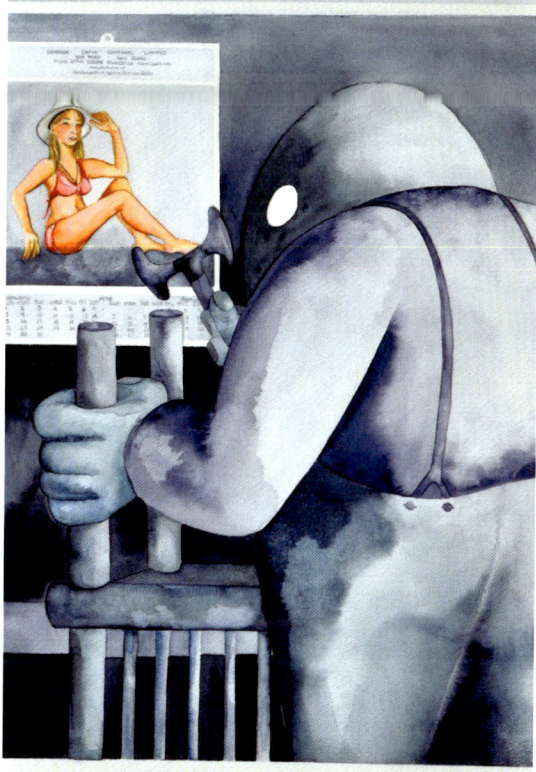

Calendar

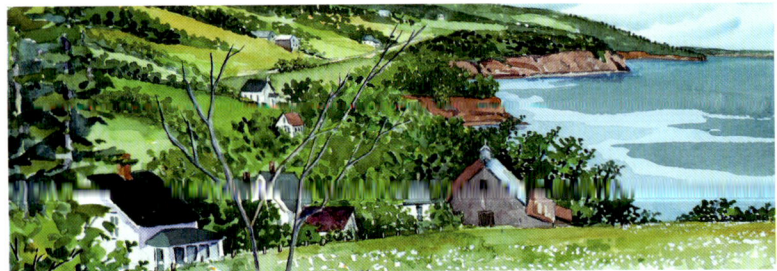

Soleytown 45.3989 -63.9956

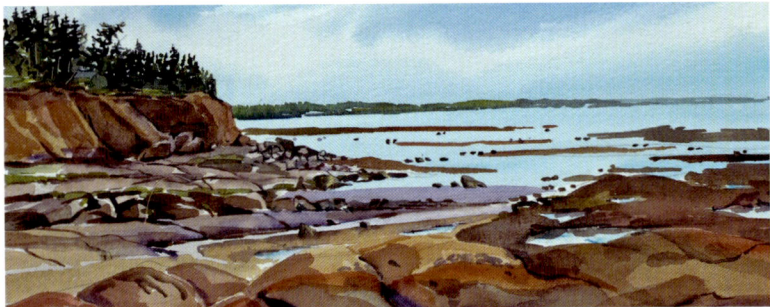

Thomas Cove

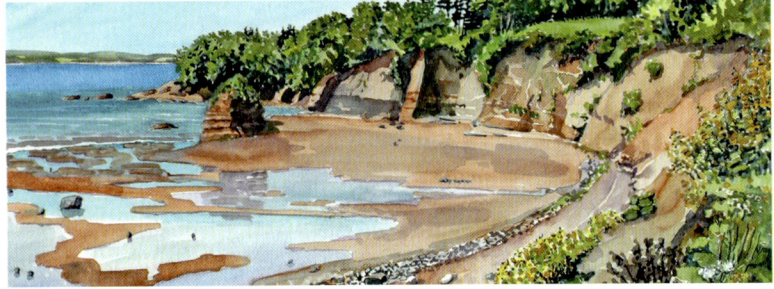

Soley Cove

3 In Nova Scotia, we call these little standing towers of sandstone "flower pots." I remember when a flower pot in Soleytown was a little peninsula attached to the mainland. Often, I would take a picnic out to the end and sit and enjoy the view. By the time my children were born, it was no long safe to walk out on the eroding land bridge and eventually a flower pot was born.

A few years ago, I was sitting on the top of the cliff working on a watercolour of this beautiful bit of sandstone, topped with a few trees, surrounded by mud and water. Suddenly the wind picked up my big plastic palette and blew it over the cliff. I couldn't safely leave my easel, the painting, or my chair in the very strong wind. I stowed everything away in the trunk of the car. Then I looked over the cliff. There was my palette about halfway down. These big palettes hold a lot of paint and there must have been a couple of hundred dollars' worth in it. (We artists are notorious for spinning out a penny.) Then I noticed a large rope tied to the guardrail. Kids must have used this rope to get down to the beach. I climbed over the guardrail, grabbed the rope, and lowered myself down the cliff to the palette. This wasn't very hard. I had gravity to help me and two hands on the rope. Coming back up, however, was very hard. I couldn't climb the cliff with only one hand on the rope, so I was forced to push the palette a little way up the cliff and then climb with both hands. With difficulty, I pushed and climbed, pushed and climbed and eventually reached the top of the cliff. Two tourists taking photos were startled to see an old woman's head (mine) popping up from below.

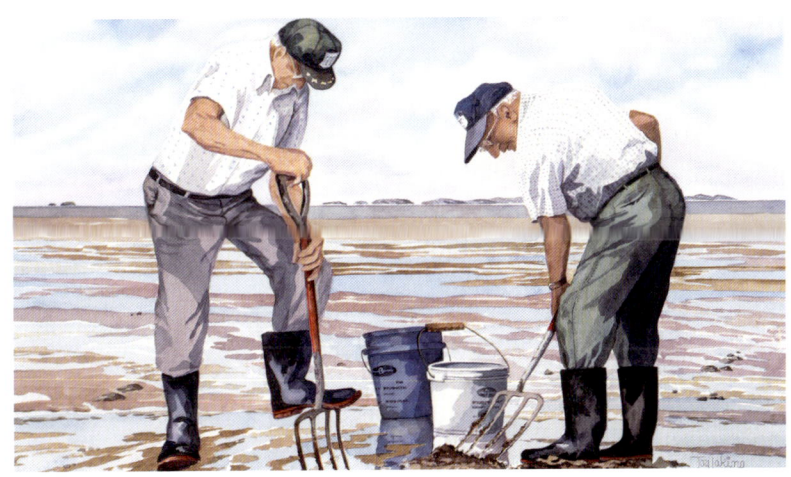

Men Clamming

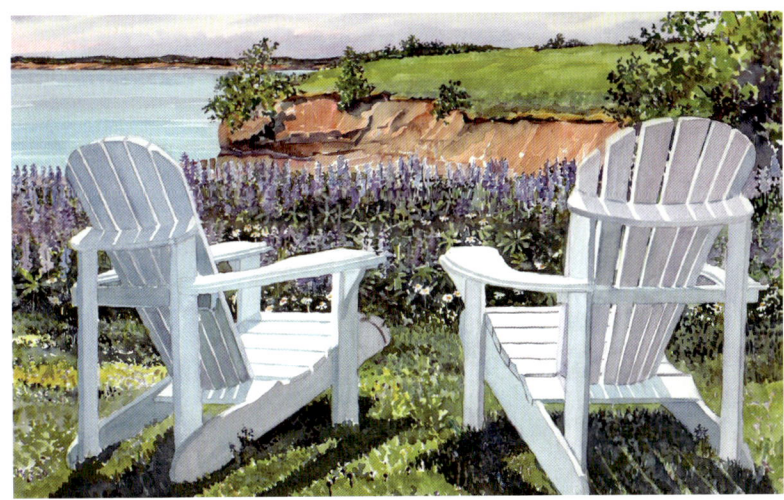

Chairs and Lupins

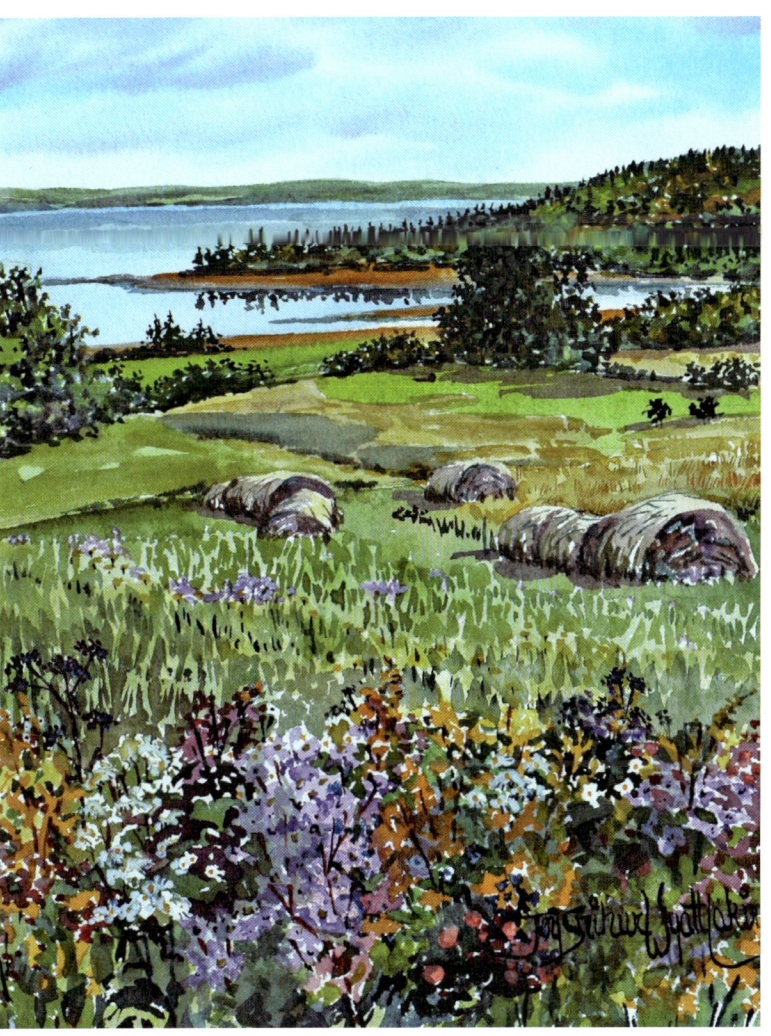

Wildflowers and Hay Bales looking towards Economy Point

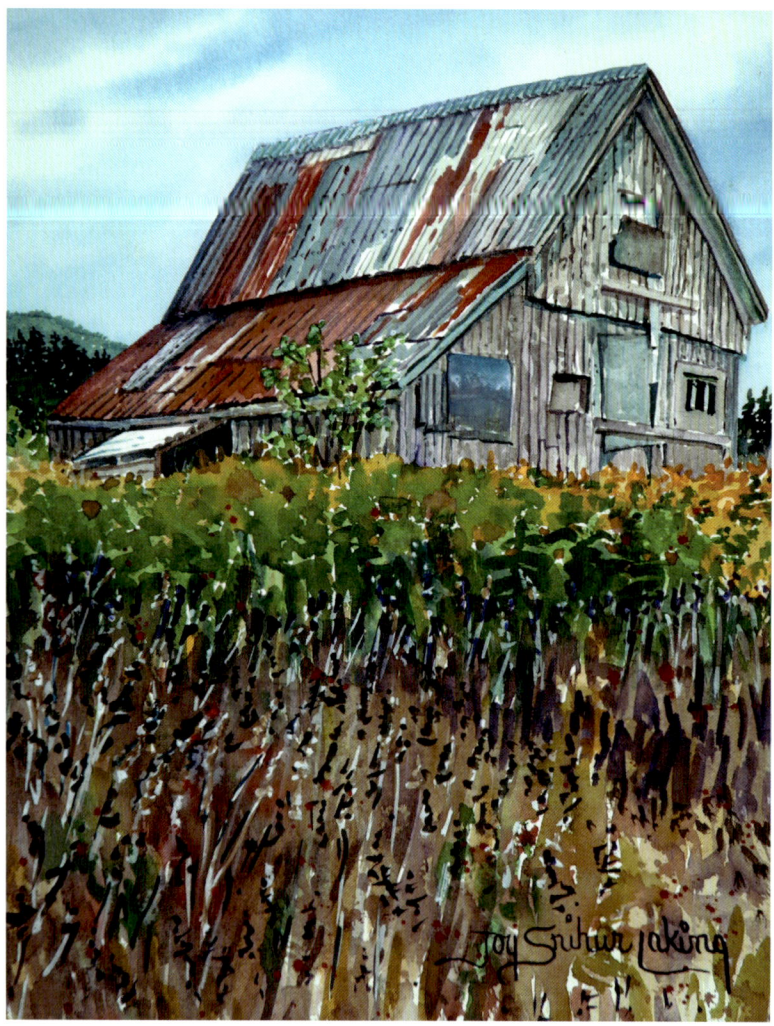

Old Barn in Five Islands

4 A few years ago, Jim and I set off by car with our sleeping bags and a little tent on a trip from our house in Nova Scotia to the west coast of Canada and then north to Alaska. Before we left, I dyed wool in different colours and packed it in the front seat of our car with a big piece of burlap and my hooking frame. When we departed, there was nothing done on this mat. When we returned two months later, "Full Moon and Starry Night over Five Islands" was finished. I had had so much fun. Because of the whimsy of the stars and the water, I was making creative decisions all the way along, while enjoying the moose, the bears, the buffalo, and the magnificent scenery. Over time this mat has inspired me to do the occasional oil painting with a colourful invented sky.

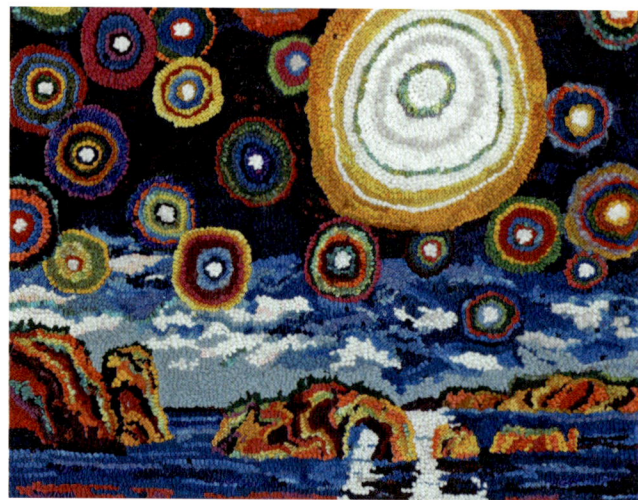

Starry Night, Five Islands (hooked wool on burlap)

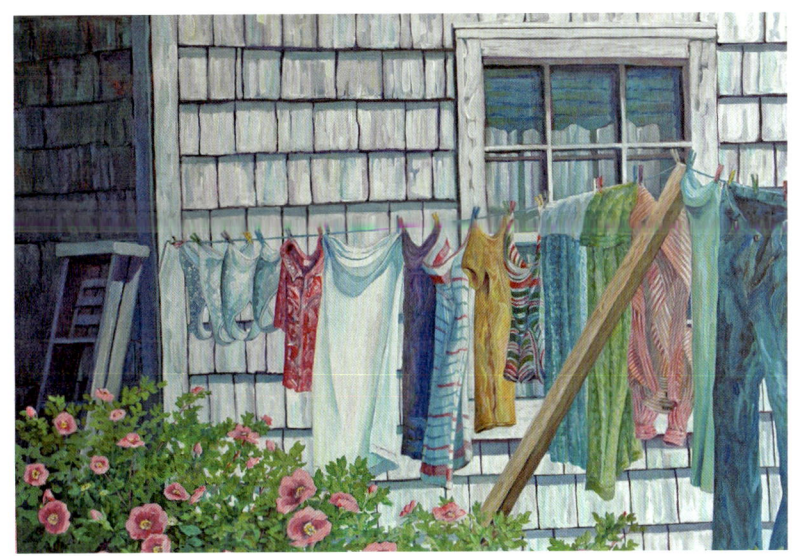

Wild Roses and Laundry

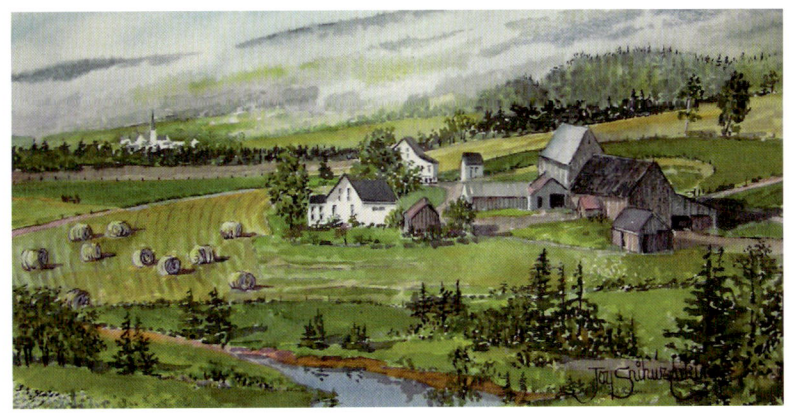

Chester's Farm 45.4085 -64.0127

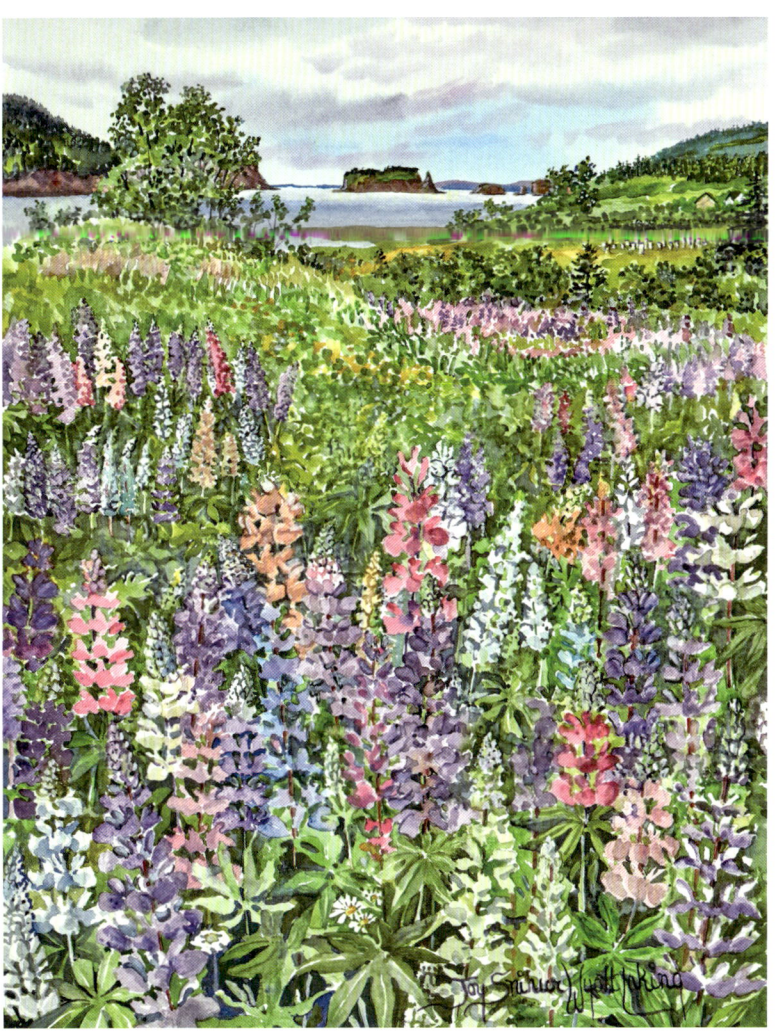

Lupins and Five Islands

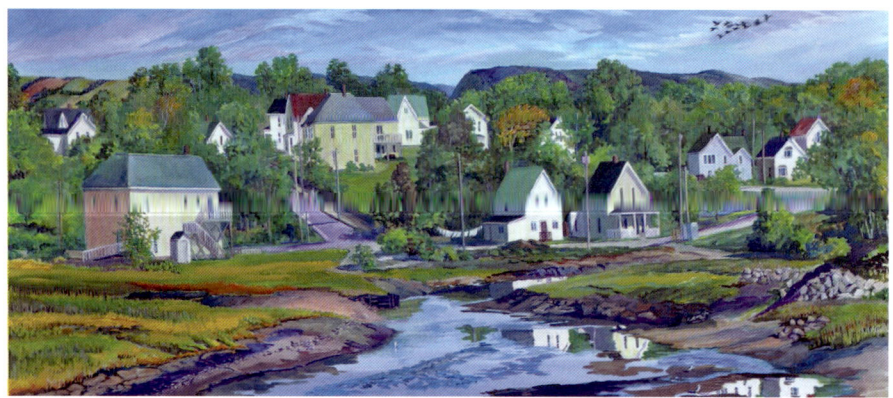

Four Days in September

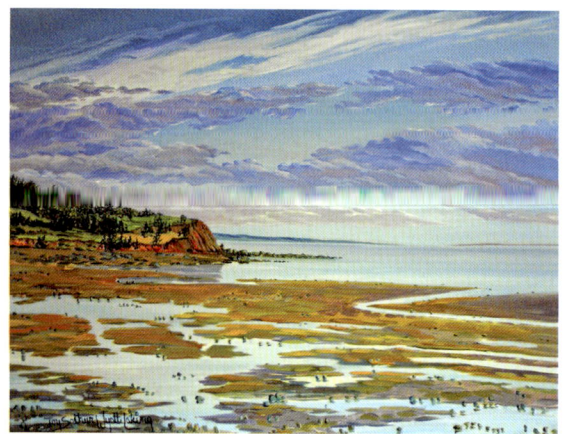

Low Tide

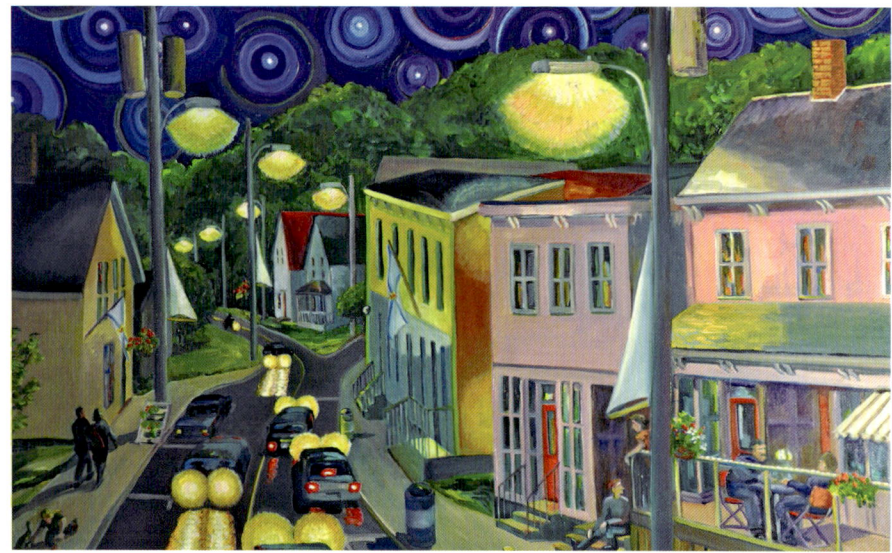

Starry Night on Main Street, Parrsboro

5 Thunder rolls in the distance.
The first drops of rain fall.
In the haze, the sky meets the sea.
Large sandstone cliffs frame the harbour.
The tide is low.
The flats gradually disappear
As tiny meandering rivulets
Swell and become pools.
In a few hours,
The boats at the wharf will float again.
Right in front of me,
On a long stony peninsula,
The lighthouse sits and waits;
No light, no foghorn,
But it is at the ready.

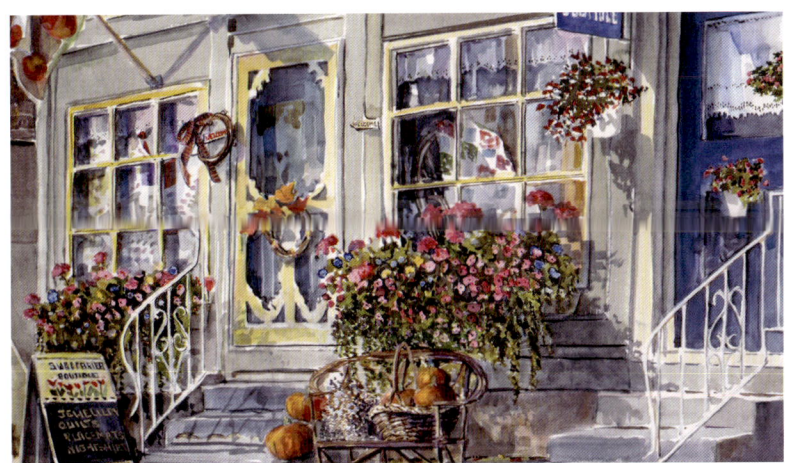

Joan's Shop 45.4036 -64.3262

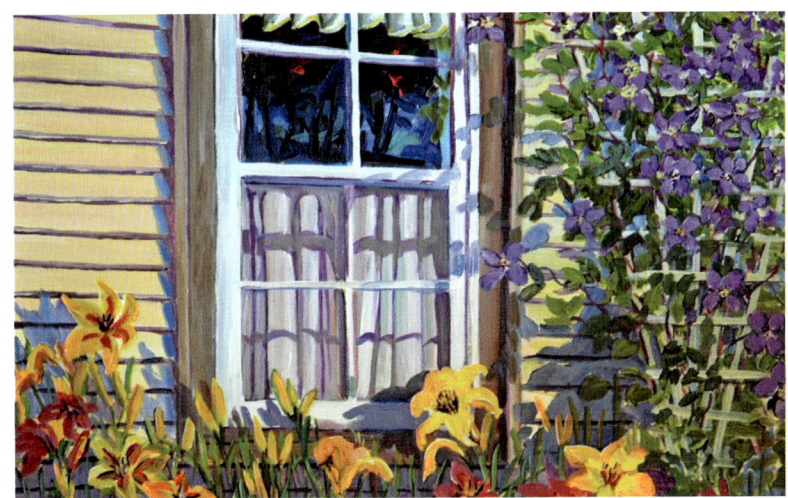

Flowers and Window

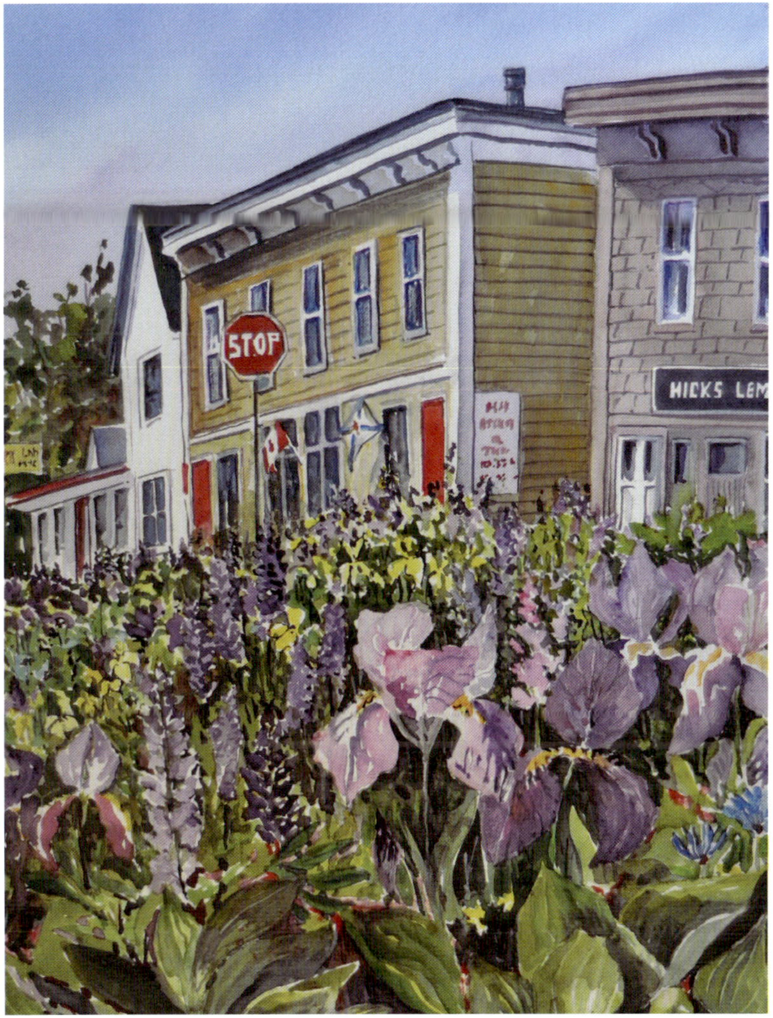

Near the Parrsboro Cenotaph

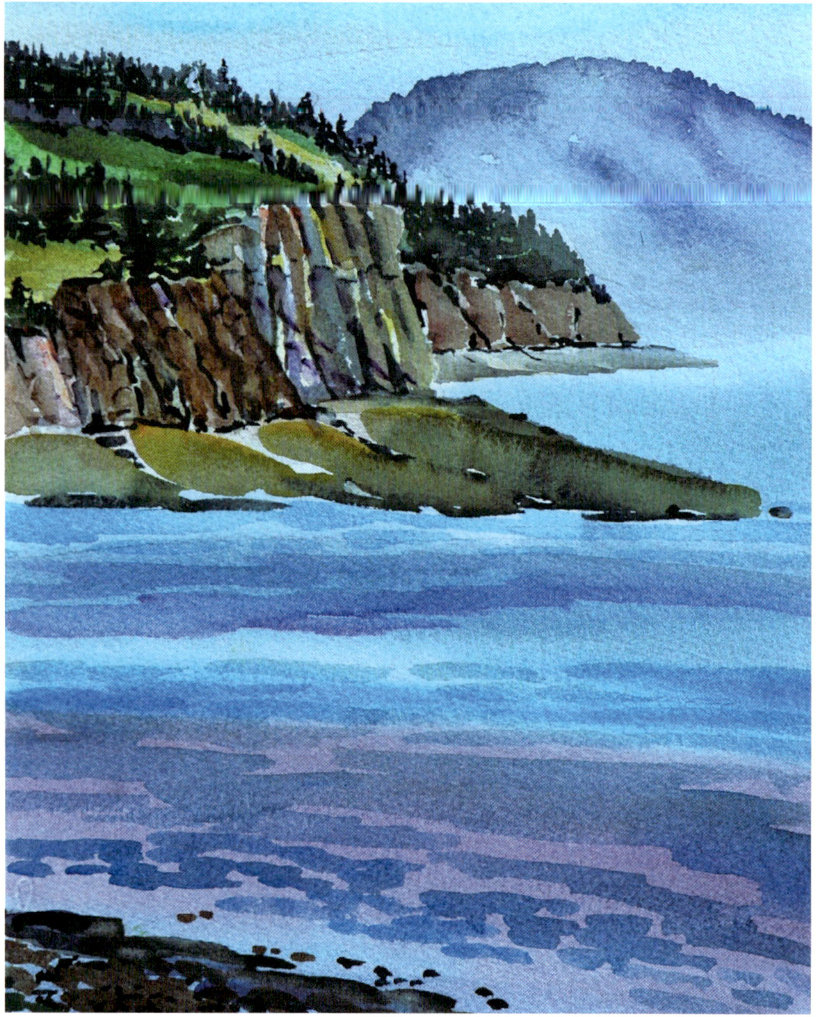

Misty Morning

 On Partridge Island
The steep wooded cliff front
Is connected to the mainland
By a narrow gravel bar.
Next to it, a distinctive circular fish weir
Curls like a tail out into the water.
Cycles of freeze and thaw
Erode the cliffs
Exposing agate, amethyst, geodes, fossils.

The back of Partridge Island,
Barren rock,
Is visited mainly by seals and seagulls.
It sits solidly, proudly in its surroundings:
The Minas Basin
And the huge dark headlands
Of Cape Sharp and Cape Split.

As the tide goes out,
Tidal pools shrink to little streams,
Then disappear.
As the tide comes in,
It covers the marsh grasses I am painting.
Sometimes it is the lighting that is transient.
Fog obliterates almost everything,
Then burns off to glorious sunshine.
No matter what the conditions,
Partridge Island feels like home.

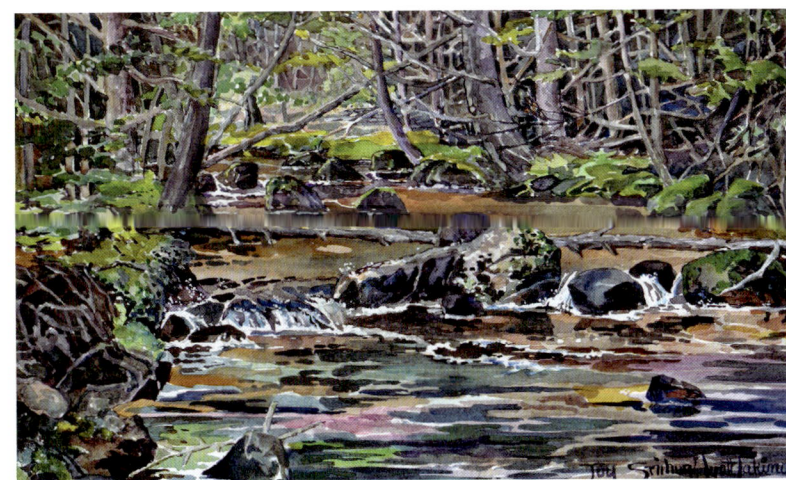
Stream near Hidden Falls

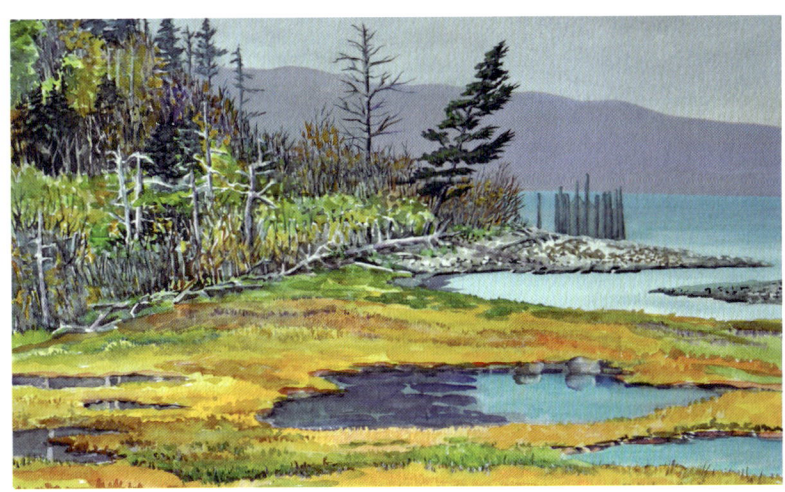
Partridge Island 45.3699 -64.3343

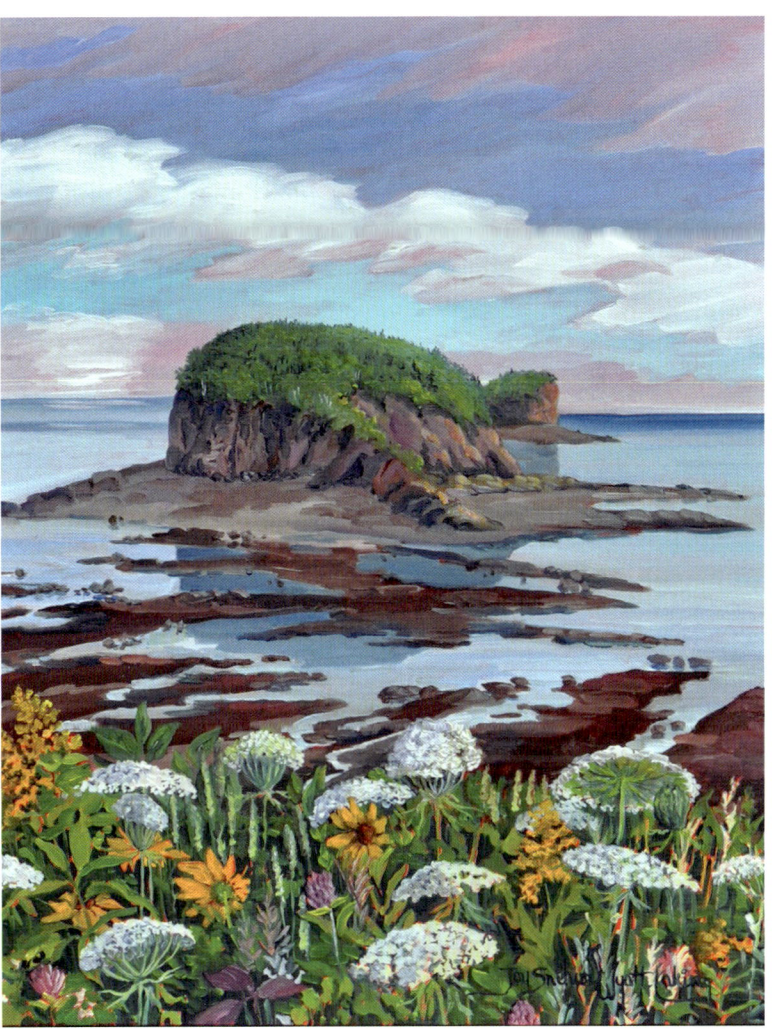
Two Islands

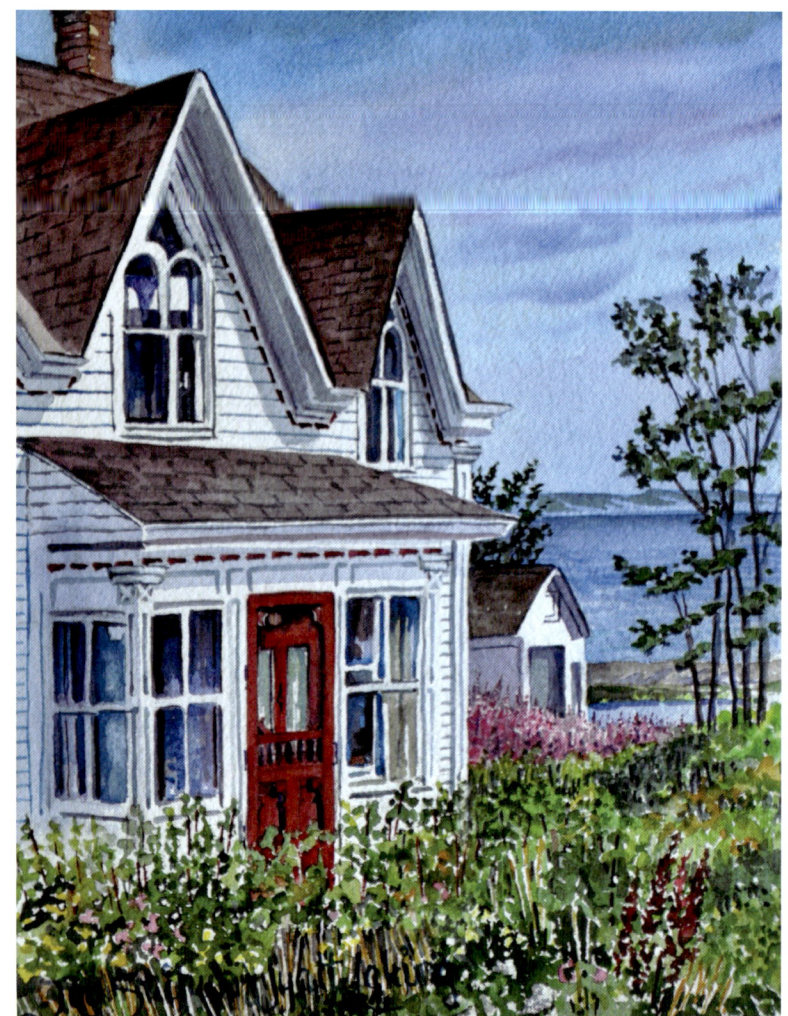

Spencer's Island 45.3551 -64.7123

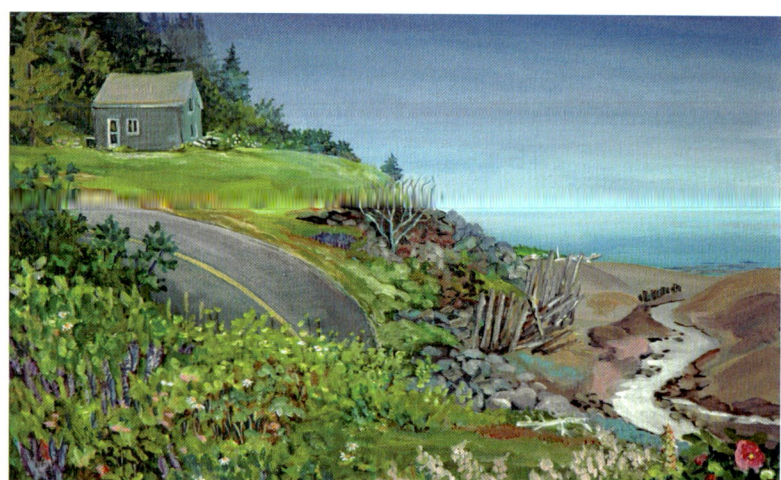

Before the Thunderstorm

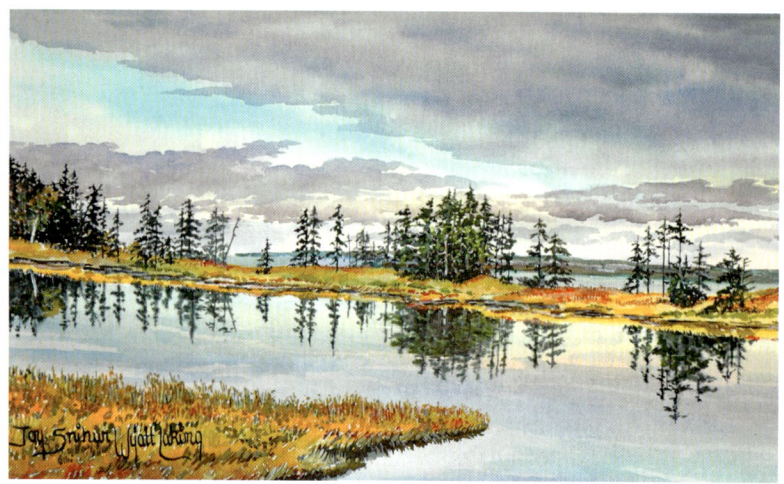

Autumn, West Bay

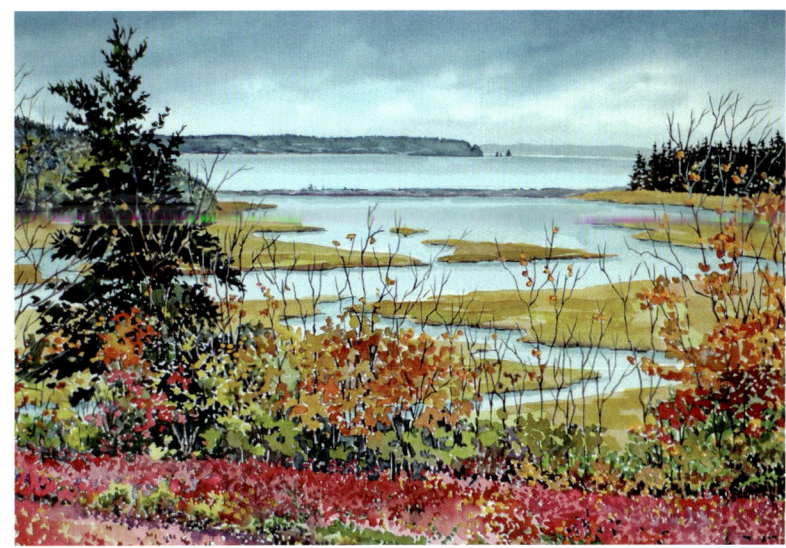

Cape Split from Diligent River

 Nova Scotia has many blueberry fields. Every other year after a heavy frost, the fields turn the most magnificent magenta. When painting these with watercolour, I do not put a wash of red over the field area. Instead, I build it up with little dark red patterns. I leave white paper in between these little areas. It is easy at the end to add light red or orange or a little water, or to tone down some of these white sections and make the field more cohesive. I use this same approach with doing foreground grasses. There is no green or yellow wash over the area. I start with dark green or deep yellow and work towards the light tones.

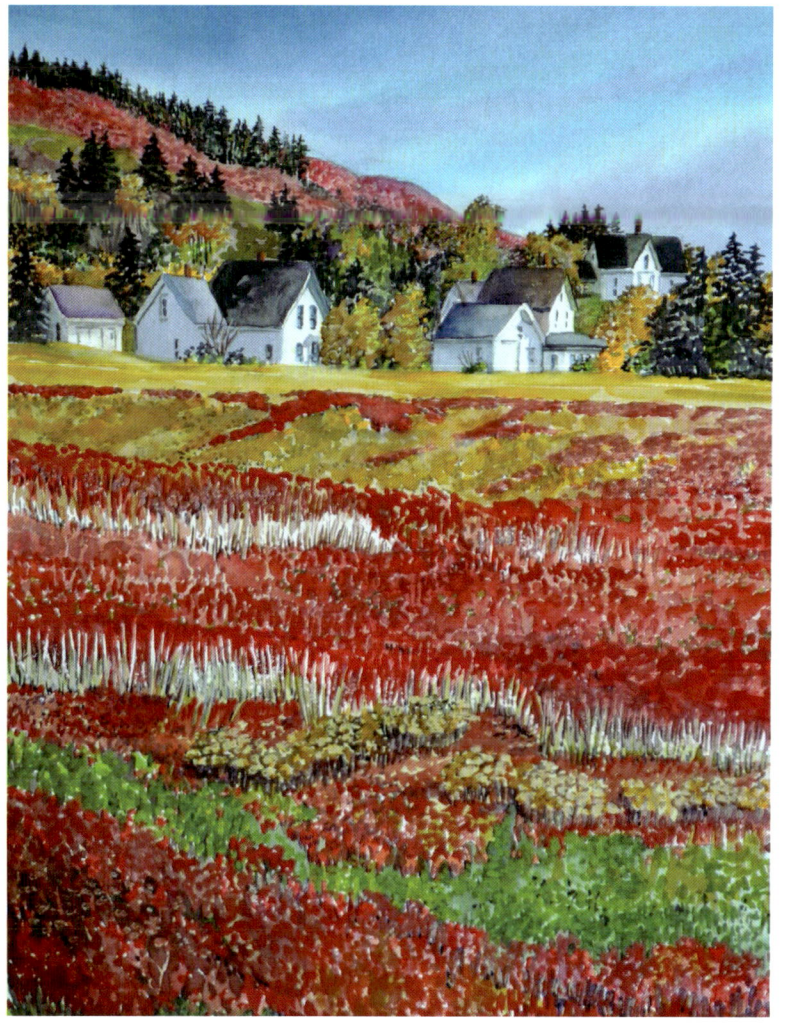

Diligent River

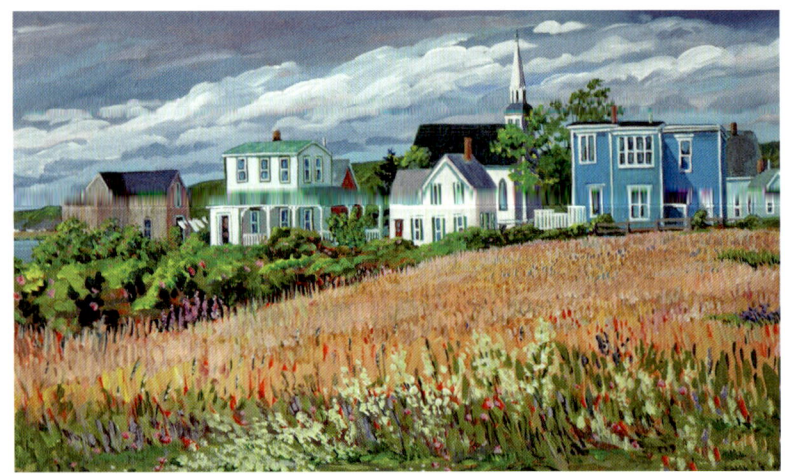
Advocate

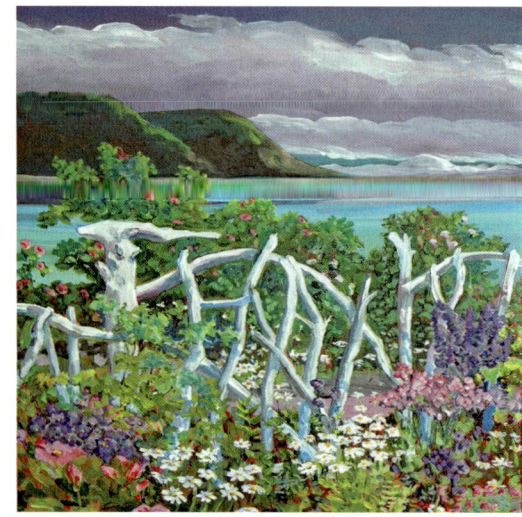
Advocate Garden

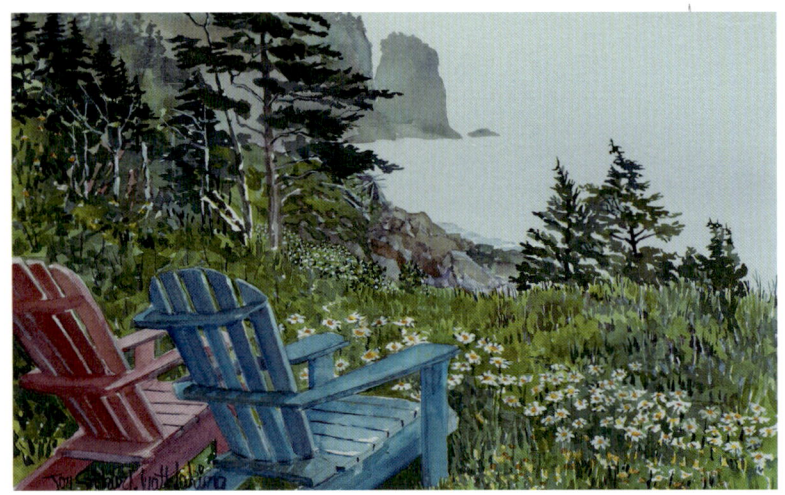
Chairs at Cape D'Or

When I set out by car to go painting, I usually have no idea what I am looking for. The first decision is to go left or right at the end of my lane. Then, I just drive along, waiting for something to call out to me. When something catches my eye, I am usually beyond it. I turn my car (Malorie) around and go back to take some photos. At this point, I am assessing the spot. I continue doing this until I hear a clear loud "Paint Me." If I reach Advocate, a good hour and a half from home, I stop waiting for something to call out to me and I go in search of something to paint. Advocate never disappoints me. There is always the view of the village and the bay from a cemetery on a hill.

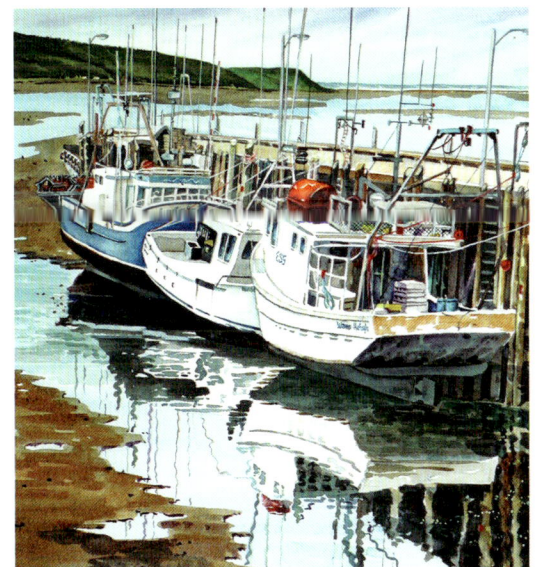

Boats at Advocate Dock

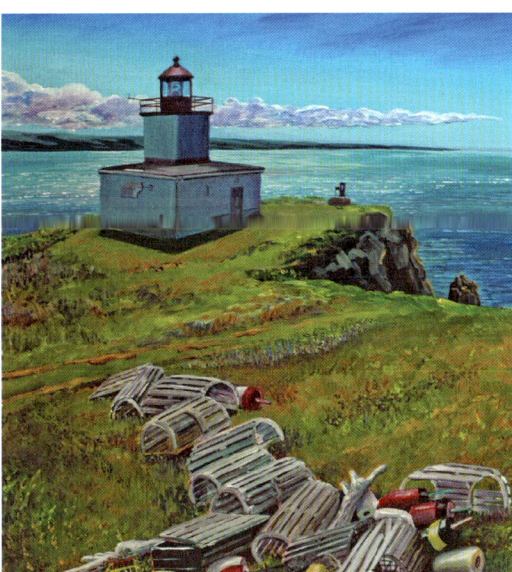

Cape D'Or 45.2913 -64.7741

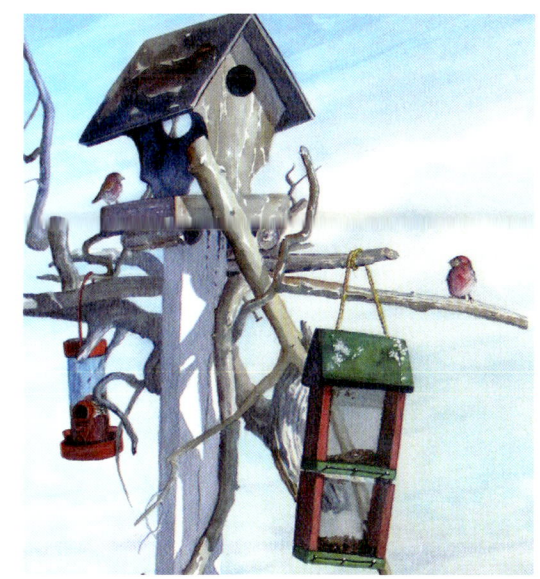

Advocate Bird Feeders

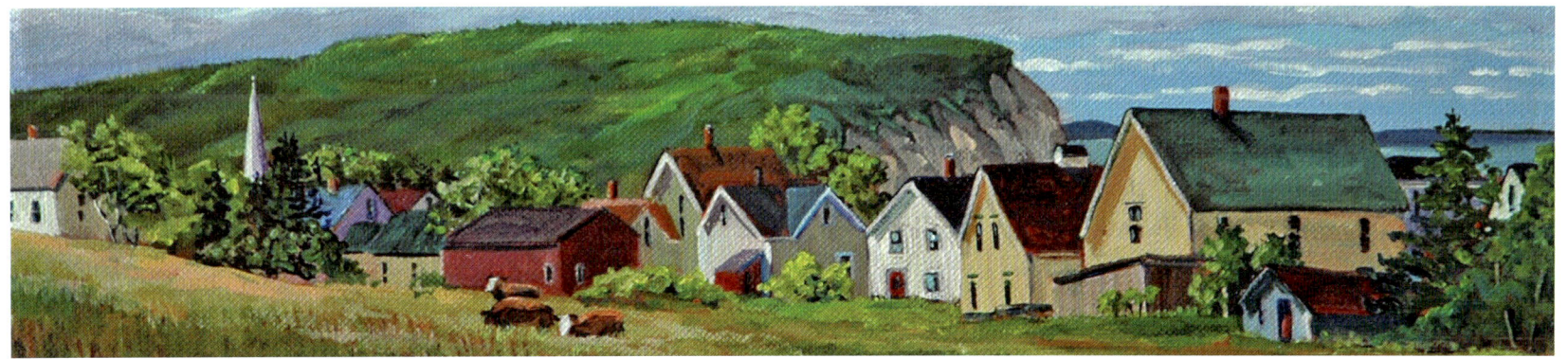

Advocate from the Cemetery

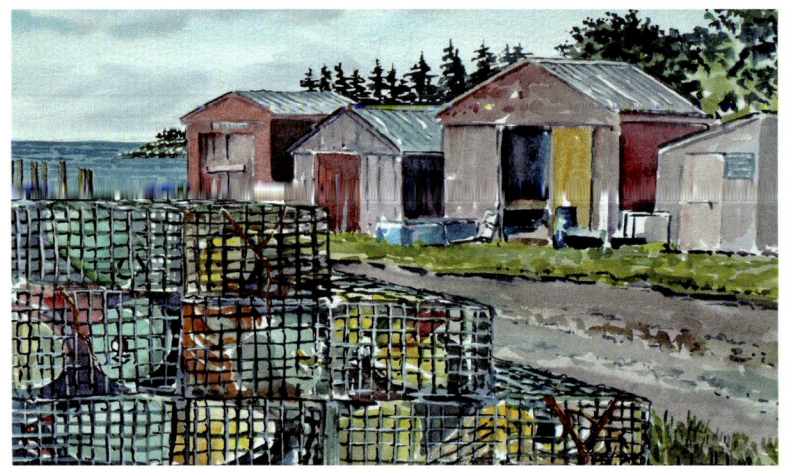
Fish Sheds and Traps, Northport

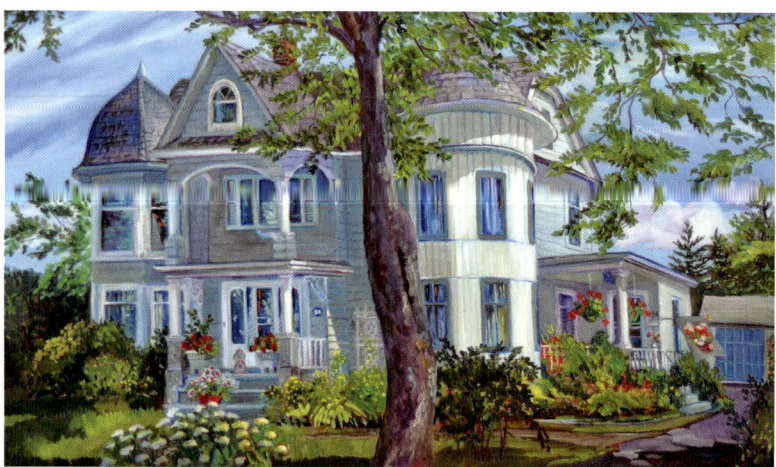
House in Amherst

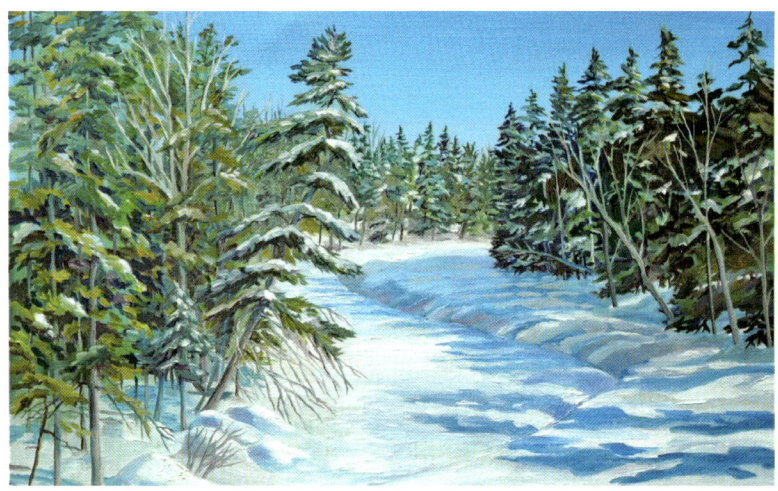
Winter Stream in Malagash

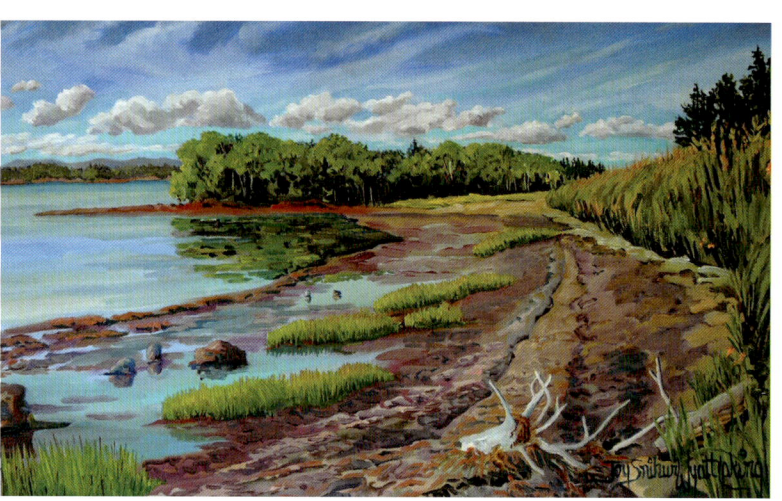
Malagash Beach

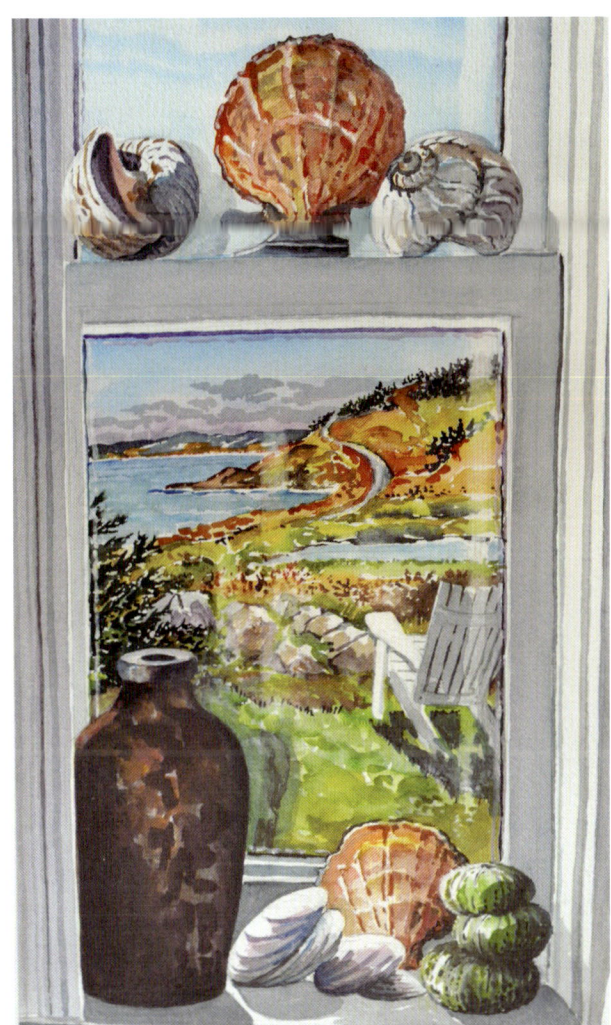

Window With Shells

 9

When painting outside, I try to do a quick sketch before I begin. I work on 1/16 (about 14 x 19 cm) of a sheet of watercolour paper with a permanent .5 marker and watercolour paint. The sketch is disposable so I find it easy to get started and make changes. Once the lighting and the composition are established, much of the painting is figured out before I start on a big piece of watercolour paper.

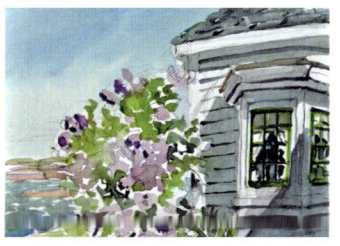

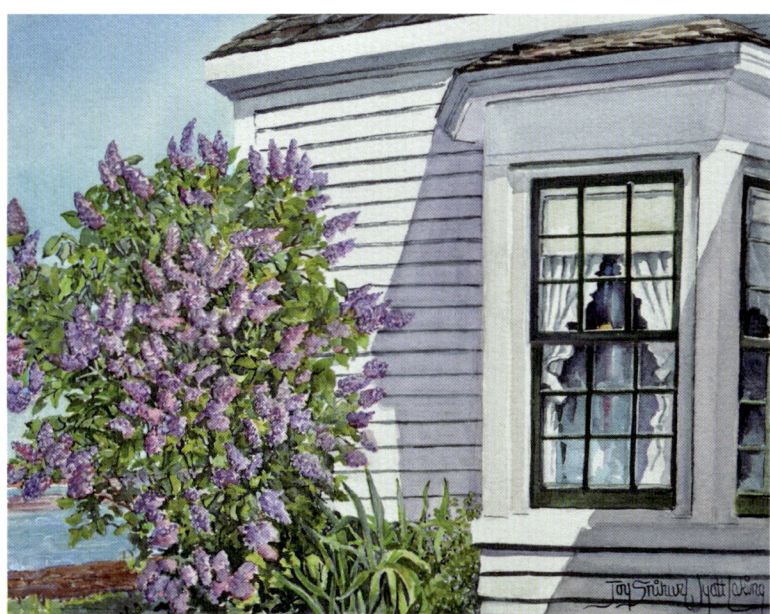

Thinker's Lodge, Pugwash 45.4213 -63.4031

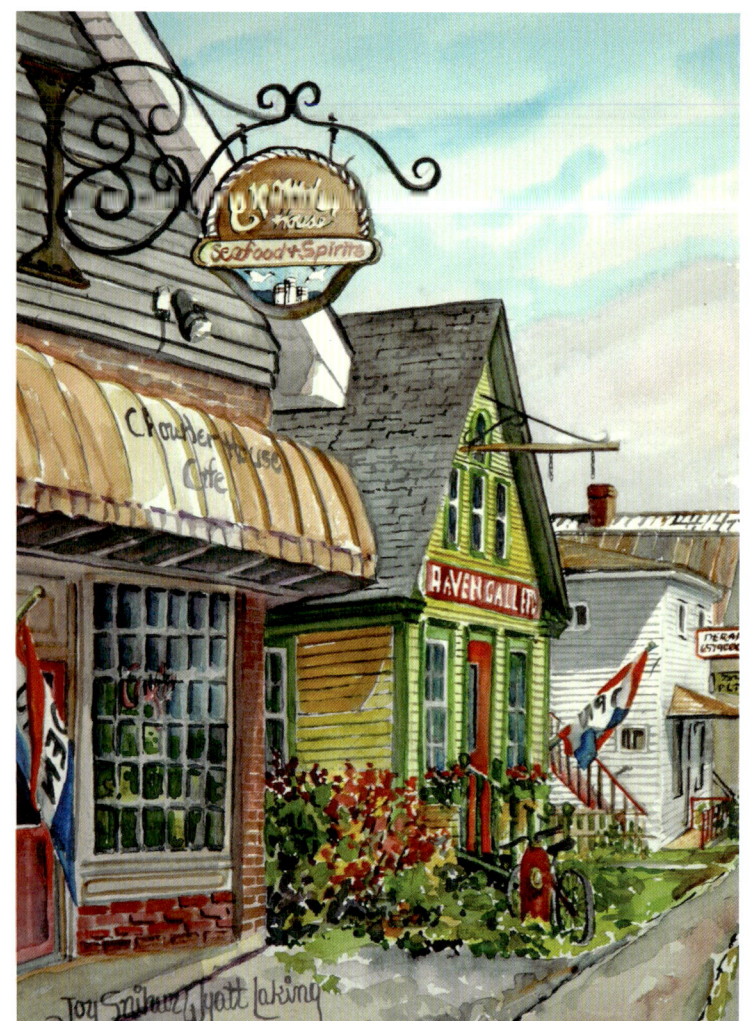

Main Street, Tatamagouche 45.7094 -63.2874

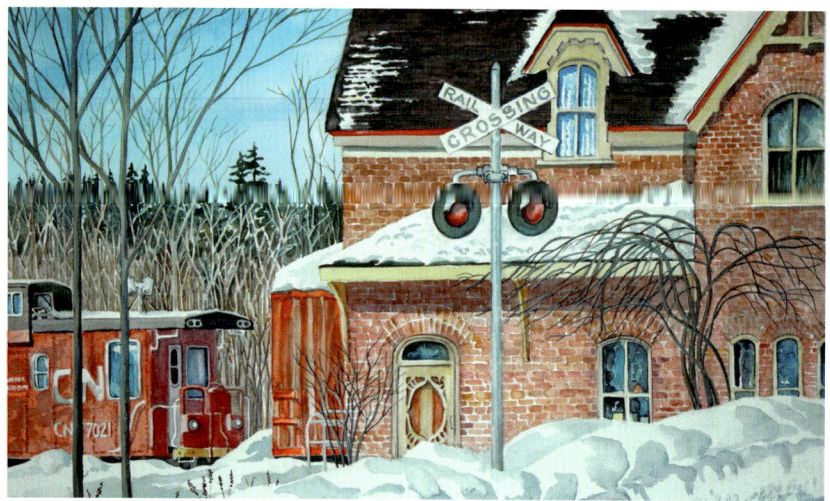

Tatamagouche Train Station

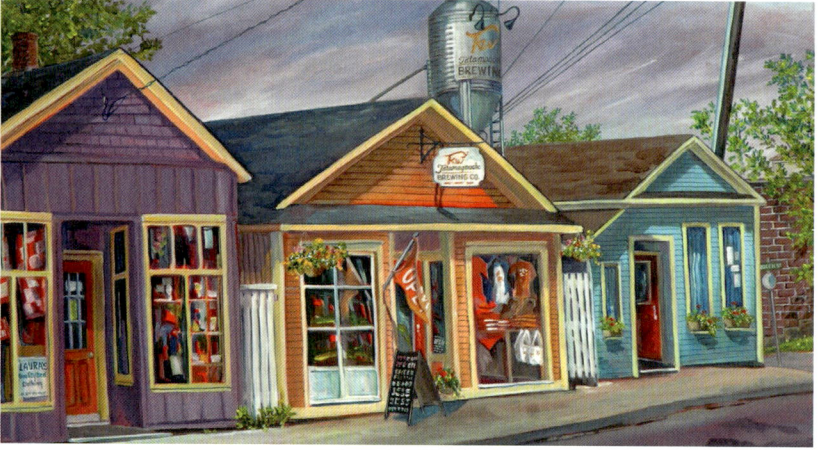

Tatamagouche Brewing

10

The clothesline was inspired by one that we had at McLeod's Cottages in Brule. On my created clothesline, I put stuff that I wanted to hang out to dry (i.e., think about and discard). The bra is made of sticks and stones and represents male and female. So much tension and unhappiness from my first marriage is hung out to dry. The panties are made entirely out of stuff from my junk drawer. I am committing to less junk in my life. The trousers are woven out of plastic grocery bags. I am committing to less plastic in my life and fewer pre-packaged foods. I had problems with the sweater. I dyed wool fabric different colours, each representing a different tension or worry in my life: money, health, death, etc. As I knotted each piece around the wire armature, I tried to visualize shedding the knots of worry that are in my own life. When I finished, the sweater looked like a giant cat toy. I gave it a haircut. Still a cat toy! Then I dyed wool and added the collar and cuffs. Finally a sweater! Then all I had to do was whittle the little clothes pegs.

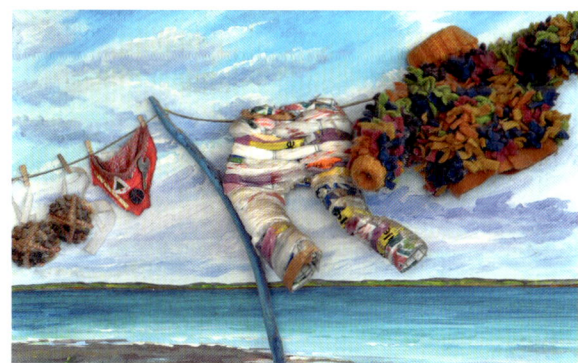

Clothesline (sticks, stones, silk, grocery bags, dyed wool)

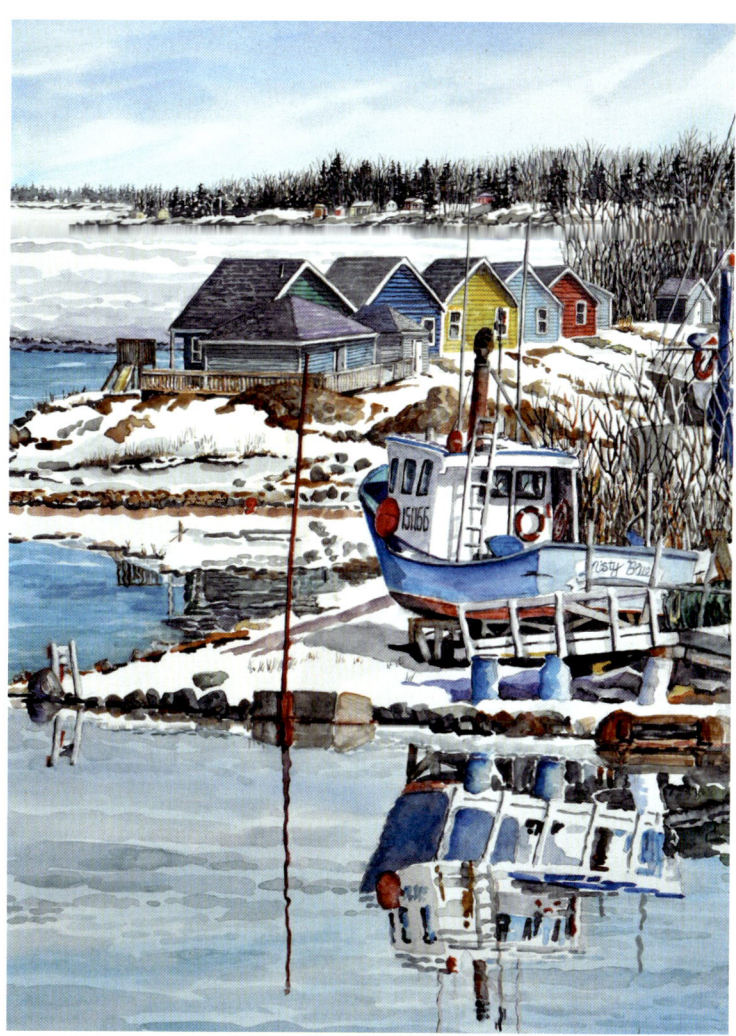

Barrachois Harbour

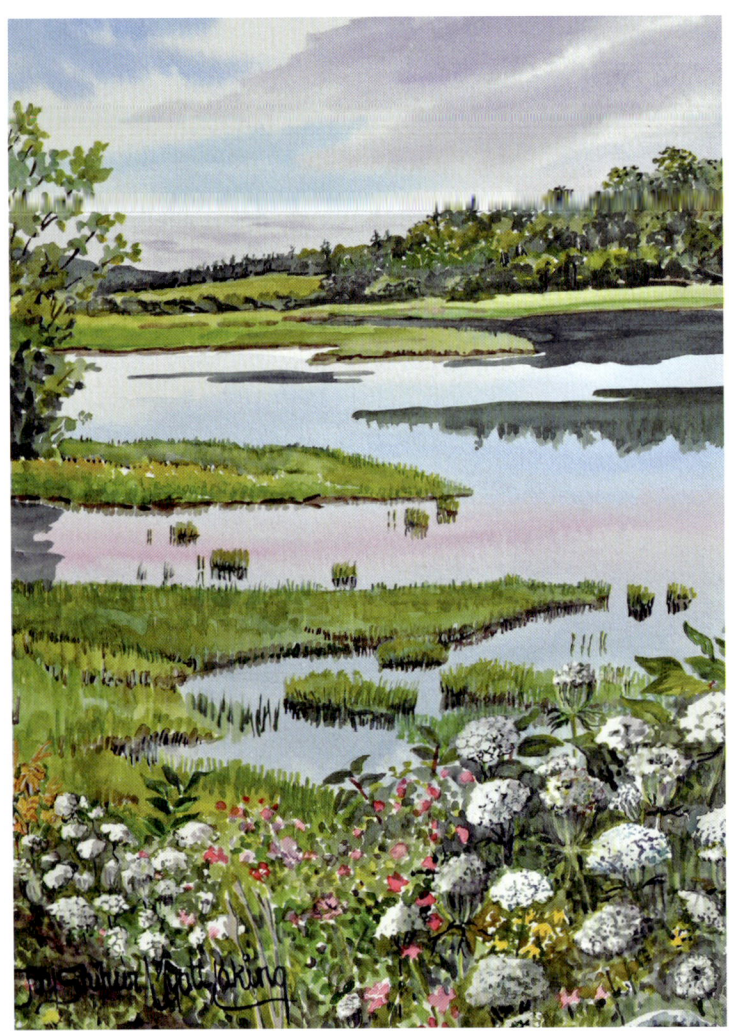

Early Morning, River John

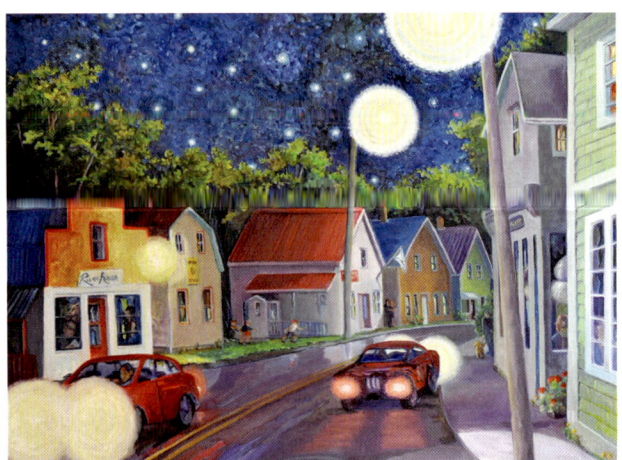

Starry Night in River John

11 I was enthralled by the lights of New York when I visited there fifty years ago. Afterwards, I painted a series called "Leaving the City" for a university art class. Forty-eight years later, I am still intrigued by lights within a painting. This painting of River John was inspired by a week's painting trip there. One night during this trip, I got up at 3 a.m. and drove downtown in my pyjamas. I did a preliminary sketch in watercolour and took some photos. The actual scene was eerily quiet. When I came home to the studio, I did the under-painting for *Starry Night in River John*, an oil painting with a sky full of colourful circles. A year later, I got back to work on this painting. One of the advantages of oil painting is that you can paint over anything and try stuff different ways. The circles in the sky went and tiny stars appeared. Rather than "Leaving the City," in this one I am embracing our villages.

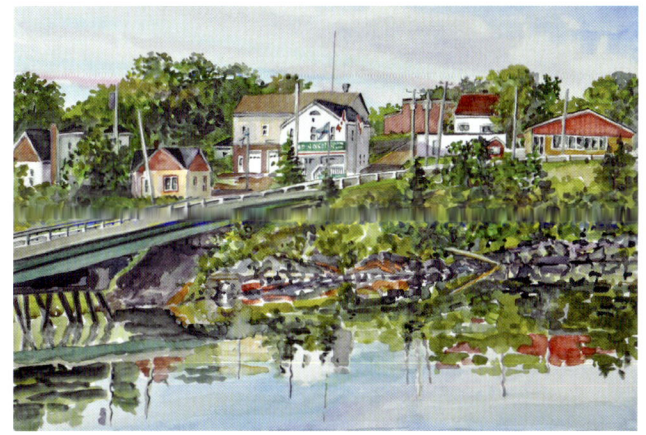

River John 45.7411 -63.0597

House and Laundry, River John

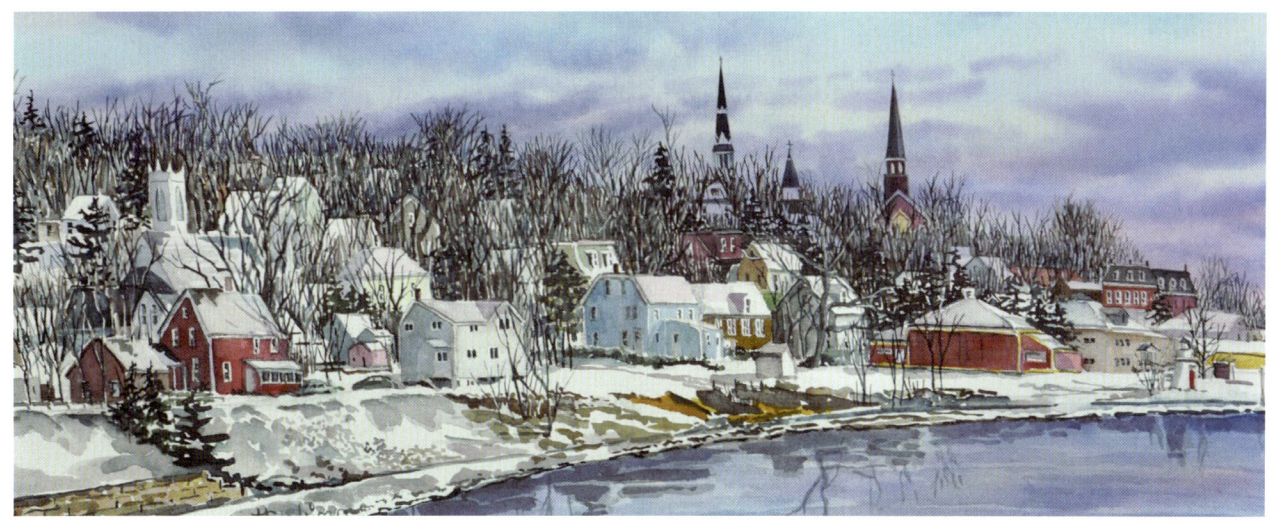

Pictou

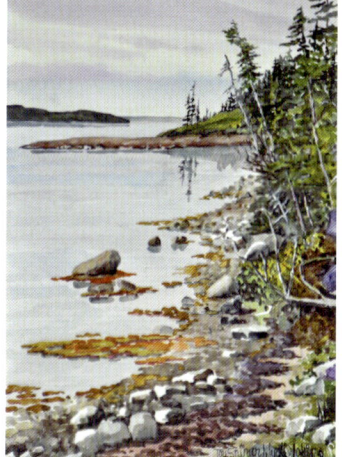

Cape John

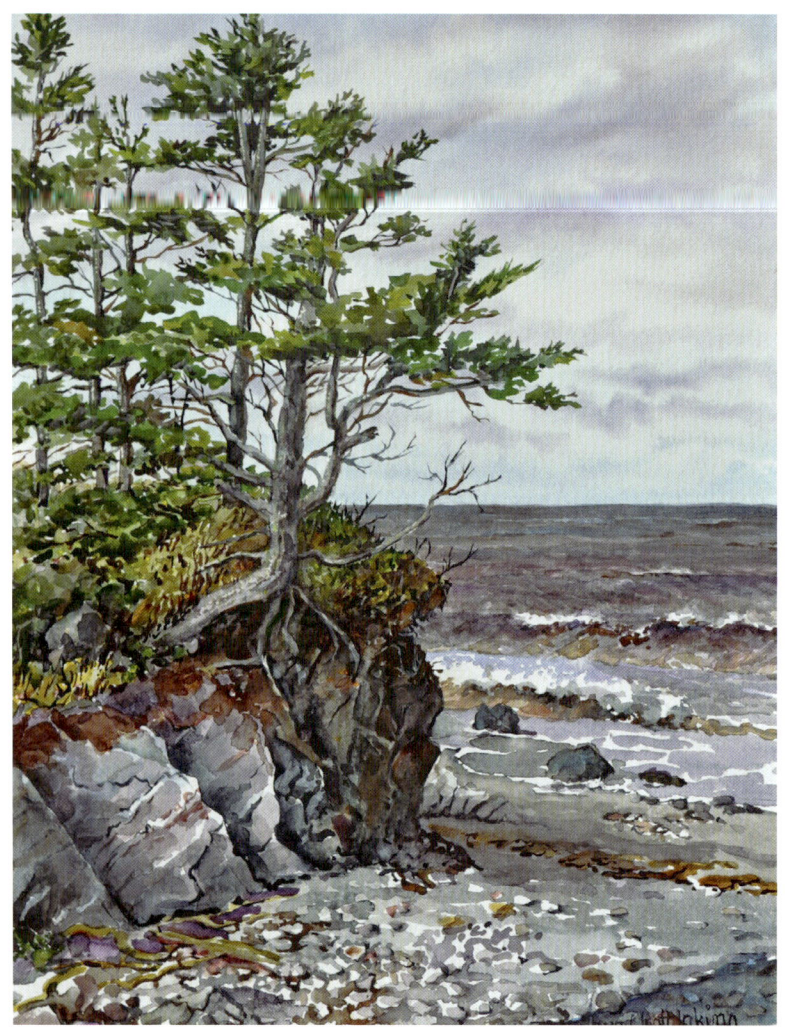

Bent Tree at Arisaig

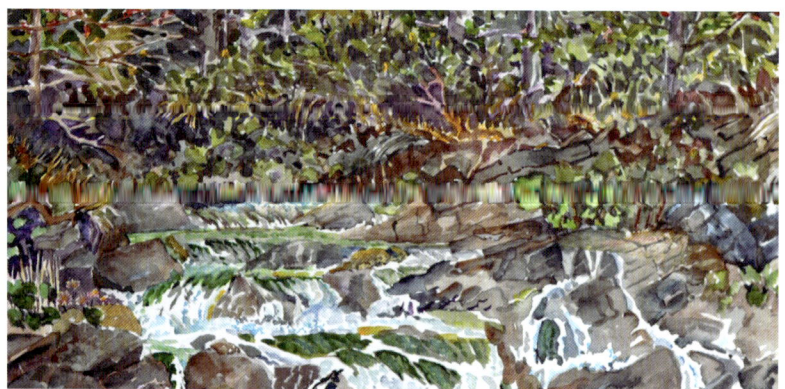

Stream at Arisaig

12 The day Hurricane Dorian was forecast to hit Nova Scotia, Susan Paterson and I were planning to go to Arisaig for a week of painting with our friend, Jaye Ouellette. Did Susan and I postpone our trip? No, we moved it ahead a day, to ensure we would get there. Needless to say, we had a couple of interesting days with no power and a wild ocean. I had brought lots of wine and we made coffee on the barbeque. For two days we painted inside. On the first day it wasn't raining, we were painting outside. I took photos of the development of the Ballantynes Cove painting. I always do the sky first because it is so easy to mess up the wet-on-wet technique. If it doesn't work out perfectly, I just turn the paper over and start again. On my website I have done a little demonstration of all the steps for doing wet on wet. After the sky is in, I start laying in the darks and gradually work toward the lights. (Jaye's website: www.jaye.ca)

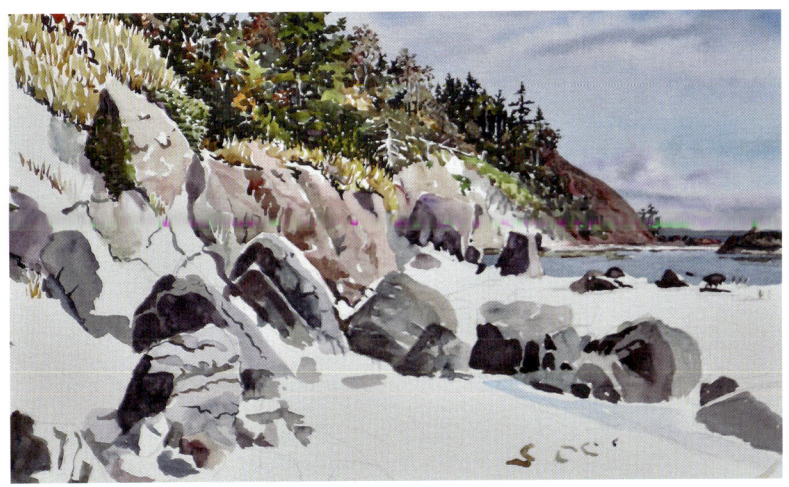

Ballantynes Cove, step one

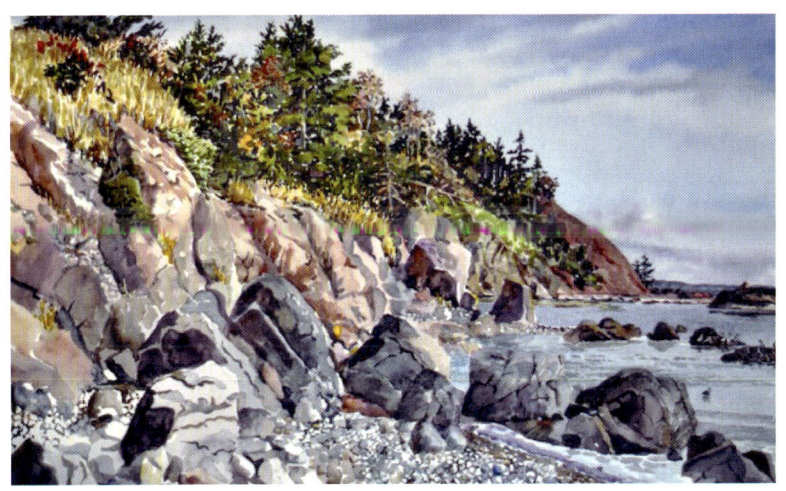

Ballantynes Cove, step three

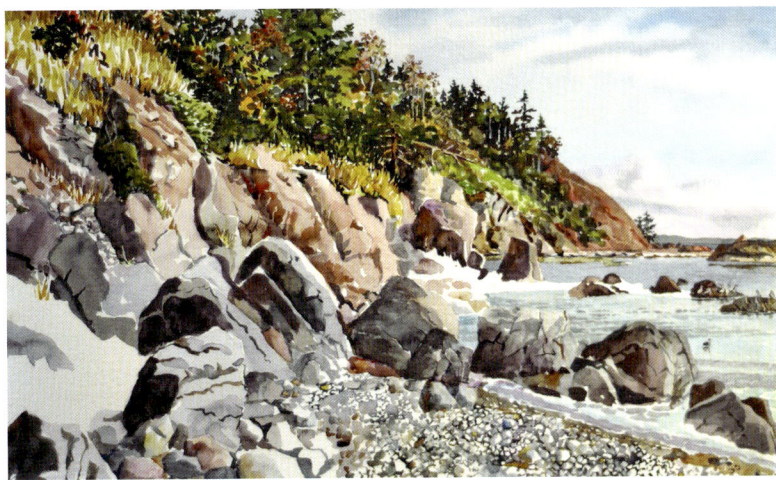

Ballantynes Cove, step two

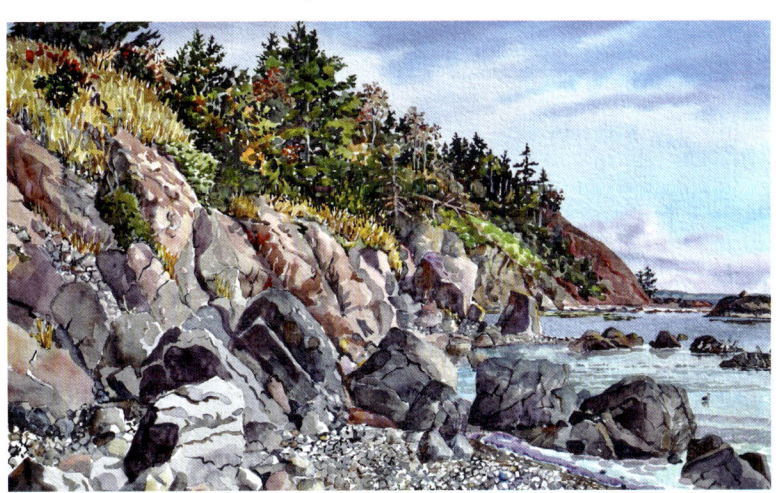

Ballantynes Cove 45.8603 -61.9163

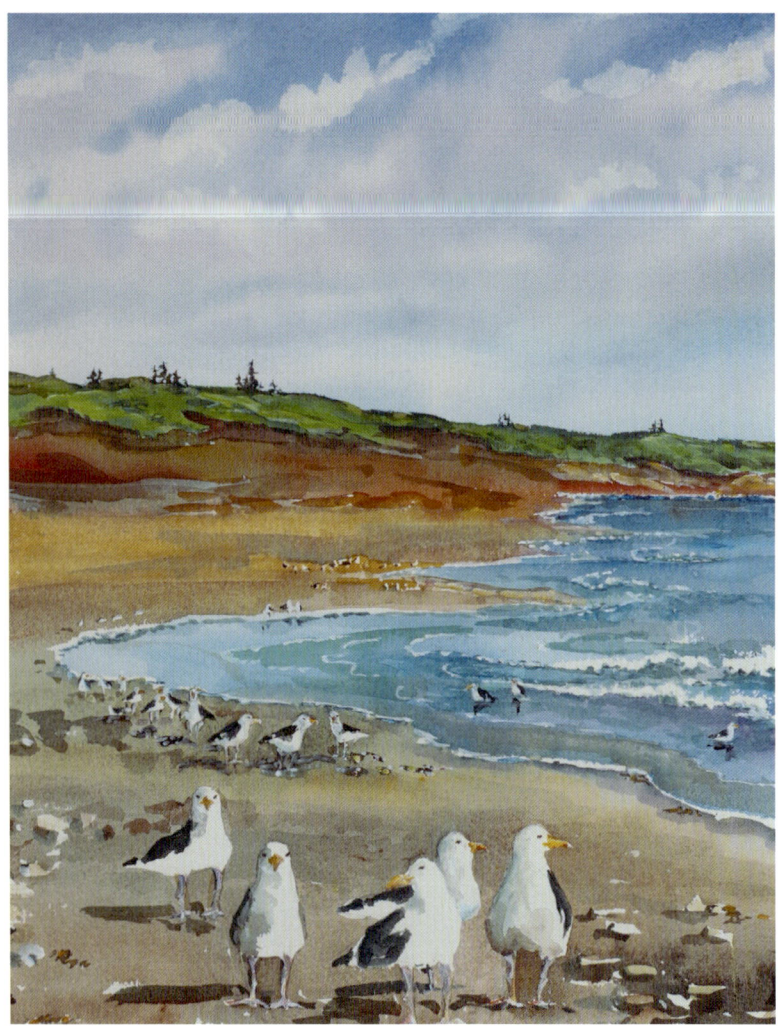

Seagulls

My grandfather and I had a friend, Herman the Seagull. Everywhere we went Herman would be waiting for us. I am an old lady now, my grandfather long gone, but Herman still waits for me in almost every season and every country.

Herman and his seagull friends flap and swoop overhead. Their raucous voices call back and forth. When they catch an updraft, they lock their wings and glide, riding the wind, at one with the sky.

He and his friends fish in shallow waters and rest atop roofs and chimneys. They cock their big white heads and stare with unblinking eyes.

It is when I scatter chips, crumbs, and crackers, just like my grandfather first showed me, that they congregate in front of me. They edge closer and closer, their hooked yellow bills almost smiling as they grab my tasty treats.

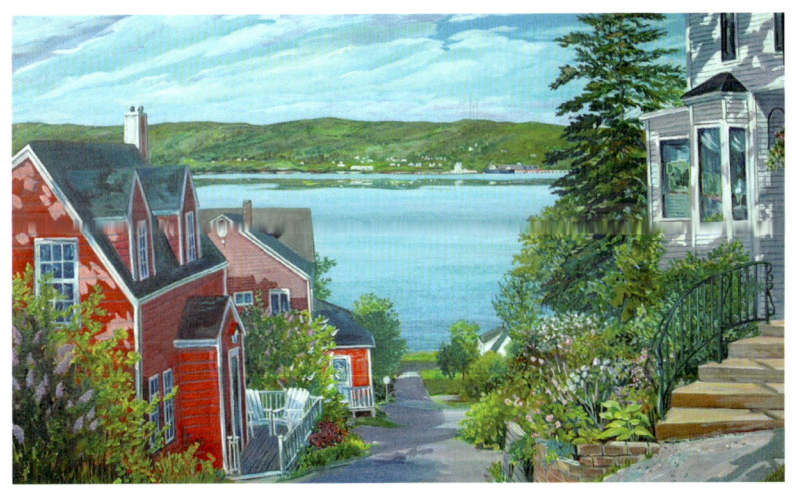
Early Morning, Philpott Street 45.3702 -61.2152

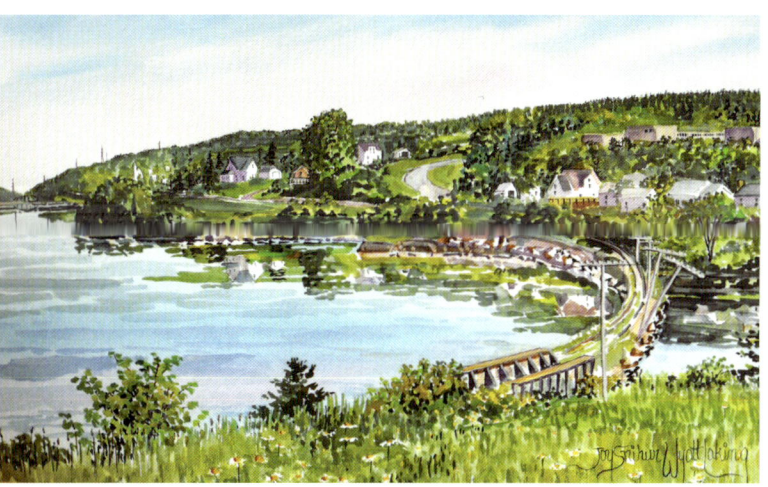
Train Tracks in Port Hawkesbury

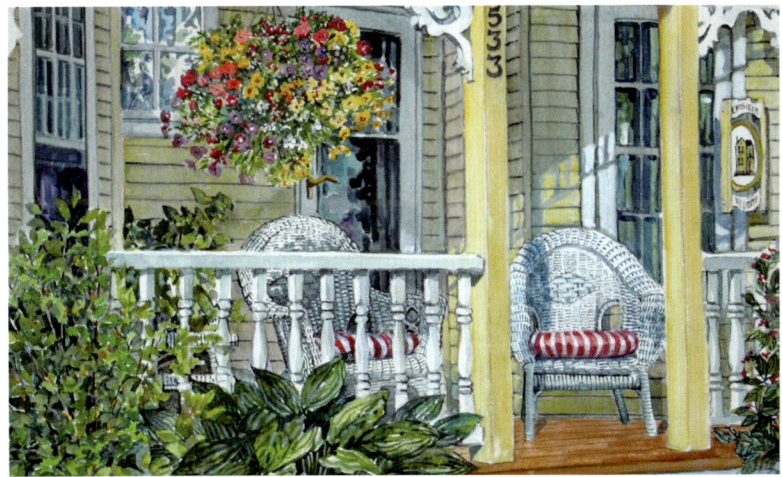
Porch with Flowers, Port Hawkesbury

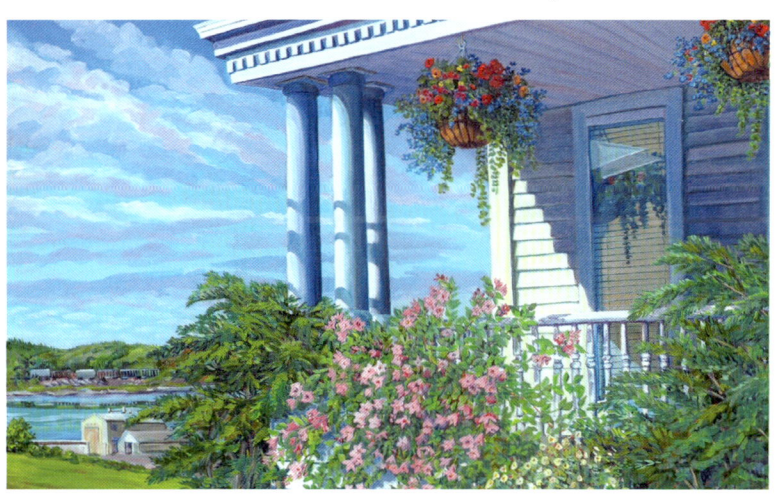
Flowers and Columns, Port Hawkesbury

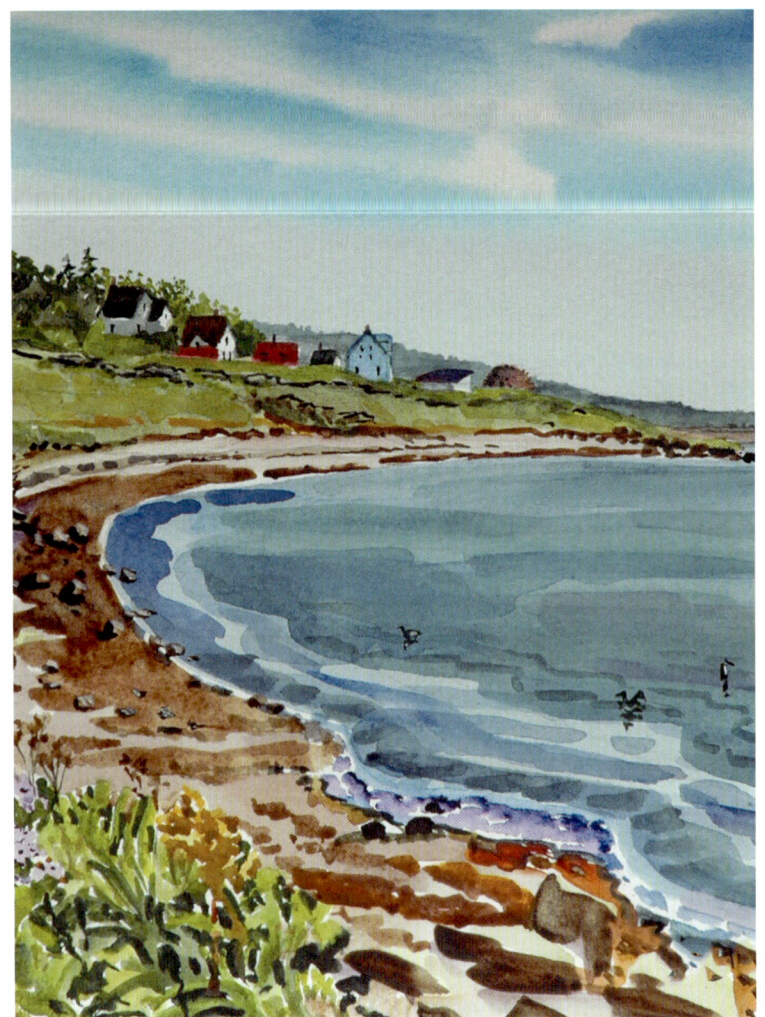

Port Hood

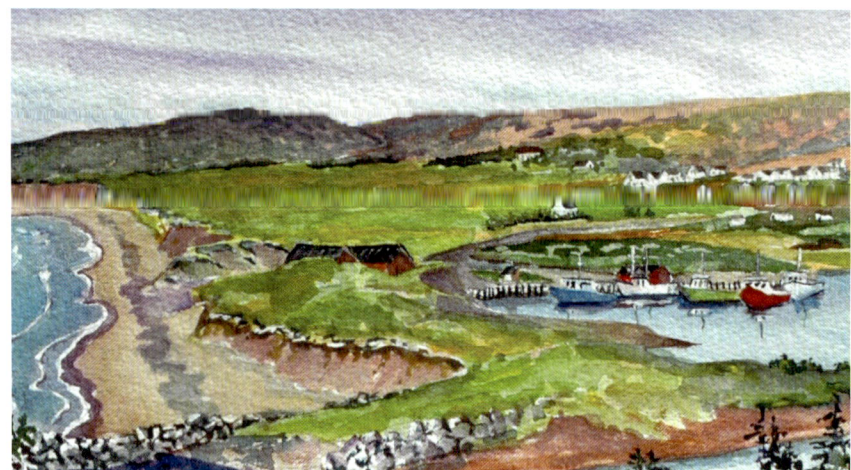

Inverness 46.1337 -61.1929

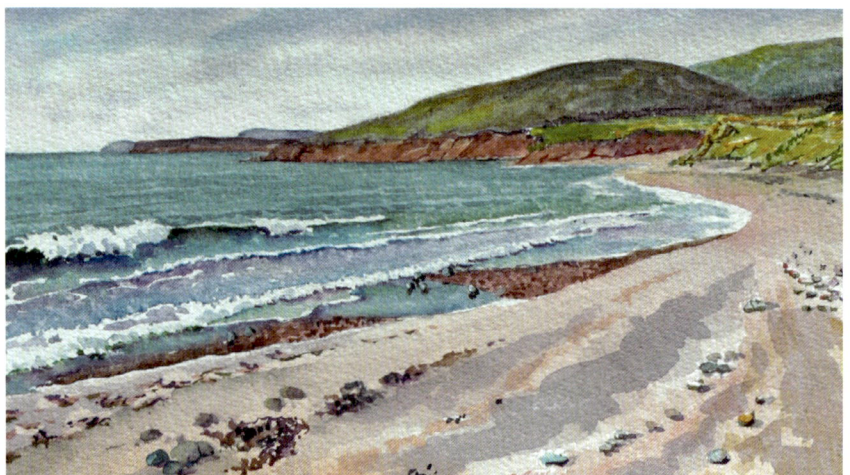

Inverness Beach

Susan Paterson and I love to go painting together. Every year for the past half-dozen years or so we have had a week or two painting on location. Susan loves to paint waterfalls. This is something that I had never tried before meeting her. When we were painting in Cape Breton, we heard about Egypt Falls. We got directions and headed in. The path was steeply downhill and I was recovering from a broken leg, but I made it. However, when we got to the base of the hill there was a cliff and rope in order to actually get to the falls. I knew I couldn't do the cliff with the rope, so I sat on the top and painted this close-up of a tree and moss. If you look really carefully on the left, you can sort of see the falls. (Susan's website: www.susanpaterson.ca)

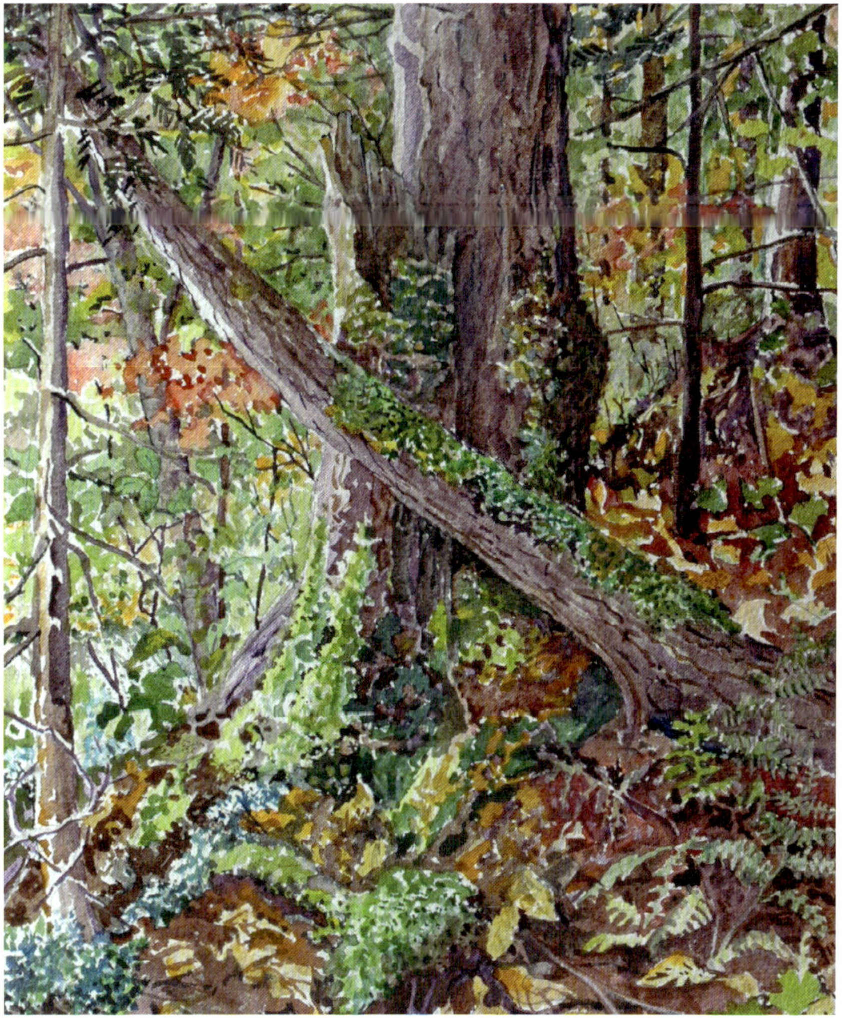

Egypt Falls

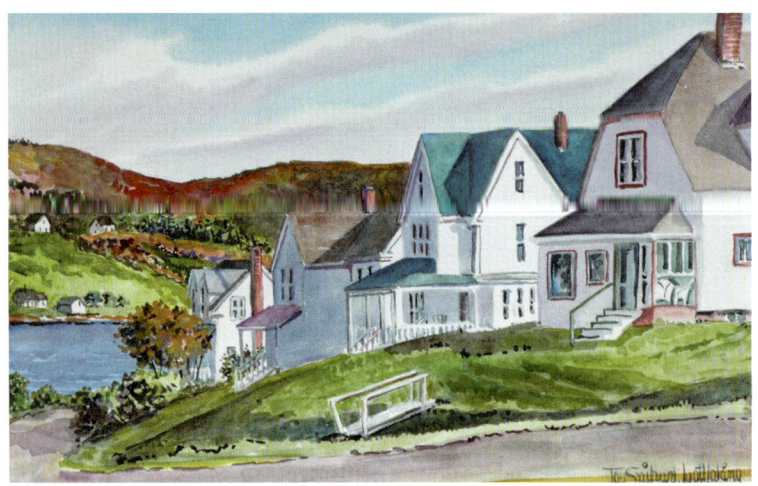

Autumn, Margaree Harbour

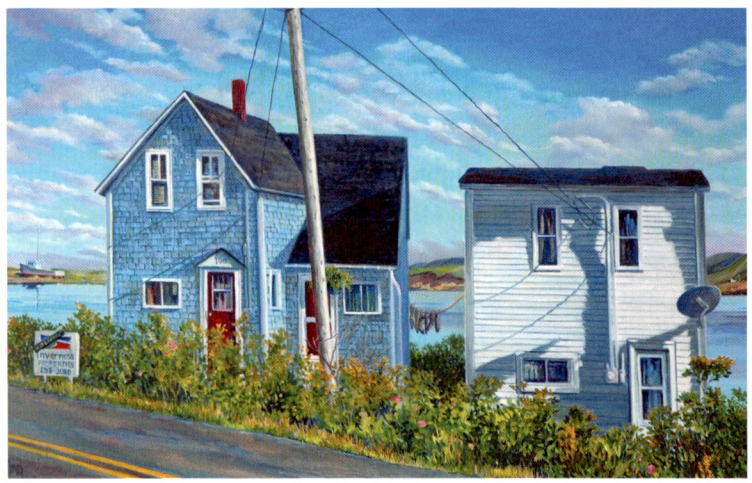

Two Houses, Margaree Harbour 46.2621 -61.0633

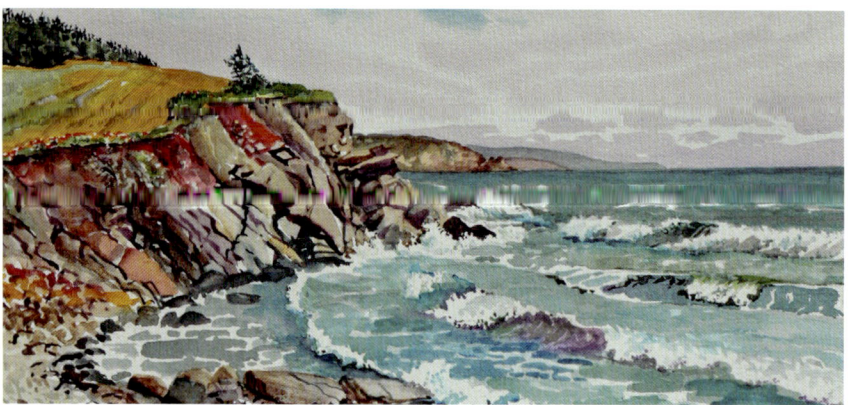

Surf at Dunvegan

 15

Early in the day,
Before the sun has cleared the cliff,
It is the performance art of waves,
The combination of sound and sight,
That soothes my soul.
A dark line rolls in
Across the pale sapphire sea
Toward the beach.
It builds into a mighty viridian concave wave.
The razor top edge glints with morning pink.
Then a thundering collapse
Of glorious surf and sound
Rolls along the entire shore.
When the energy is spent,
Only quiet flat froth remains,
Until the next wave arrives.

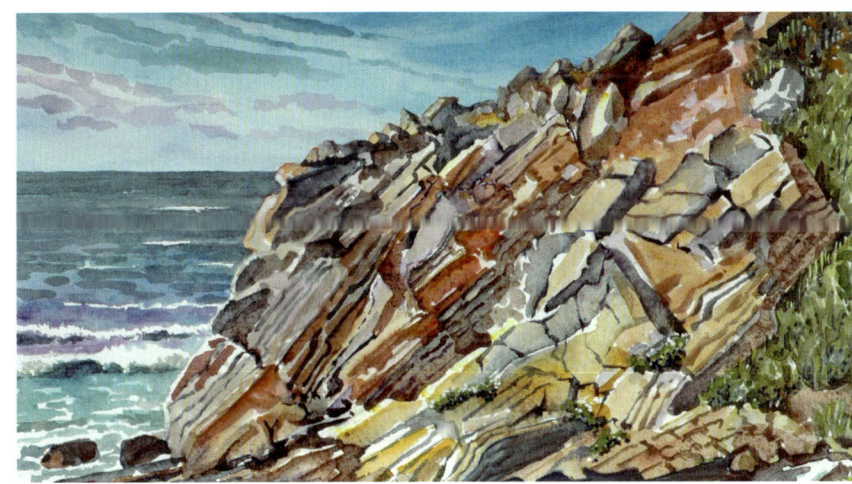

Rocky Shore

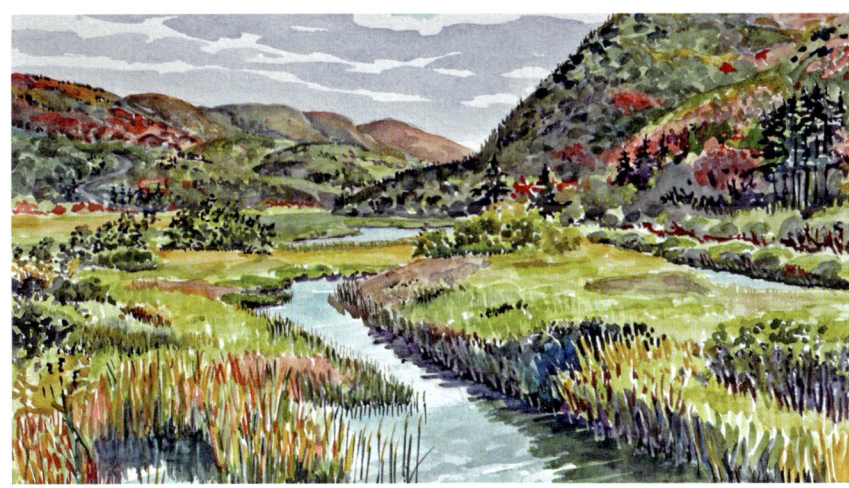

Margaree River

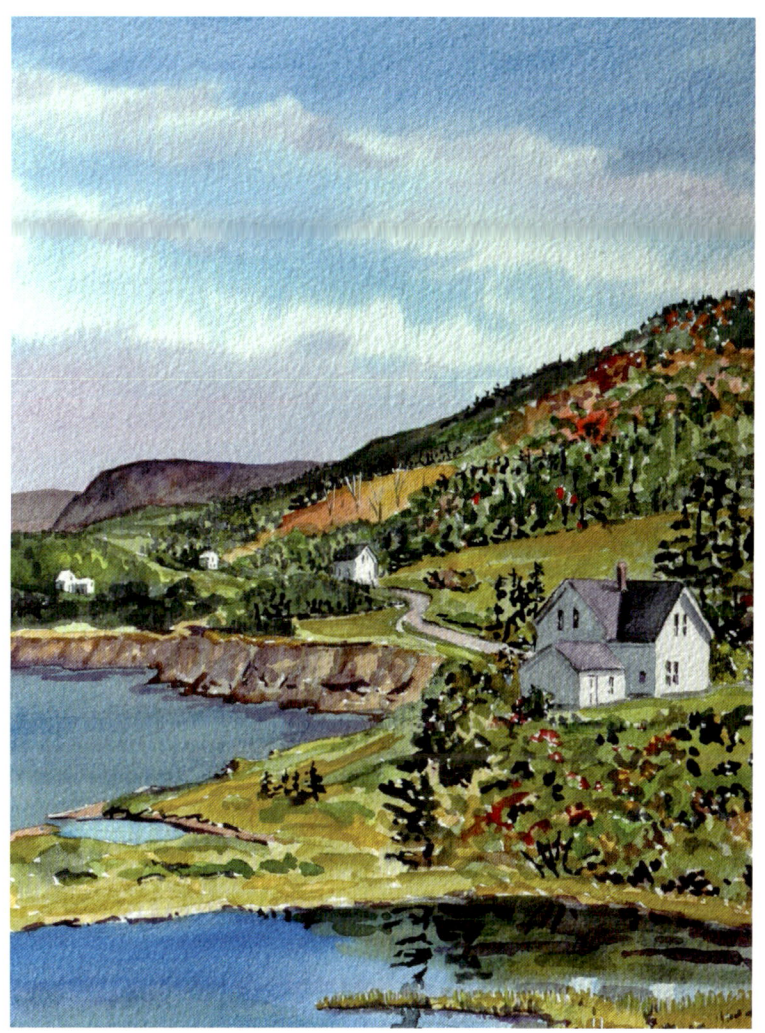

Whale Cove

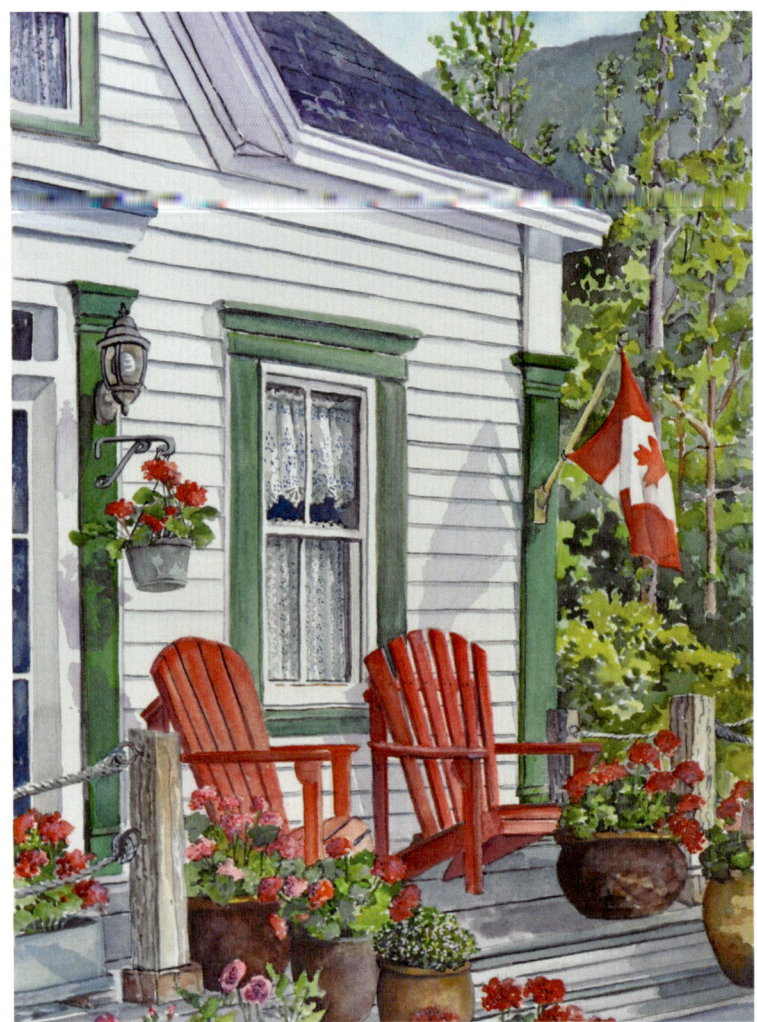

Four Mile Beach

16

I learned a lot from my mother, an artist. She always told me, "Be anything but do not be an artist. Be something reliable." So what did I become? An artist.

Another thing I learned was to never put off until tomorrow something that could be squeezed in today. My mom was the perfect 1950s housewife. While she still painted every week, the majority of her time was spent raising us and volunteering to make the world a better place. She intended to get back to her art full-time when we were grown, but she died young of breast cancer.

Before I had children, I read a biography of Georgia O'Keefe. Her husband, Alfred Stieglitz, told her that you can be an artist or you can be a mother. You can't be both.

When I had children of my own, I was determined to be a great mom and to continue to be a professional artist. I have always thought that the most necessary trait for an artist is tenacity. You have to believe in yourself when nobody else in the world does. I got up every morning at 5 a.m. and worked in my studio until 9 a.m. Then the kids got up and I made breakfast and we had wonderful mornings together. In the afternoon, I painted while the kids had naps. When they got older, they played just outside my studio in the play space for two hours. When I was in the studio, I was available for emergencies but nothing else. As soon as I came out of the studio, all of my attention was on my kids. My dual roles as mother and artist enhanced each other.

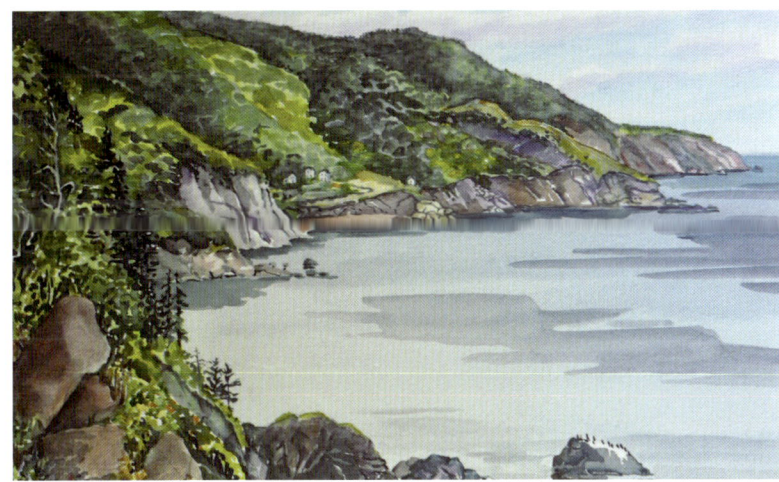

Meat Cove 47.0131 -60.5861

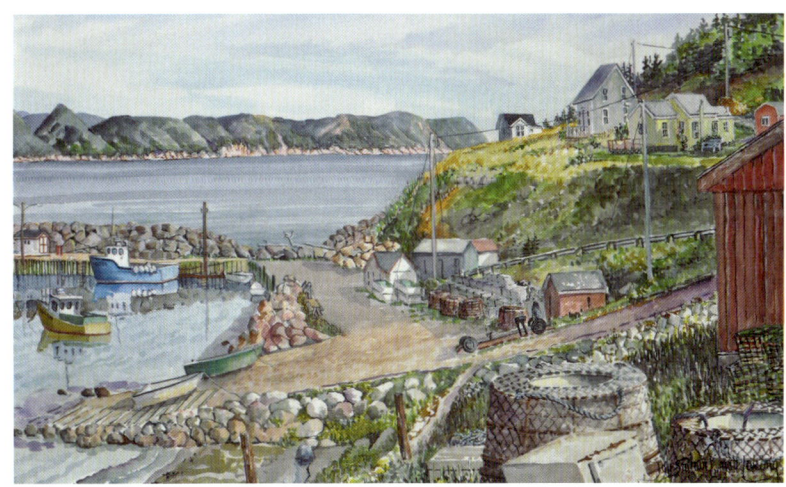

White Point, Cape Breton

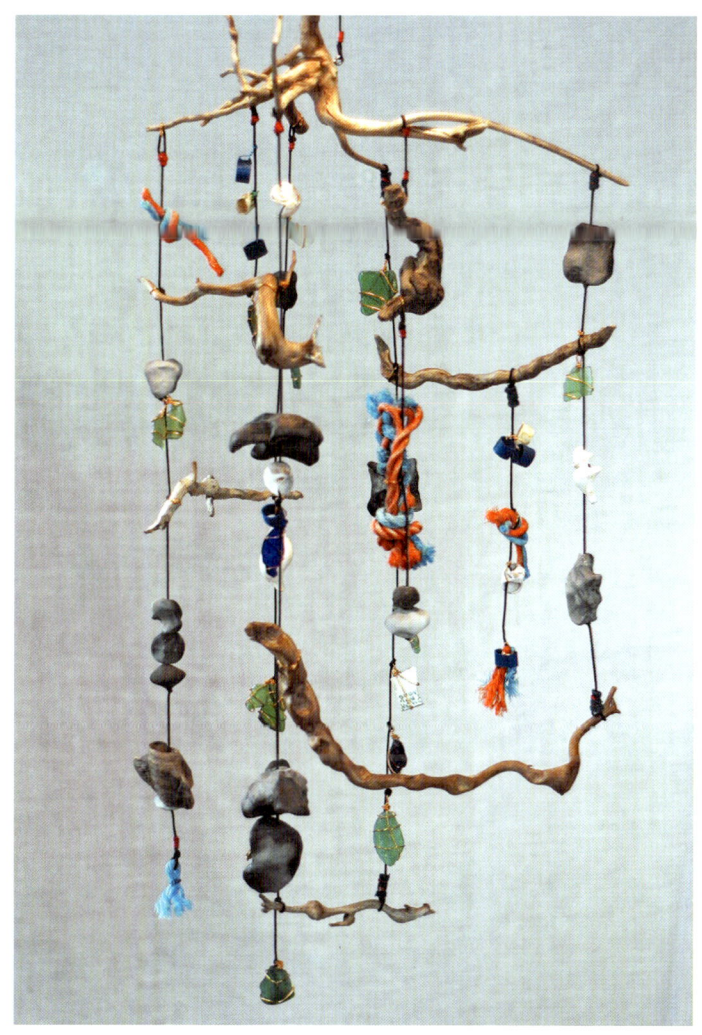

Sea Mobile (pit-fired beach clay, glass, shells, rope & driftwood)

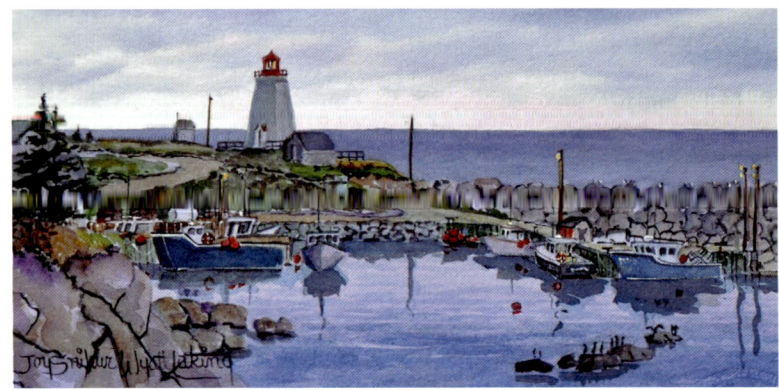

Neil's Harbour at Dusk

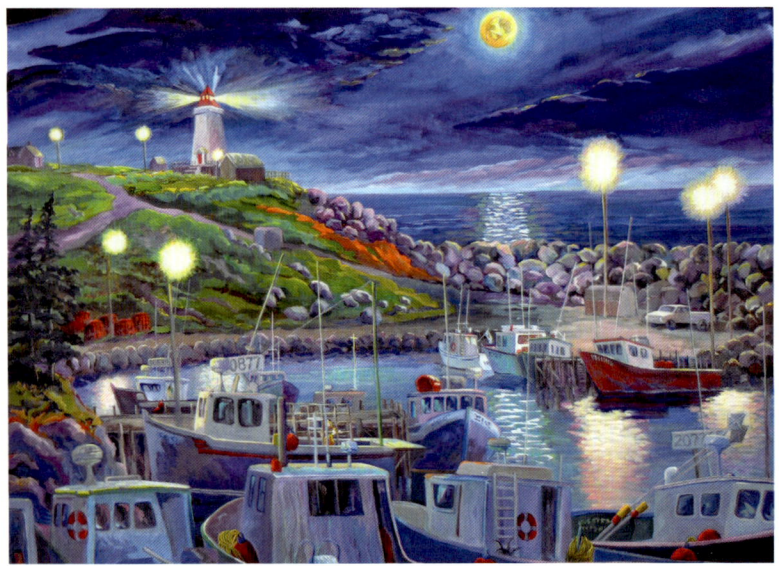

Full Moon at Neil's Harbour 46.4829 -60.1922

More than thirty years ago, every year in January, I used to organize a one-day painting workshop for my forty adult painting students. I would invite an artist whose work I loved to teach my students for the day. We met in the local school gymnasium. The potluck lunch was delicious.

This is how I met Chris Gorey of Ingonish and we have been friends ever since. Last year, we even had an exhibition together along with Susan Paterson. It was called "Outside" because the three of us all love to paint outside on location and each of us paints in our own distinctive style. To generalize, Chris is a master of capturing atmosphere in the traditional watercolour style. Susan loves painting detail. She can happily sit all day by the roots of an old tree doing a phenomenal pencil drawing on neutral paper and then adding lights and darks.

And I love painting stuff: old porches and buildings. It wasn't until my dad came visiting from Ontario and he and I went painting together that I realized this. Each time, we found a place to paint, Dad would say, "Let's just look a little further." Finally I asked, "Dad, what are we looking for?" "Not old buildings and porches," he said. "I like to paint rocks and water." So that is what we did and I was pushed into finally discovering the beauty in painting a landscape with no man-made things. The next day my dad said, "Today we have to go painting again and today we will paint what you like."
(Chris's website:www.goreygallery.ca)

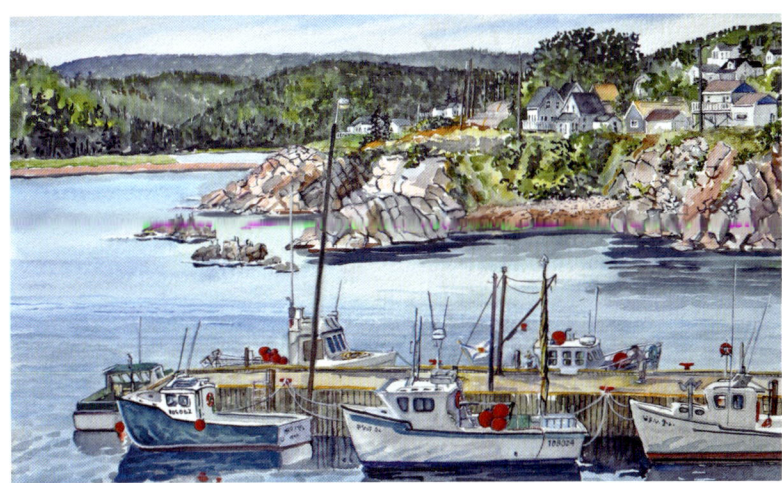

Neil's Harbour

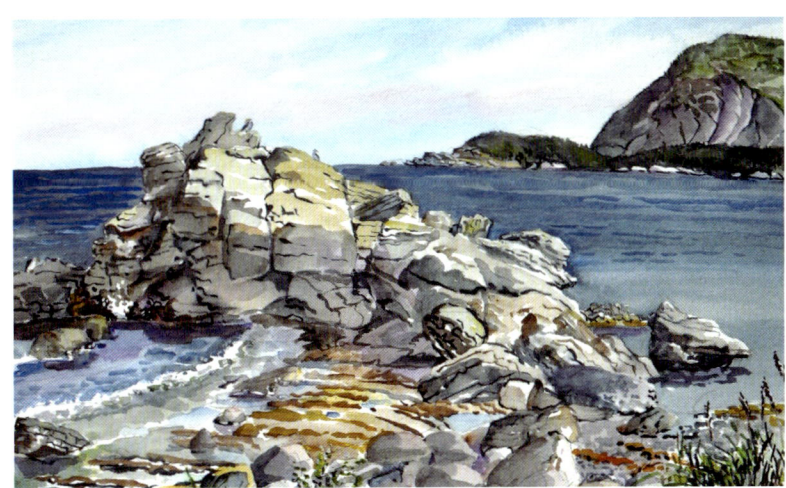

Ingonish

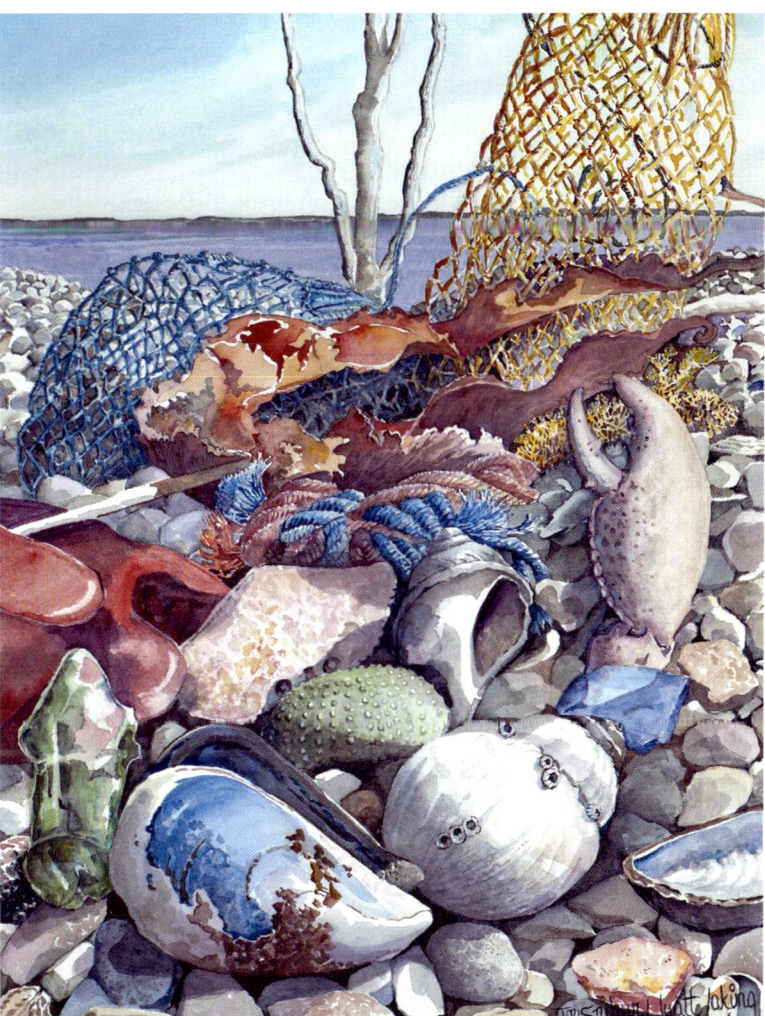

Beach Still Life

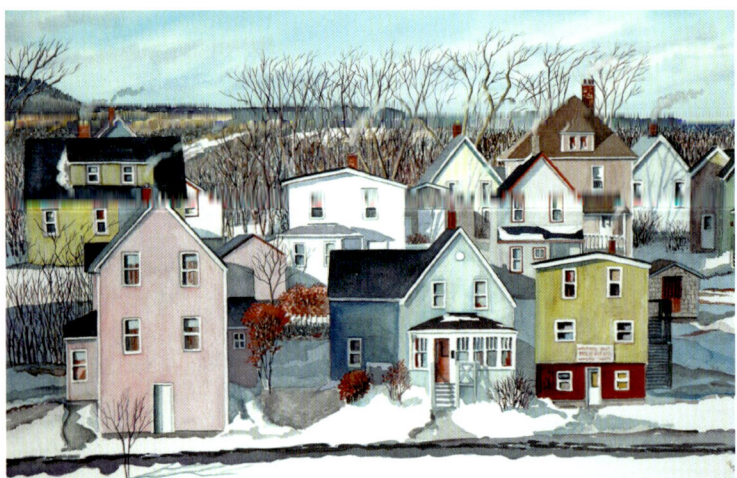
Whitney Pier

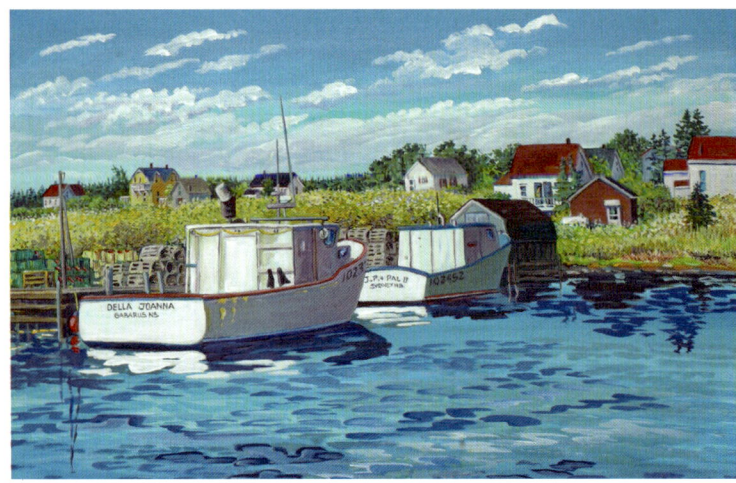
White Boats at Gabarus

18

A huge orange harvest moon to the east,
To the west a glorious rose sky
With dark mauve clouds scuttling along.
In front of me is Gabarus:
Houses perched on the headlands,
A cove filled with Cape Island boats,
Lights glowing in the fish store windows.
While the cove is a flat mirror of peace,
The raucous gulls wheeling overhead
Add an element of excitement.
I am here for a week
By myself in a small rented yellow house.

Early the next morning when I am sitting outside painting,
The villagers start to come by
With food and with stories.
"There used to be five shops and two fish plants here."
"I brought you chicken soup and biscuits for your dinner."
"The main road used to be along the shore but it eroded away.
 Now the backs of the houses face the new road."
"We brought you six cookies, a Pepsi, and a banana."
"I used to live in Gabarus.
 Now it's all changed and
 My friends and relatives are in the cemetery."
"You said that you liked my blueberry cake yesterday
 And so I have brought you another piece today."
Nowhere else have I ever received so much food.
Everyone wants to welcome me
And see what I am up to.

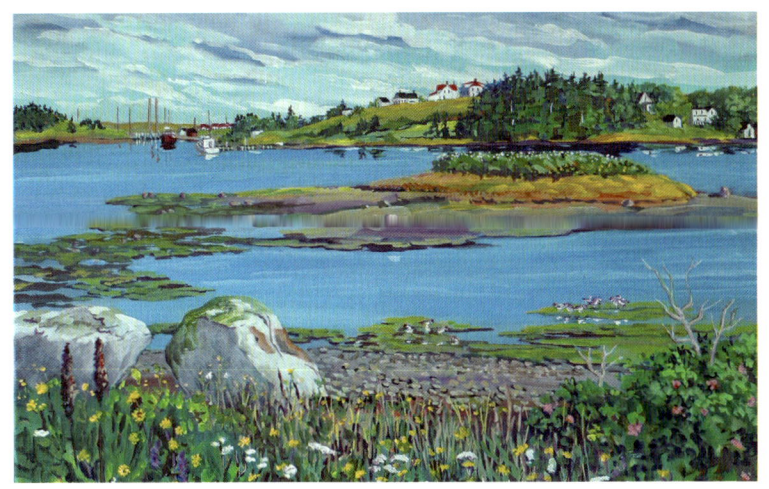
Back Bay at Gabarus

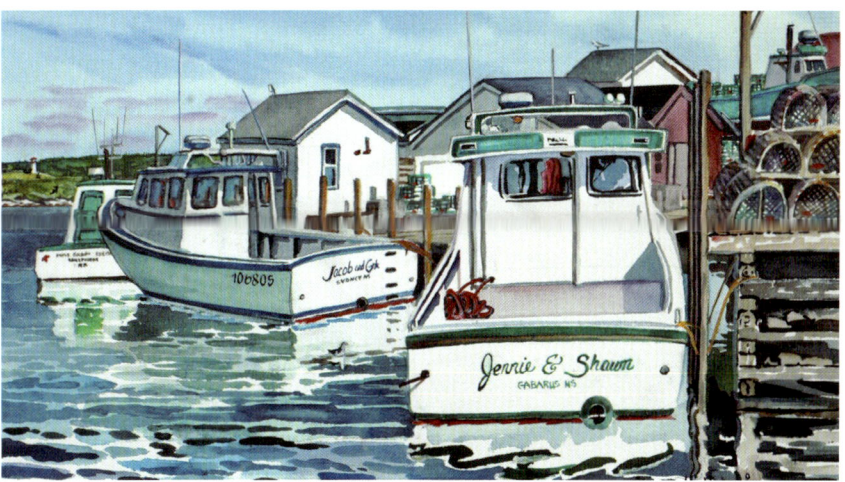
Boats at Gabarus

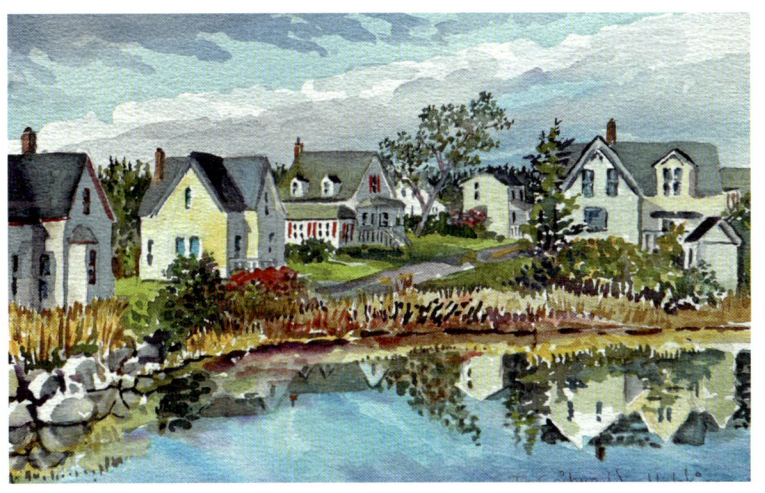
Gabarus 45.8376 -60.1373

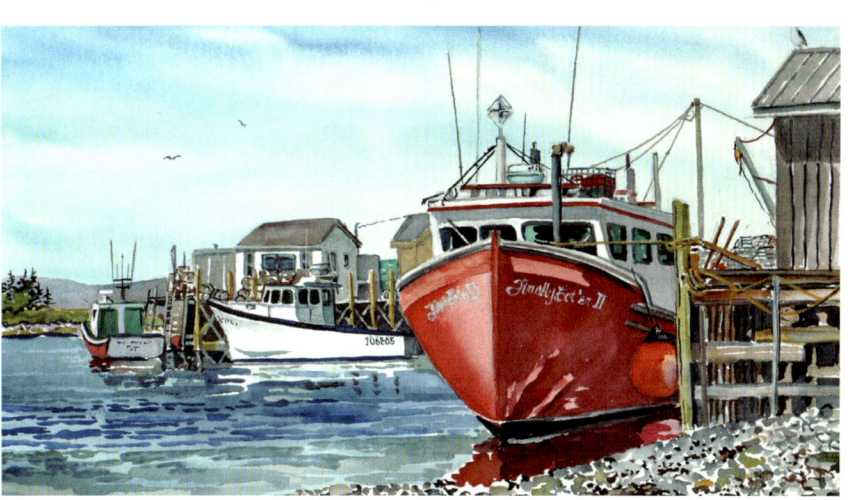
"Finally Got 'Er II"

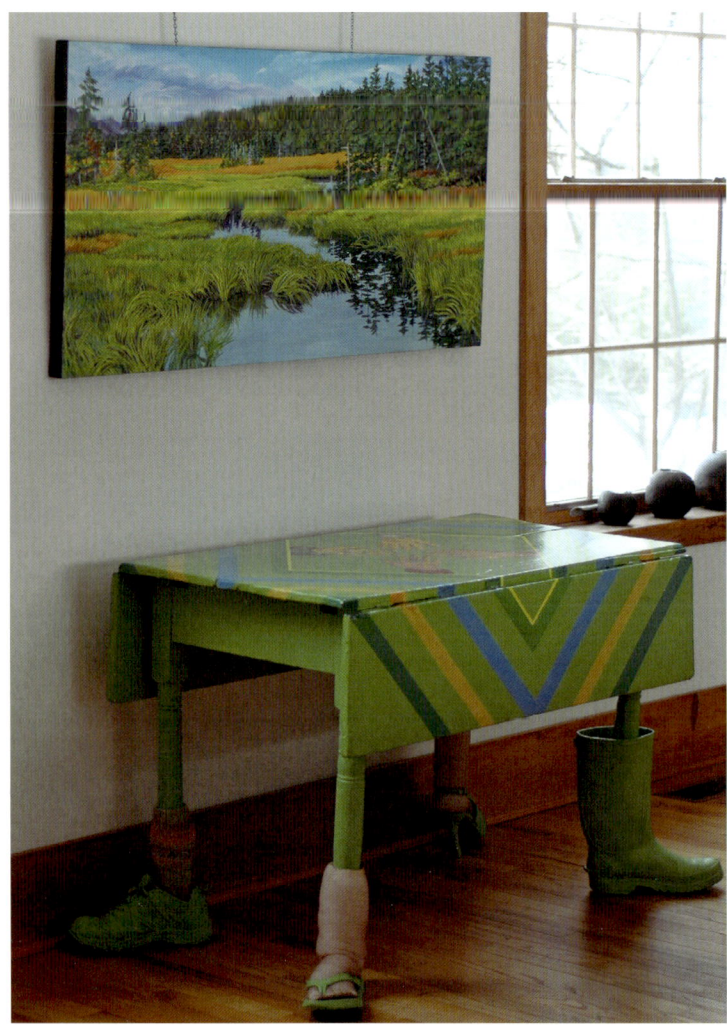

 Often a painting influences the subsequent painting by its theme, colour, or paint handling. Sometimes, a painting actually influences a totally different sort of art.

This painting of a marsh in Grand Greve suddenly got me thinking about doing a table to go with it. I just happened to have an old table that the legs had been cut shorter. I decided to add four different feet to bring the table up to eating height. I made the feet to represent each one of my three children and myself. In the centre of the tabletop I painted our four hands. Once the table was finished, I wrote a story for children called "The Adventures of Dog and Table." This led to a long chapter book and this has led in turn to a project that is in my back pocket and will take me at least six months to illustrate.

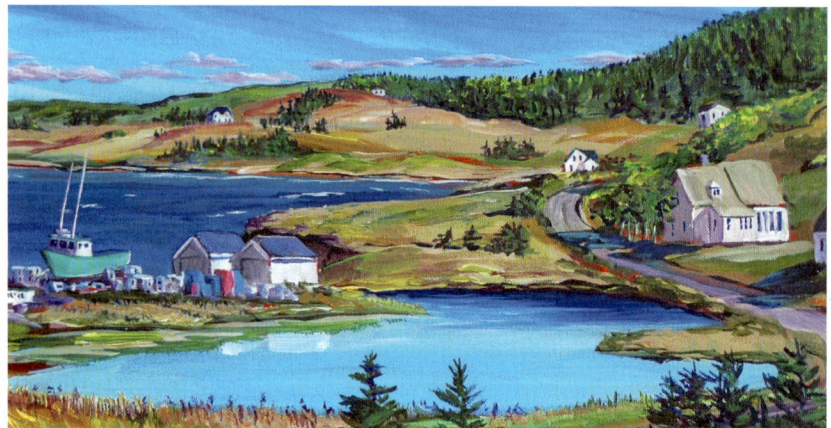

Grand Greve with Table

L'Ardoise

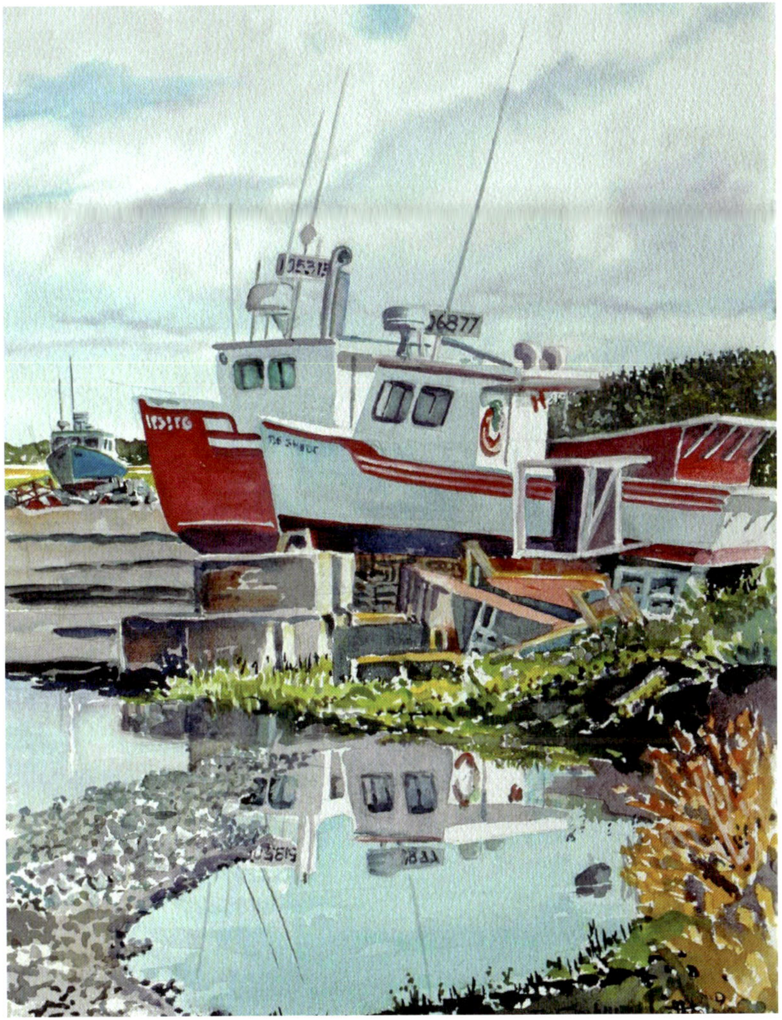

Boats at Little Harbour 45.5813 -60.7397

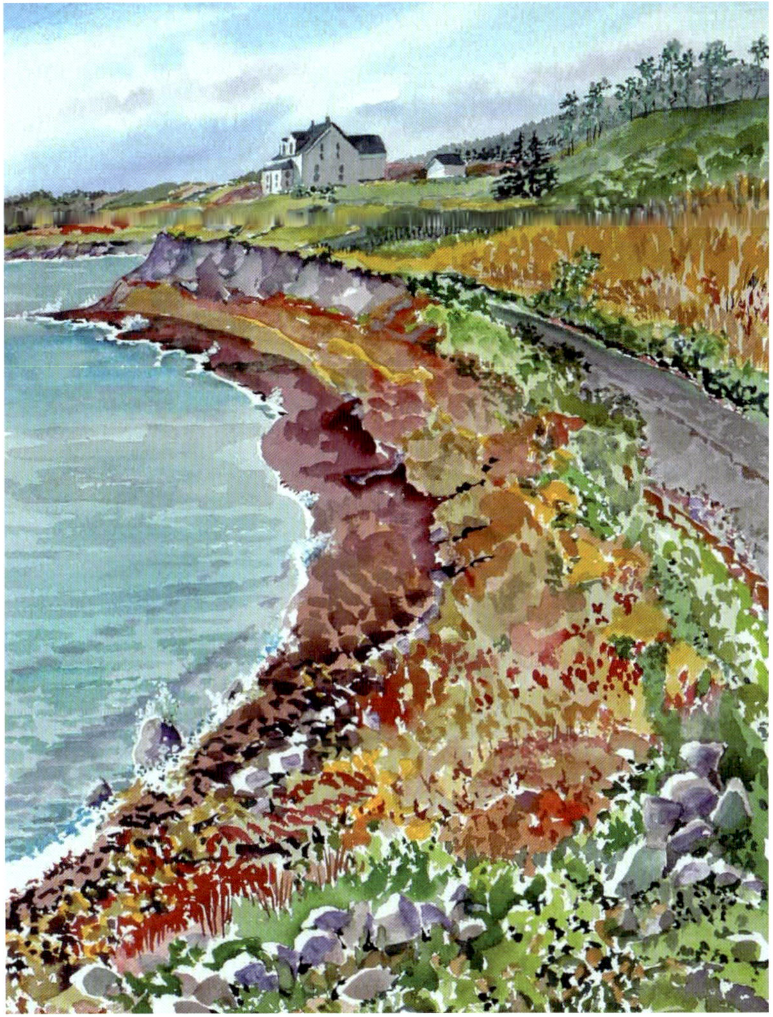

Harold Westlake's Old House, L'Ardoise

The Painted Province 49

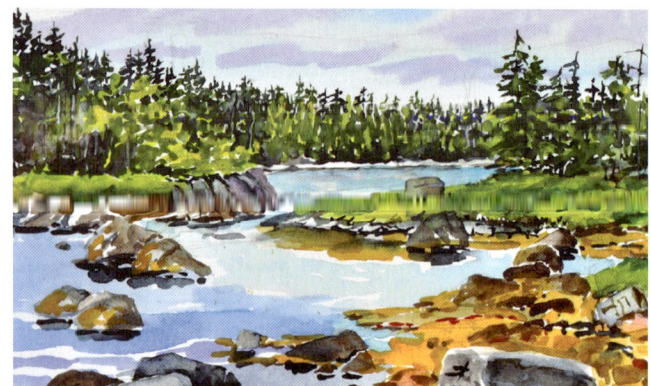
The Shanties (watercolour)

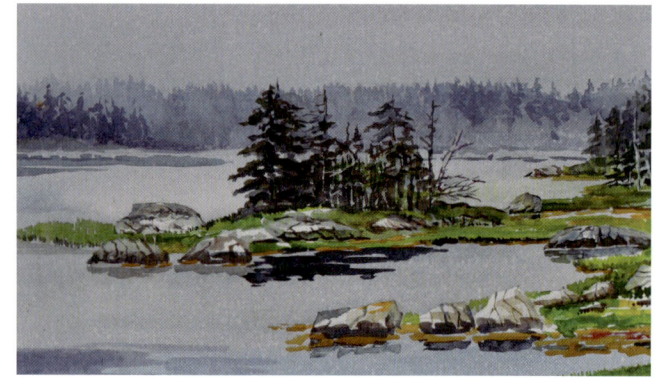
Foggy Morning 45.1023 -61.7608

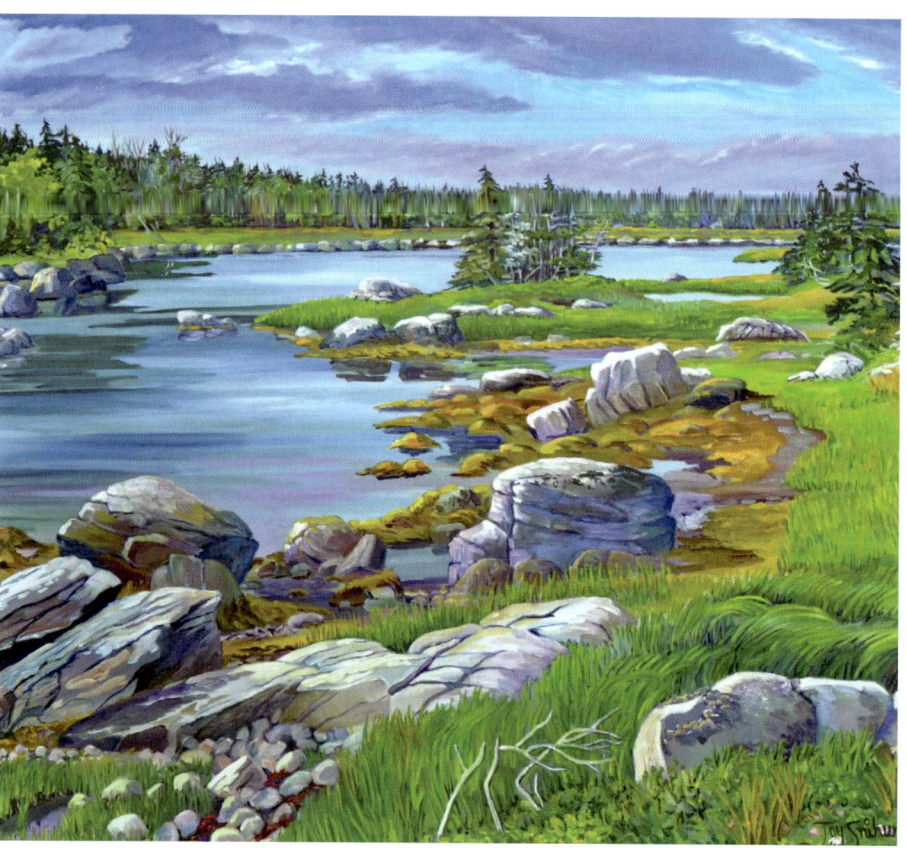
The Shanties (acrylic)

 Here are three paintings of The Shanties, all of the same view but completely different in feeling. I started out doing the sunny watercolour with the light almost glowing on the orange rockweed. By the time I was finished, the tide was high and the fog was in. A different sort of beauty and I started again to capture that. I was so in love with this spot that I went back again the next two days to do the large acrylic.

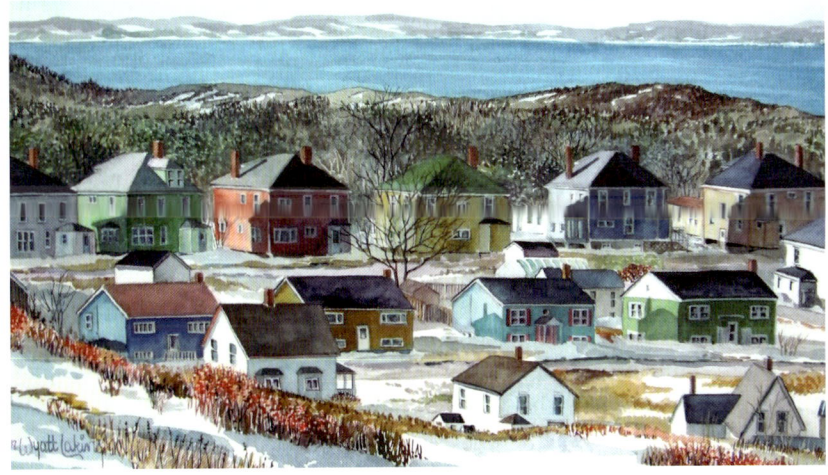

Canso

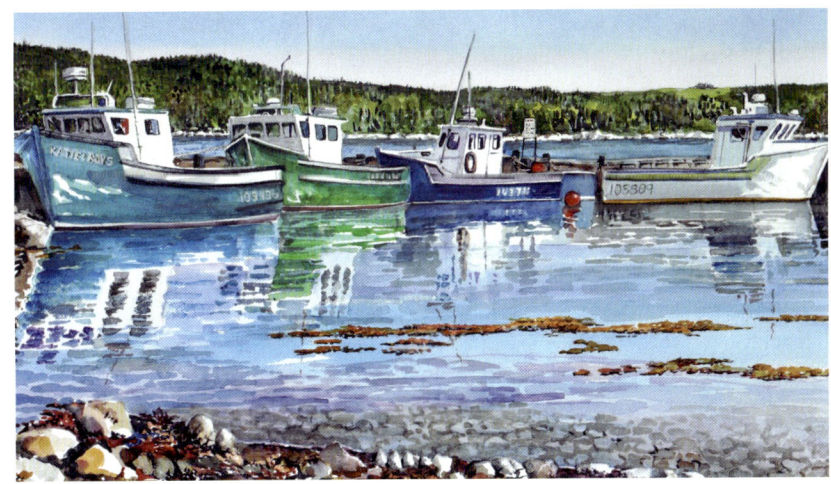

Fisherman's Cove

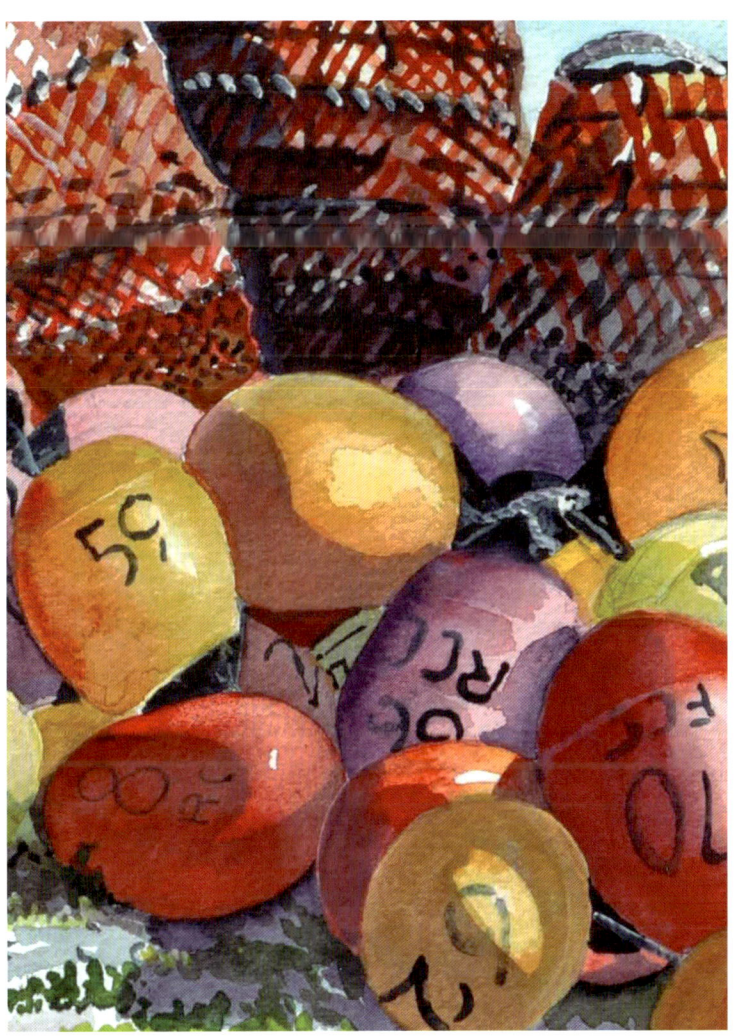

Crab Traps and Buoys

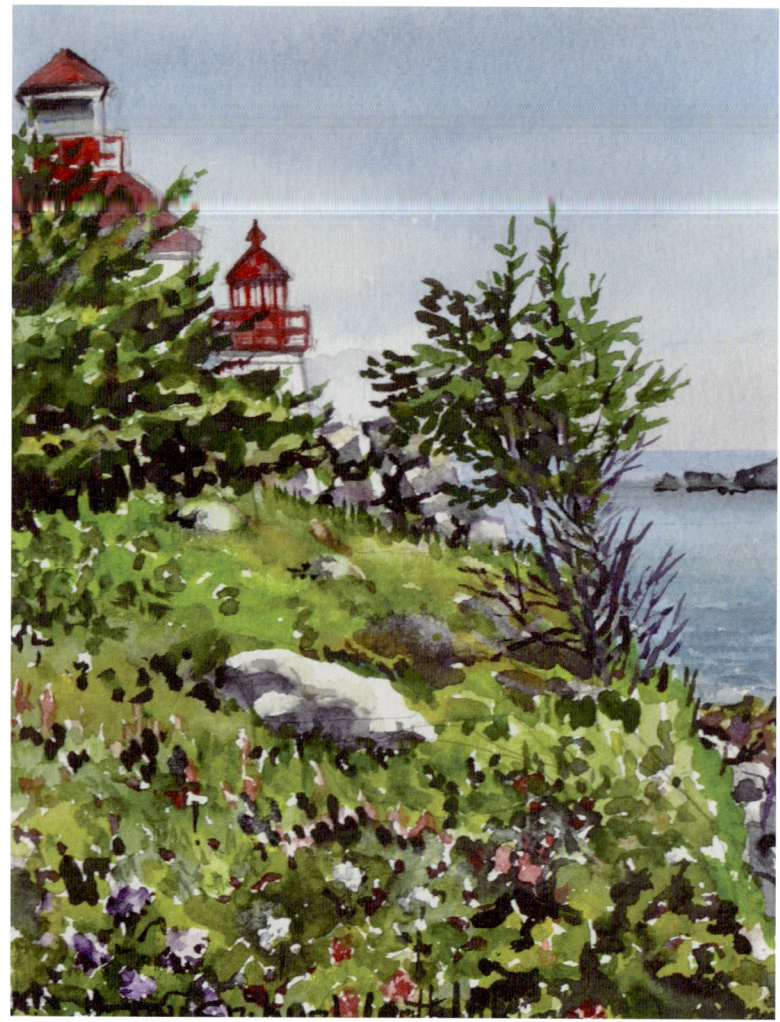

Port Bickerton Lighthouses

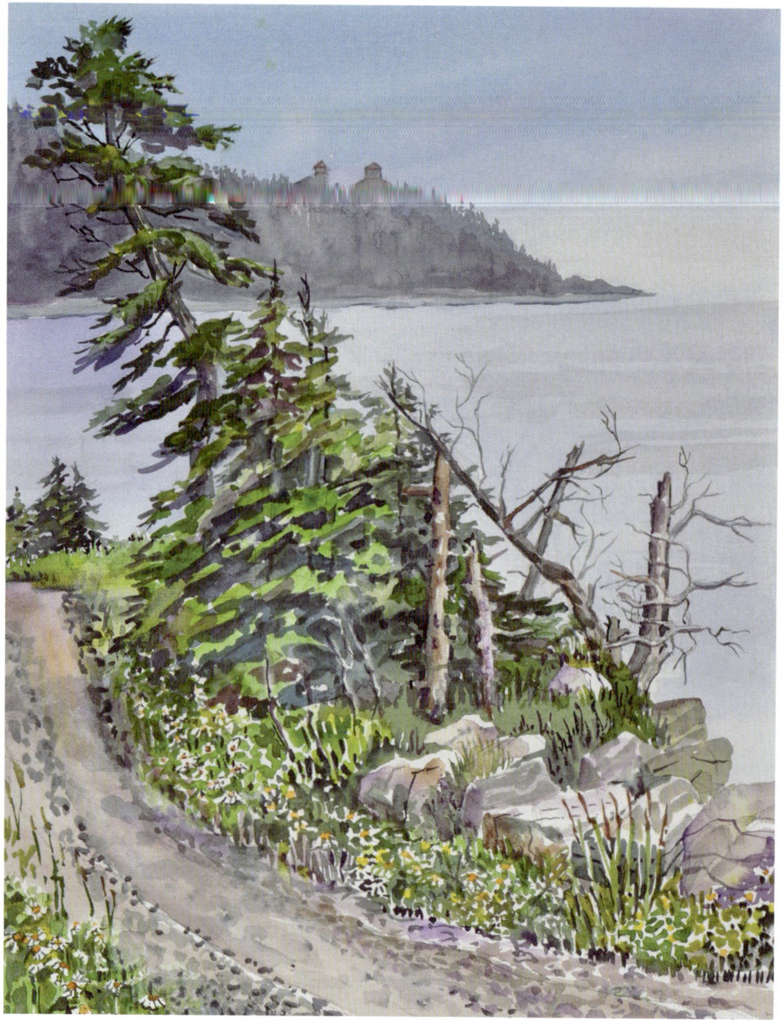

Lighthouses in the Fog

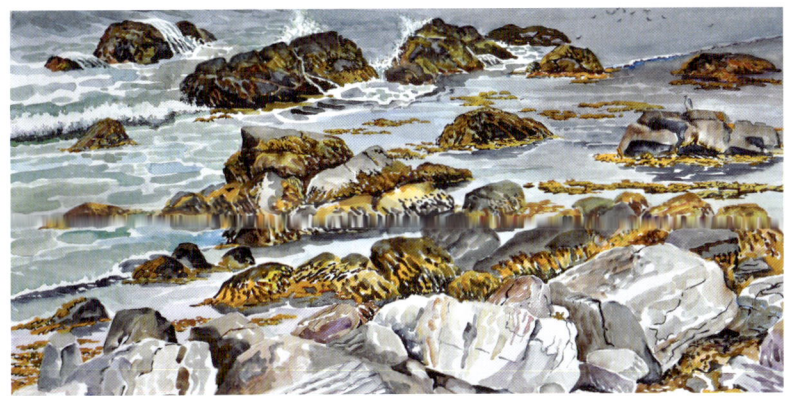

Foggy Day at Port Bickerton 45.0904 -61.7019

21

My painting chair is plunked
On a textured yellow green carpet
Of lycopodium, bunchberry, yarrow,
And a low raspberry-like runner with
Shiny red berries that taste delicious.
The odd stunted spruce leans
Like a drunken sentinel In front of me,
A willet peeps to a landing
On a wet rockweed covered rock.
Beyond the other enormous gray rocks,
A merganser glides down.
All the while, the foghorn moans
And slate gray waves roll in
Exploding on the rocks.
Their power spent,
They dissolve into quiet cerulean pools.

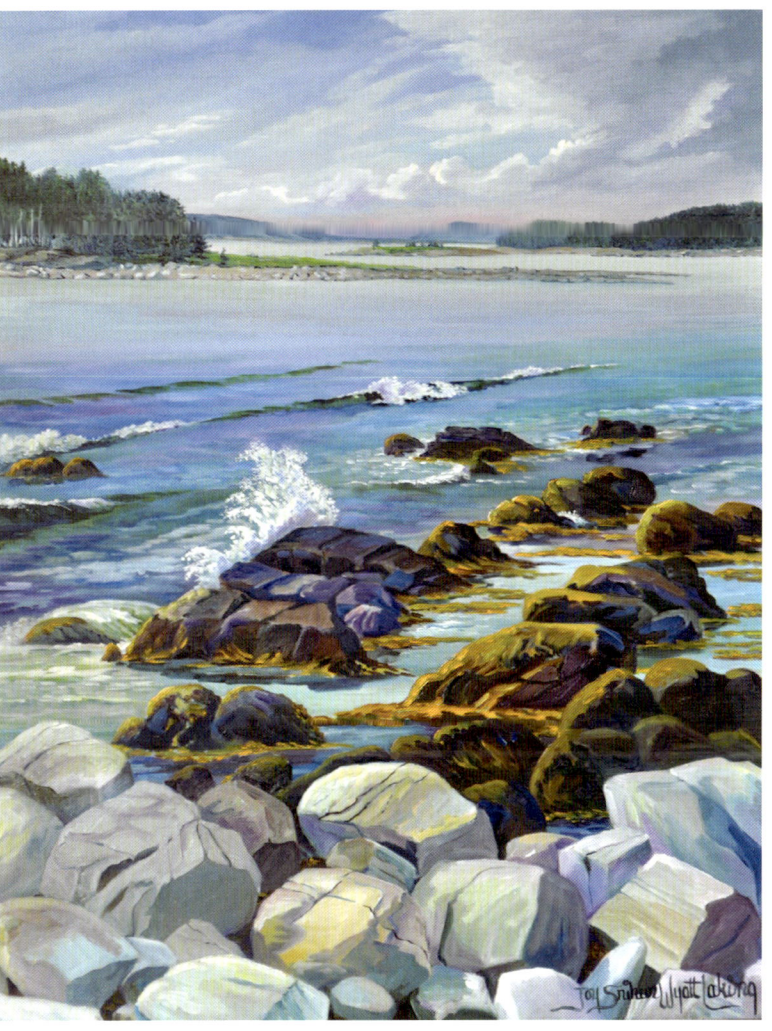

Surf at Port Bickerton

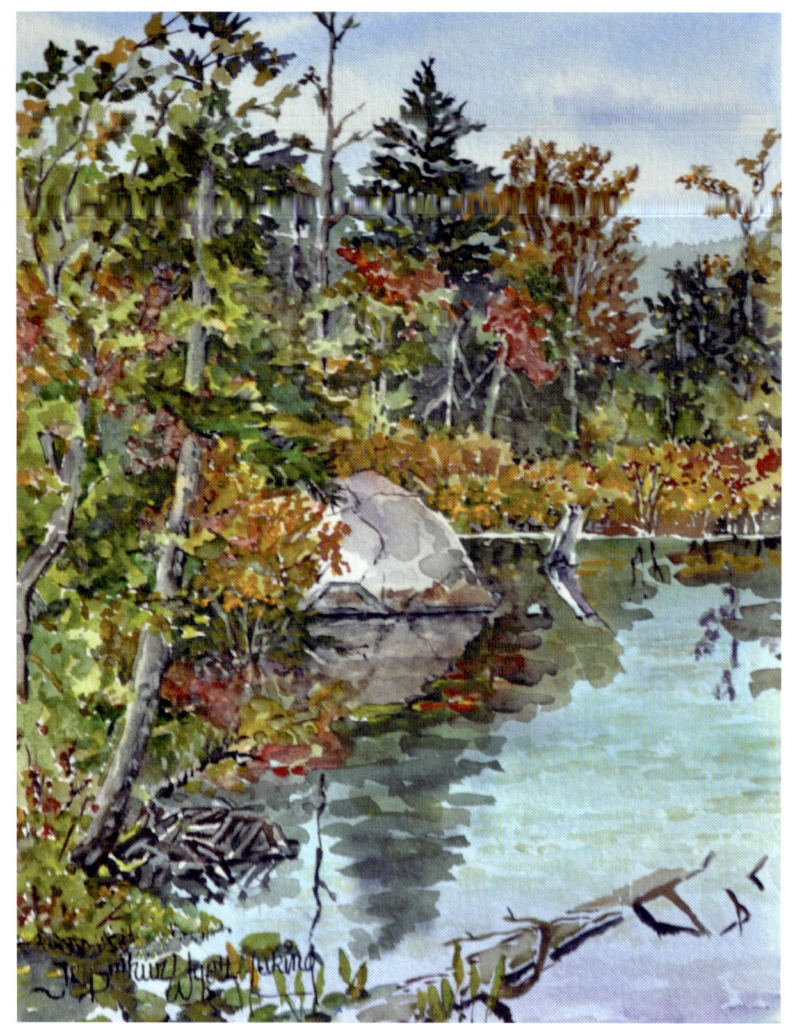

Autumn, West Chezzetcook

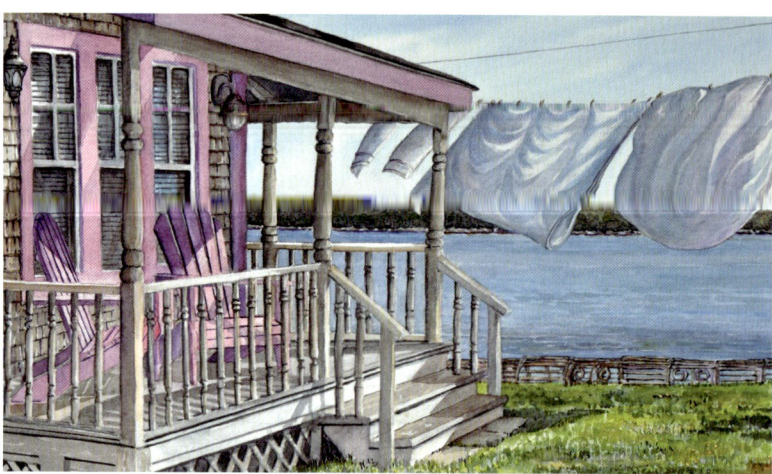

Sheets and Pink Porch, West Jeddore

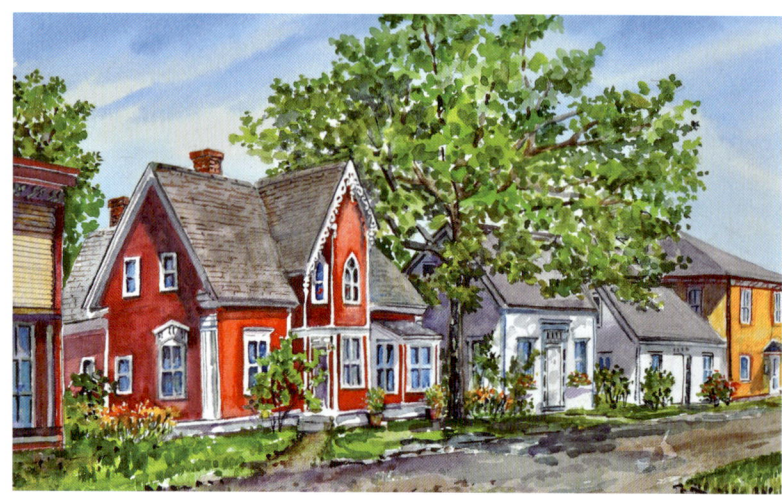

Sherbrooke Village 45.1402 -62.9844

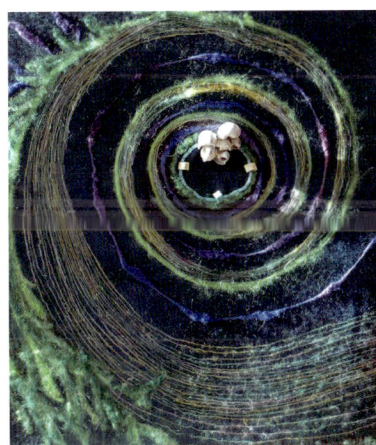

Sea Felting (dyed wool, shells, lobster bands)

22 I sat on Martinique Beach for an entire day, watching, listening to, and painting the waves. At the end of the day, I felt like I had distilled thousands of waves into one perfect painting. This feeling of complete satisfaction happens only very occasionally. When I look at these "perfect" paintings years after they are done, I still think, "Wow, I did that!"

What's the point of this story? Many of these paintings are still unsold. This particular one I eventually gave to myself and I enjoy it every day. One of the biggest challenges for artists is to paint only for oneself and not get mired in the opinions of others. As an artist, all we have is our own vision. The secret is to just keep working, just keep trying.

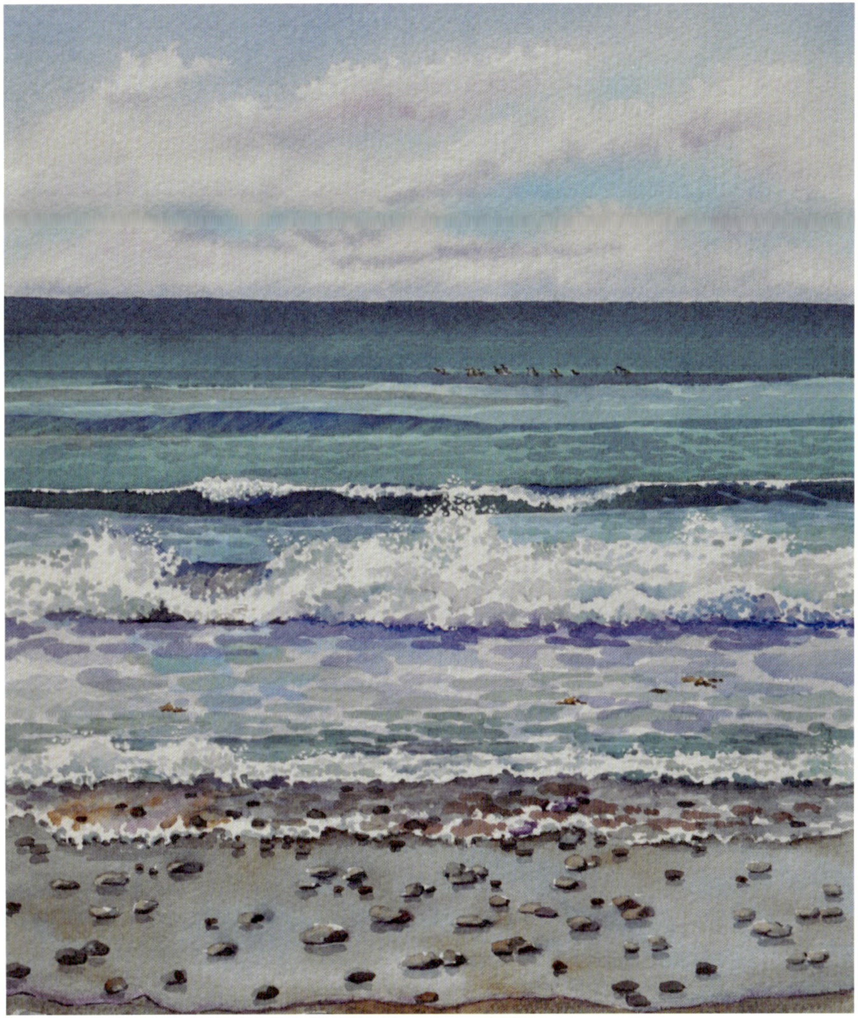

Martinique Beach

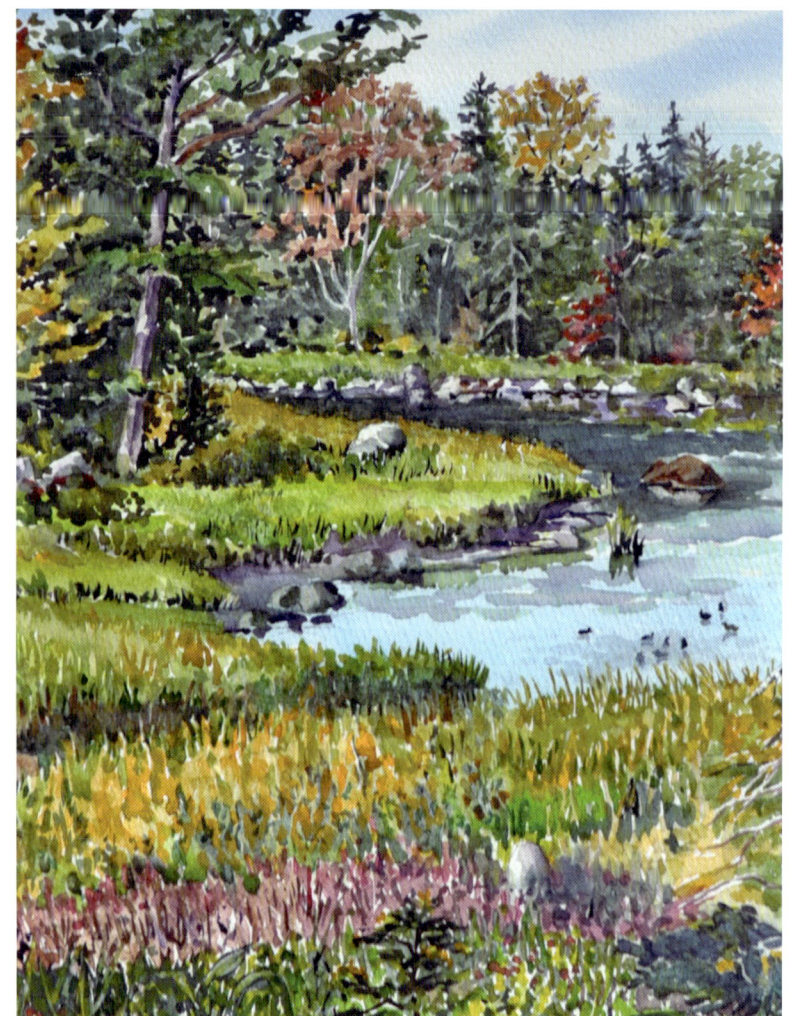

West Lawrencetown

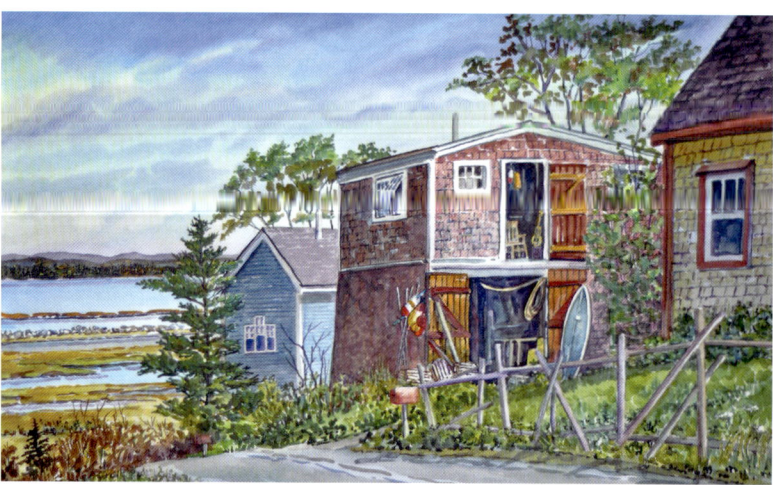

Red Shed on Dyke Road, Grand Desert 44.6917 -63.2539

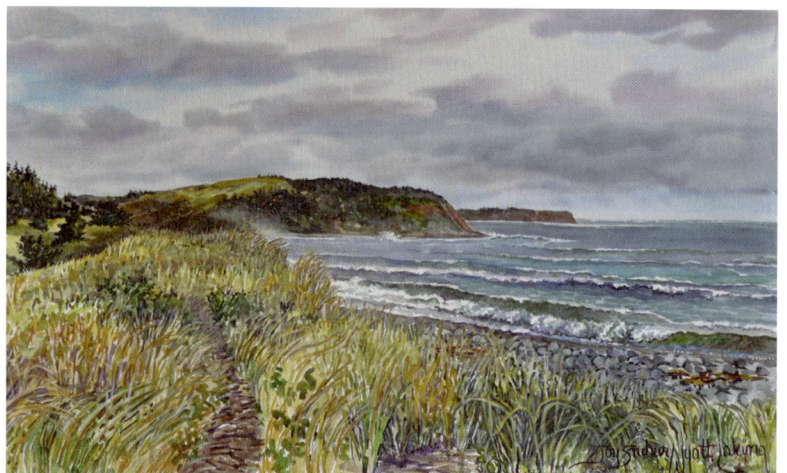

Lawrencetown Beach

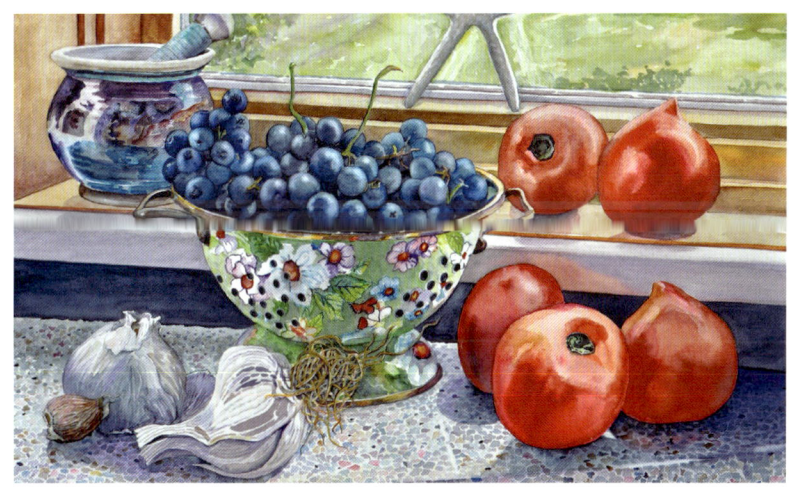

Garlic, Tomatoes, and Grapes

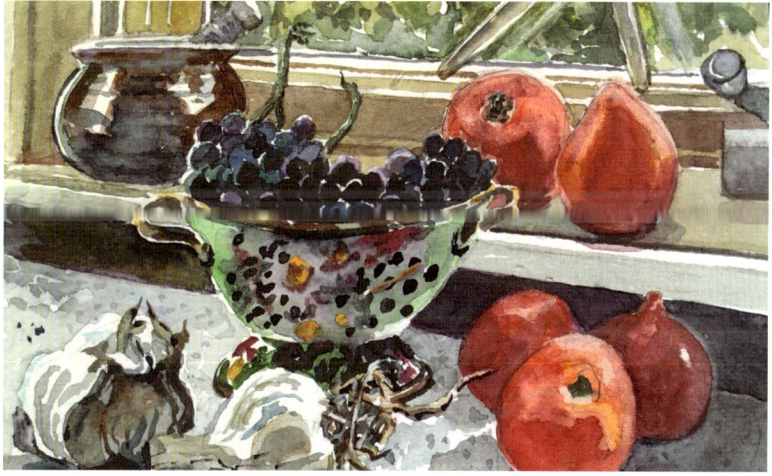

On Location Sketch for Garlic, Tomatoes, and Grapes

Often in the fall, I have a very hard time moving back into the studio instead of painting out on location. Usually when I return indoors, I start with a still life, or a view in front of me. This year, while painting in Lawrencetown on the Eastern Shore in late September, I was smitten with this still life. However, I didn't get any rainy days and I felt I had to take advantage of the weather by working outside. One morning, the lighting on the still life was spectacular. I spent an hour or so on a little sketch. I took photos and did a large pencil outline on a half-sheet of watercolour paper before heading out for the day. As a result, this fall I could hardly wait to get home and into the studio to add the paint.

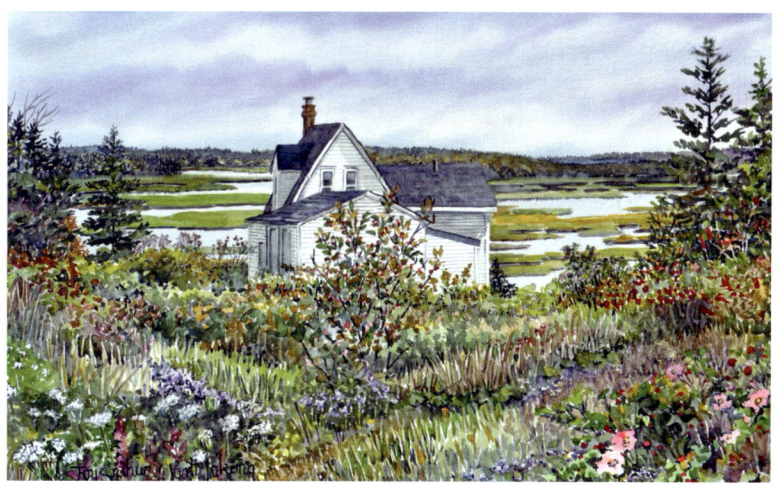

House and Marsh, Grand Desert

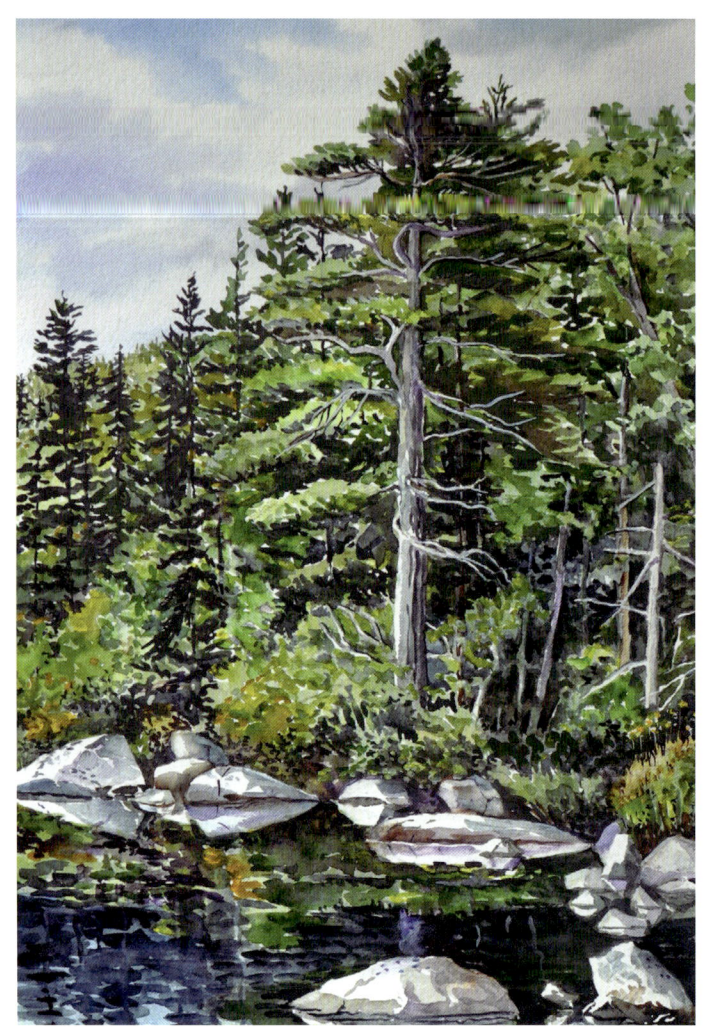

Hobson Lake with Pine

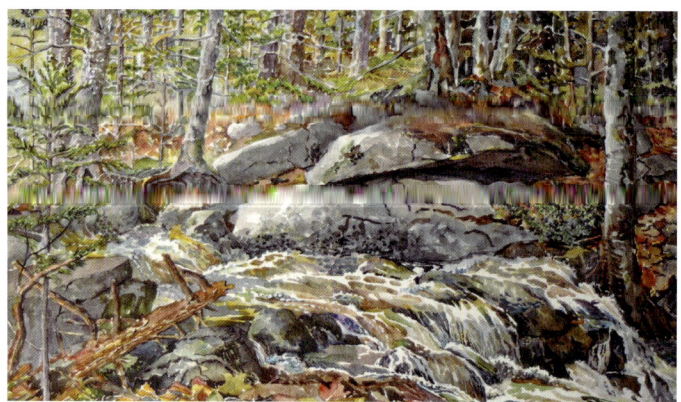

Stream near Hobson Lake 44.6947 -63.7117

24 Recently the Province of Nova Scotia made a protected wilderness area within the Halifax Regional Municipality. A small but mighty team of volunteers, the Friends of Blue Mountain-Birch Cove Lakes Society, was formed to support this project and to encourage the acquisition of the lands around it. Twice I have been guided into Hobson Lake for a day of painting. This is one of the most beautiful places in this book as well as the hardest to get to.

When I moved to Nova Scotia forty-eight years ago, I lived for a few years on Kearney Lake adjacent to this area of marvellous woods and water. Since that time, the area has experienced urban sprawl. Having additional lands protected will provide a healthy, beautiful Nova Scotia buffer to our "could be anywhere" North American city life. Even more importantly, our planet desperately needs to mitigate climate change for all of our animals, including our children and their children. (www.bluemountainfriends.ca)

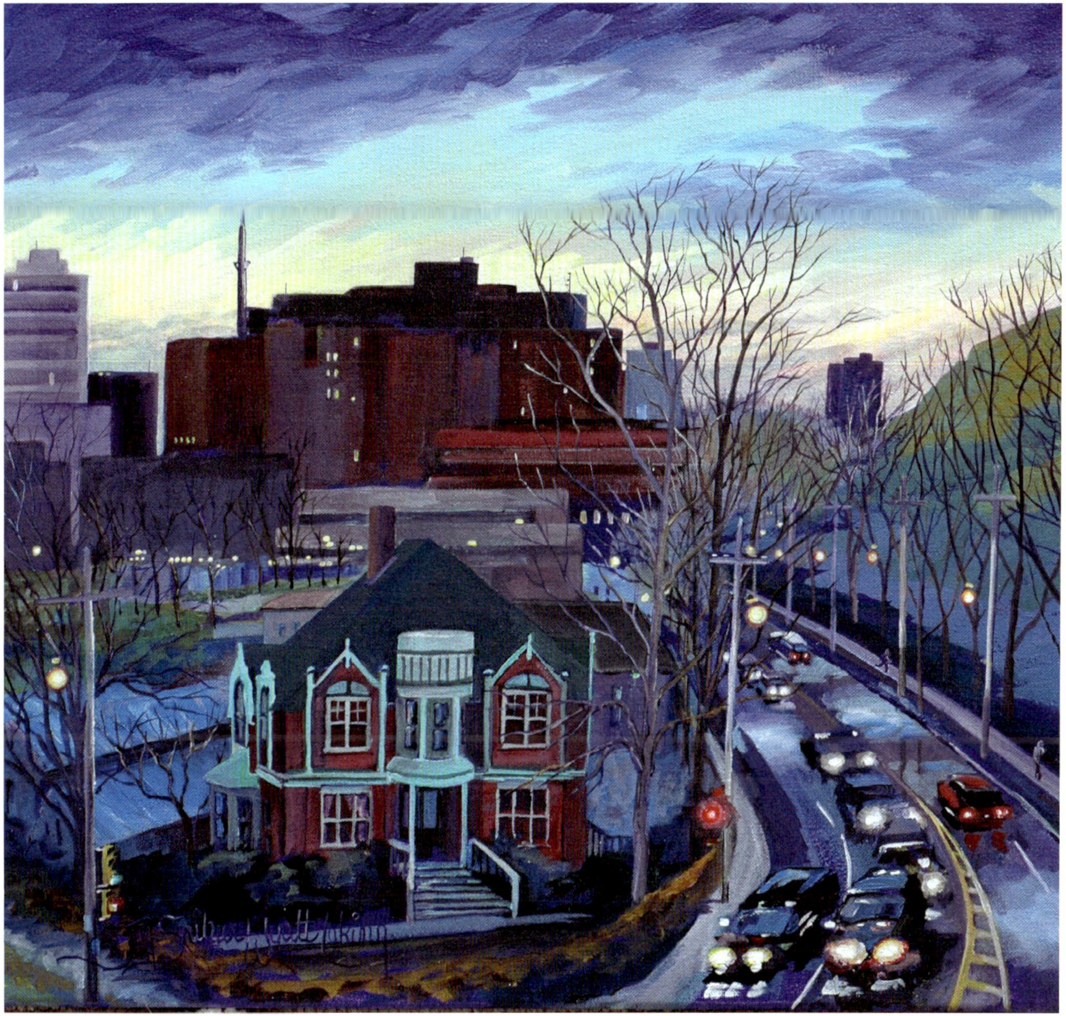

Early Morning from the old CBC Building in Halifax

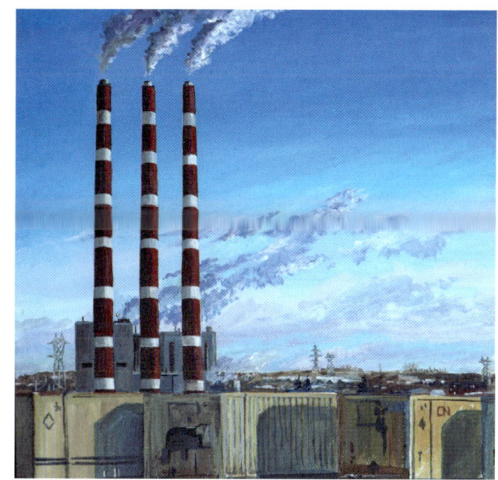

Three Stacks

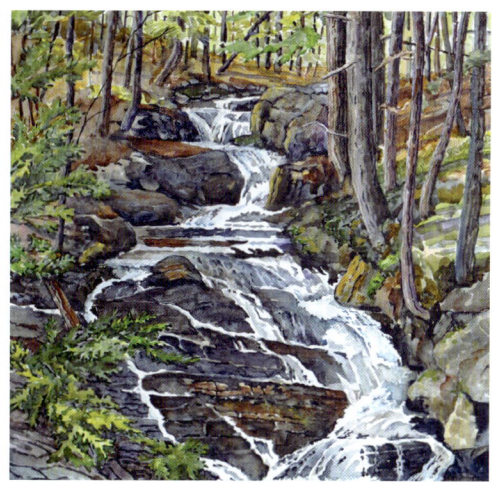

Tannery Falls, Grand Lake

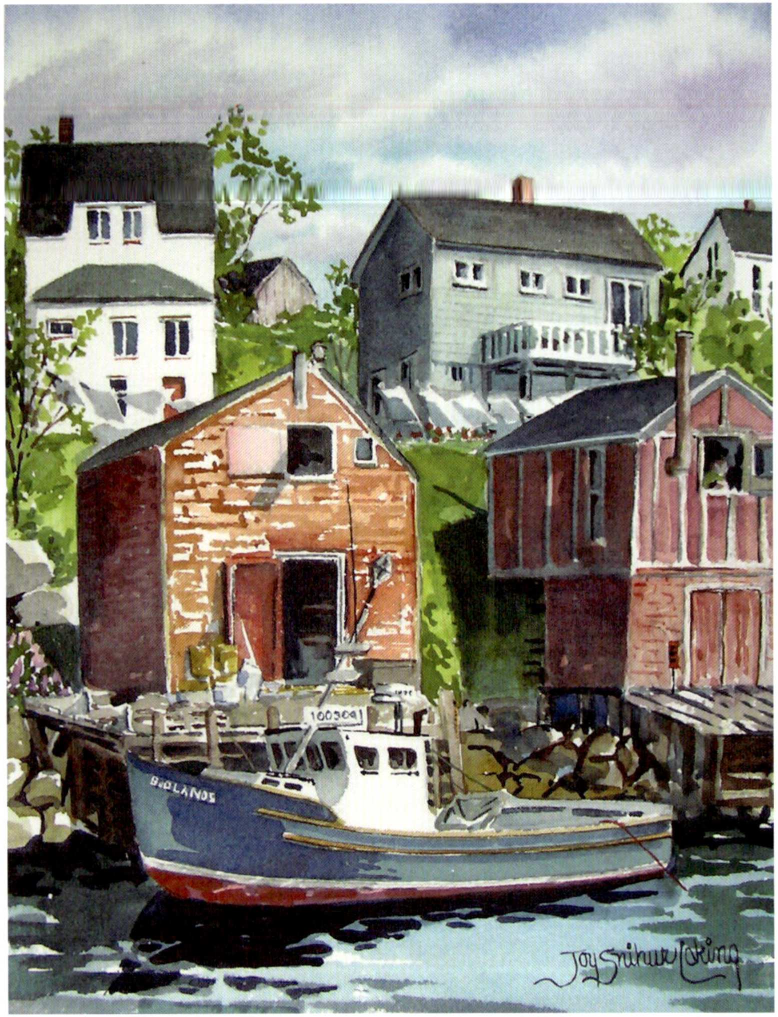

When I started in watercolour, I had finished my degree in Fine Art, working in acrylics, and I was living in artistic isolation in Nova Scotia. (No mother handy to show me how to use watercolours and no Internet to glean ideas.) I will always be glad that I am self-taught since I developed my own style. Instead of the traditional approach of starting with light washes and working towards the darks, I start with the darks and shape the entire painting by jumping around and letting dark areas dry. Darks are more luminous and intense when they are put directly on white paper instead of layered over several washes. I leave the whites empty and at the very end I might tone them down with a tiny bit of coloured wash if they seem too dominant.

Many years ago, I was at an exhibition of paintings by a friend of mine. At a distance, I admired the highlights in her painting of a lively flowing stream. When I got up close, I could see that she had cut the highlights in with a razor blade. Sacrilege, I thought, destroying the integrity of the paper. I have certainly changed my tune now. Anything goes. I happily scrape in whites with a razor blade, scrub in highlights with my tiny scrubber brush, and use white gouache when needed.

Wash Day in Herring Cove

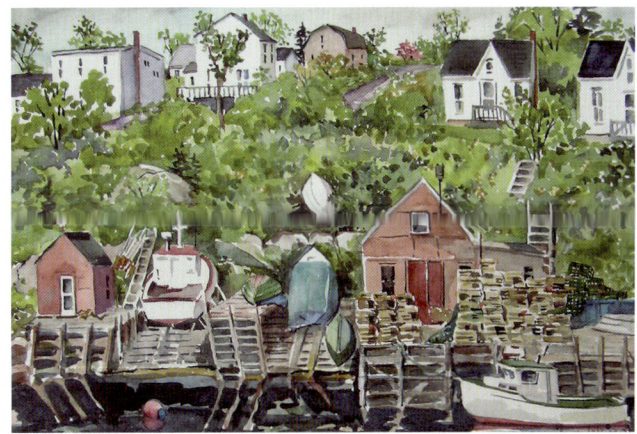
Herring Cove Sheds

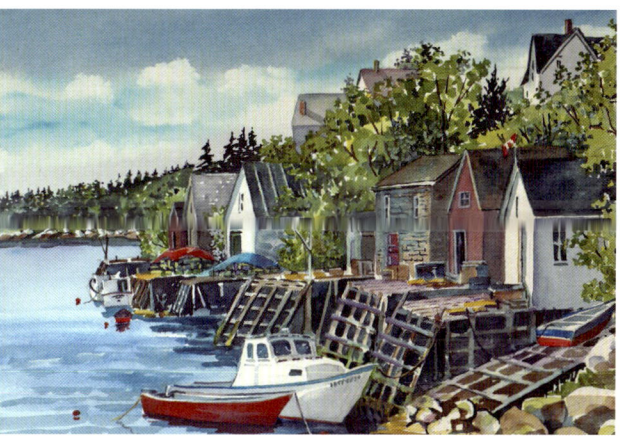
Herring Cove Harbour 44.5738 -63.5564

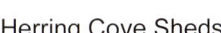
Chebucto Head

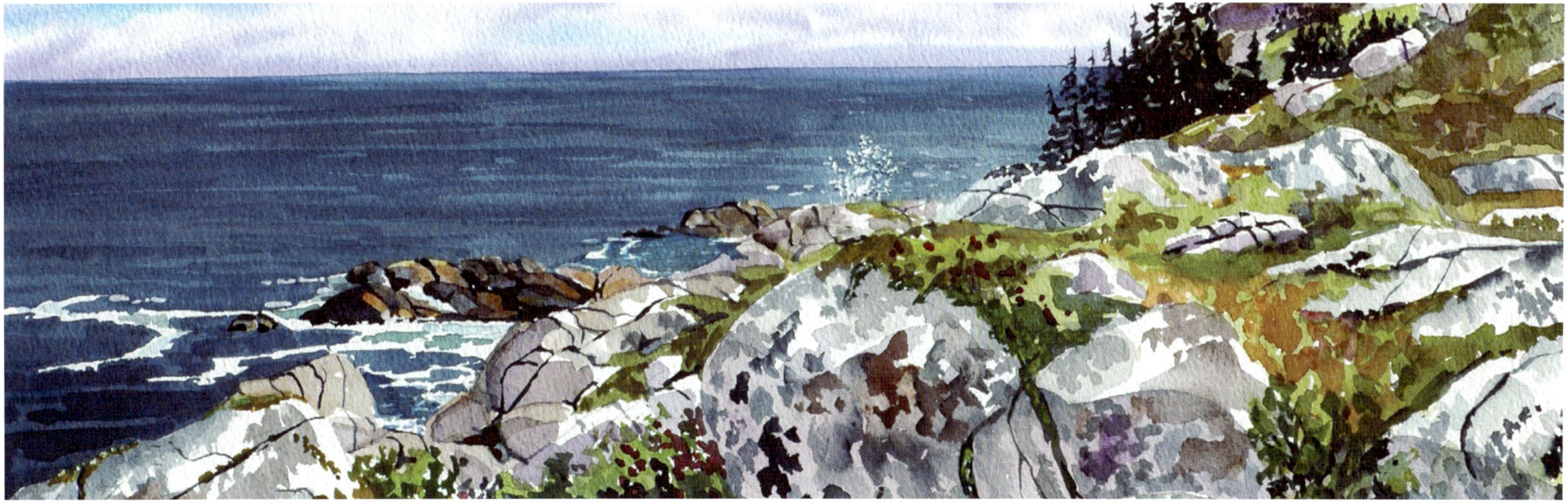

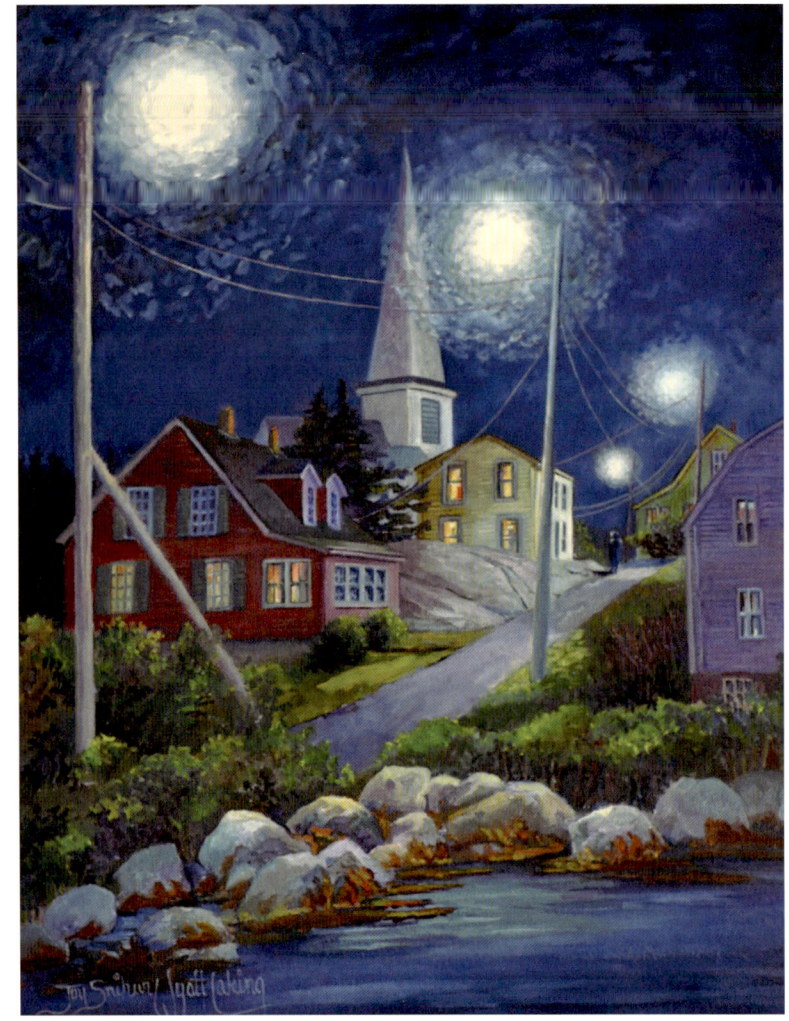

Night Time in Prospect 44.2711 -63.4330

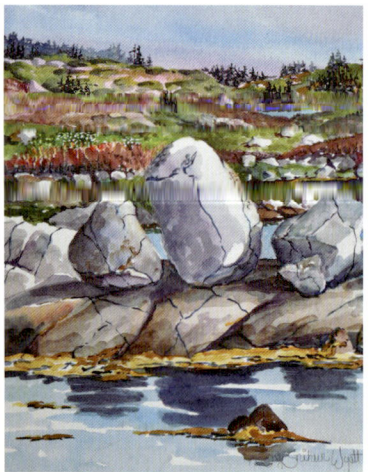

Morning Light

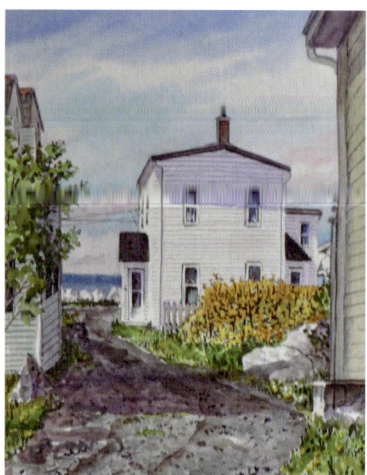

The Lane, Prospect

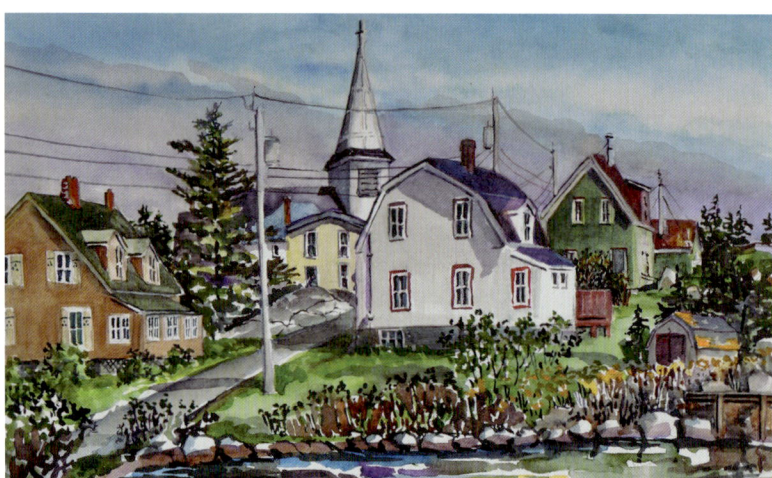

The Village of Prospect

62   Joy Snihur Wyatt Laking

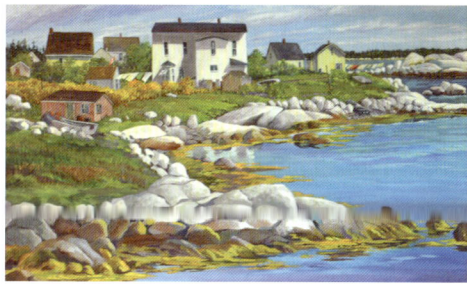

The salty air is heavy, and damp.
As the fog rolls in and out,
Gray shapes become islands.
Headlands, rock, trees,
And humps of sienna and ochre,
Appear and disappear.
Like a foghorn, a dove coos.
Two Canada geese skid down.
Swallows swoop.
Grackles, with blue heads and distinctive tails,
Play hide and seek In the wlld bamboo beside me.
Overhead, a heron slowly flaps by.
The stark white head and breast of a
Solitary standing seagull
Glows in this mute landscape.
As the tide slides in,
Amid rocks and eelgrass,
A weasel dashes out with one of its young in its mouth.
For hours, I sit, paint, write,
One more chord in this visual hymn.

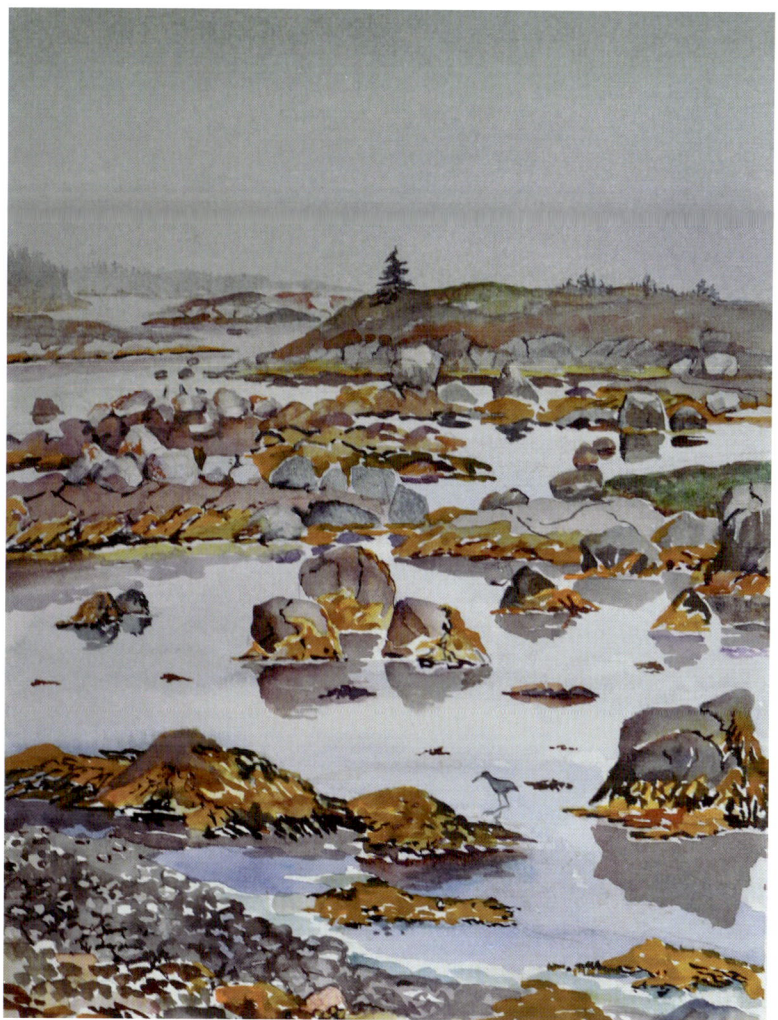

Back Bay in Prospect

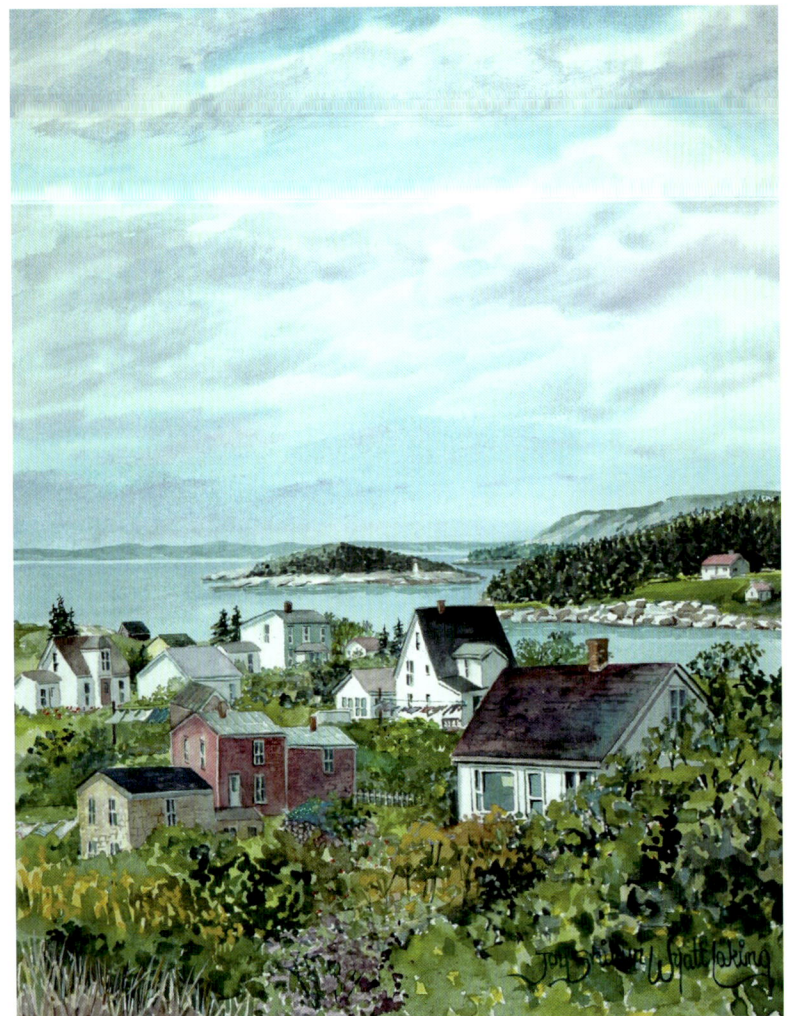

Indian Harbour

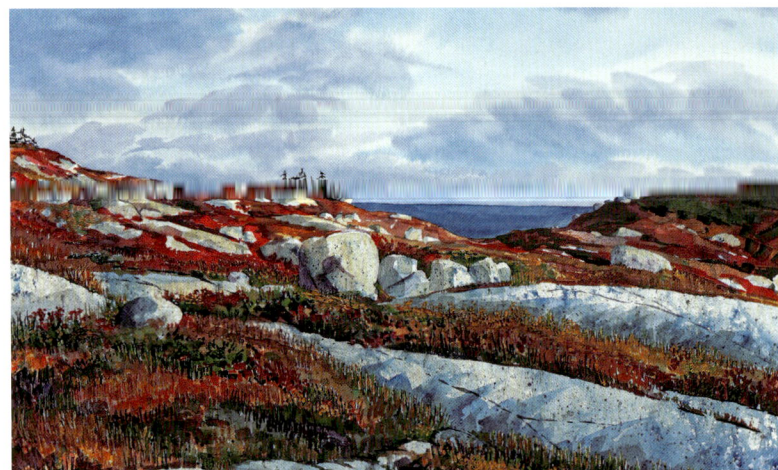

Rocks at Peggy's Cove

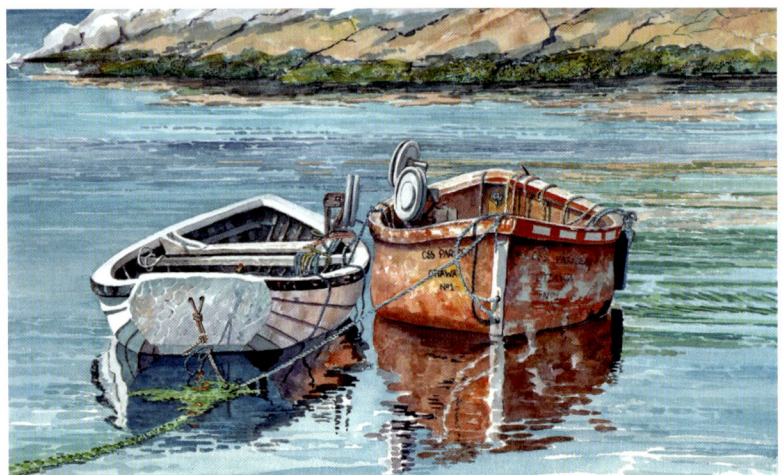

Two Boats

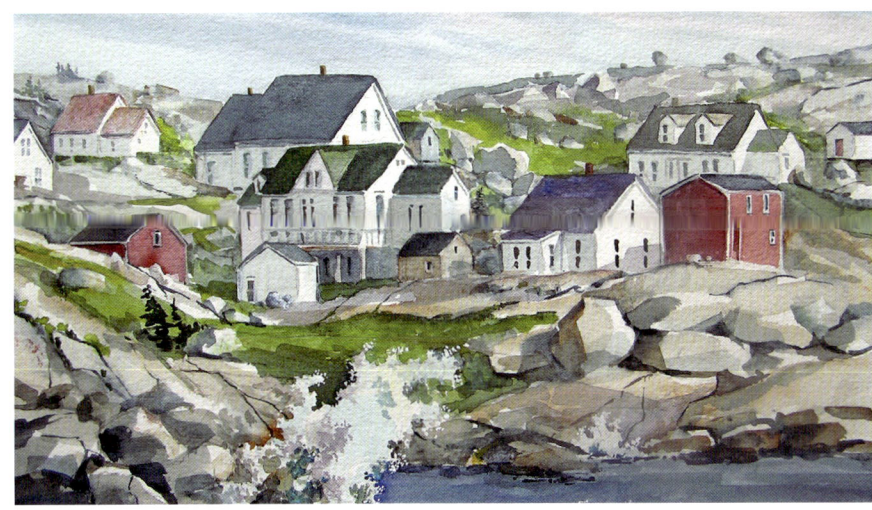

Village of Peggy's Cove

27 Peggy's Cove is Nova Scotia's most visited and photographed community. Set on bare well-worn granite, the lighthouse is a beacon for tourists and fishermen. When I was a child, my family would often come to Nova Scotia in the summer with our trailer. We would spend a full three weeks coming and going from Ontario. We travelled only the mornings. In the afternoons, my artist mother loved to paint on location. Northwest Cove was her favourite place in the world. Peggy's Cove was a close second. My dad would often sit on a rock and fish. You don't need an out-of-province fishing license to fish in the salt water. My brother, sister, and I would paint or fish or make new friends at the campground. This was my first introduction to Nova Scotia. I now feel so fortunate that this beautiful province has been my home for almost fifty years.

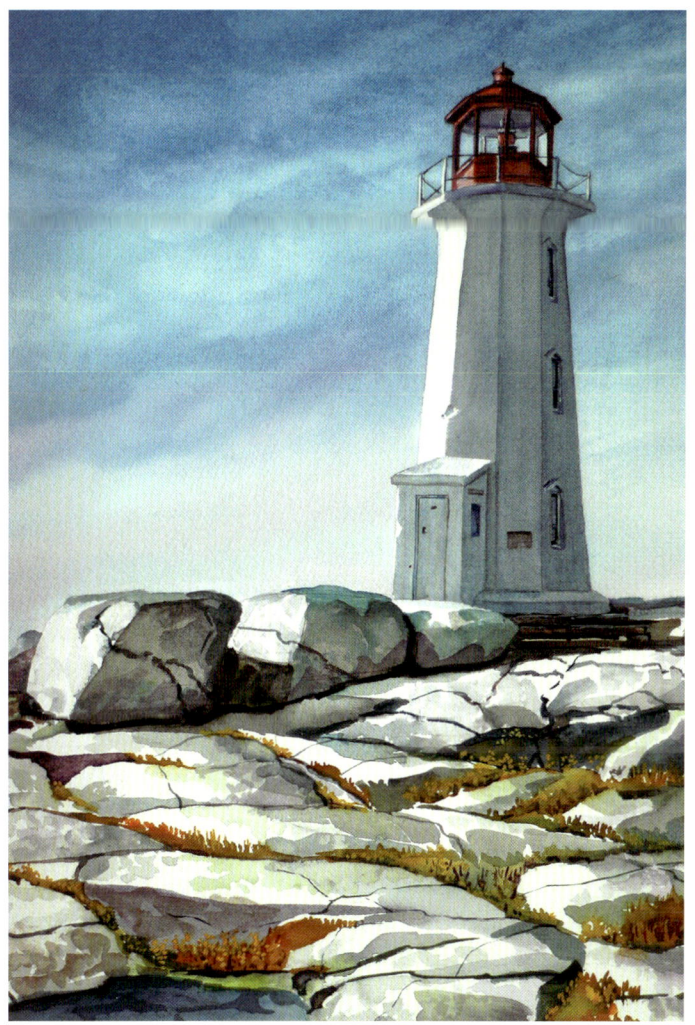

Peggy's Cove Lighthouse 44.4922 -63.9180

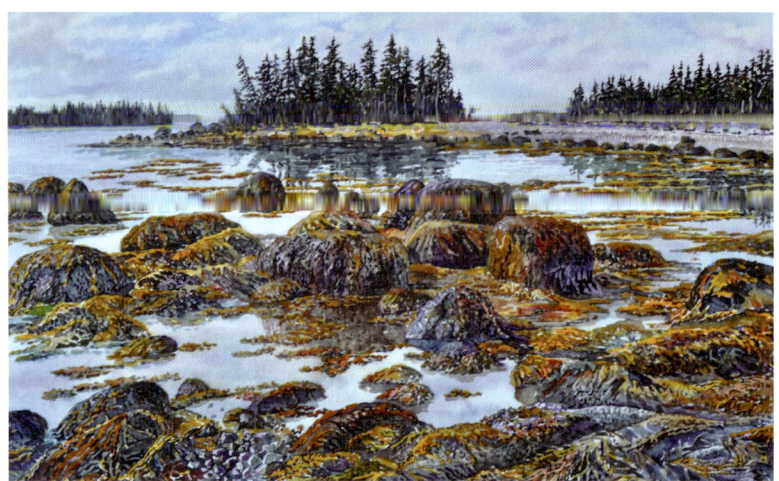

Micous Island 44.6332 -63.9361

28

It was the last day of my week of painting on the South Shore, and it was pouring rain. Never to be deterred and miss out on a painting day, I looked for a place where I could paint from inside the car. I found a driveway in Chester that looked out on this view. It was really early, not quite 7 a.m., so I didn't dare knock on the door to see if I could park in the driveway. I just parked there and got right to work.

When I get involved in my painting, I seem to zone out to the rest of the world. Suddenly, I was startled when someone knocked on my car window right beside me. A woman who spoke only a little English motioned for me to come into the house and I followed her inside. What a surprise awaited! Her husband was painting exactly the same view from inside the house. He was a professional artist from New York and he was excited to meet another artist. I still follow one of his little gems of advice: "When painting people, only look at one detail at a time." Eventually, he and I both went back to our paintings and when sun replaced the rain, I moved out of the car to paint. A little while later, the woman came with her guitar and sat down on a log near me and played me a concert of the most incredibly beautiful Spanish music while I did the last hour on the painting. Life couldn't get any better!

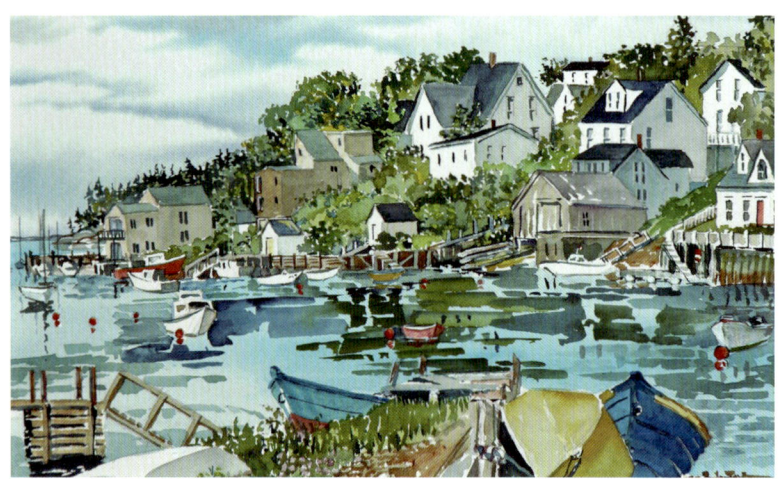

Chester

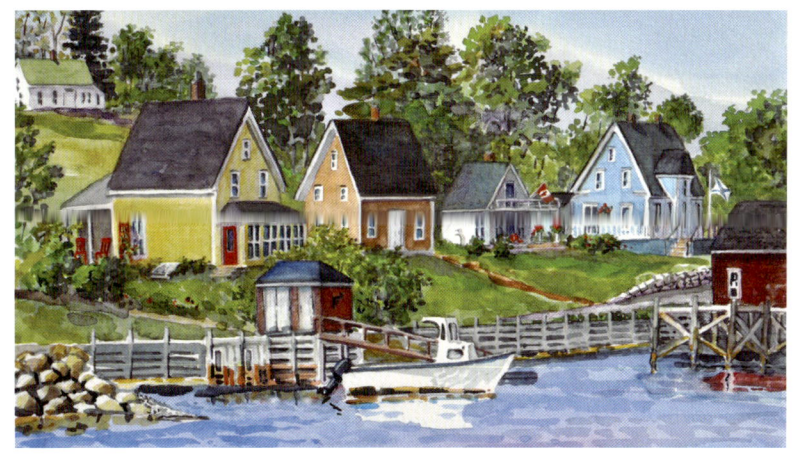

Mader's Cove

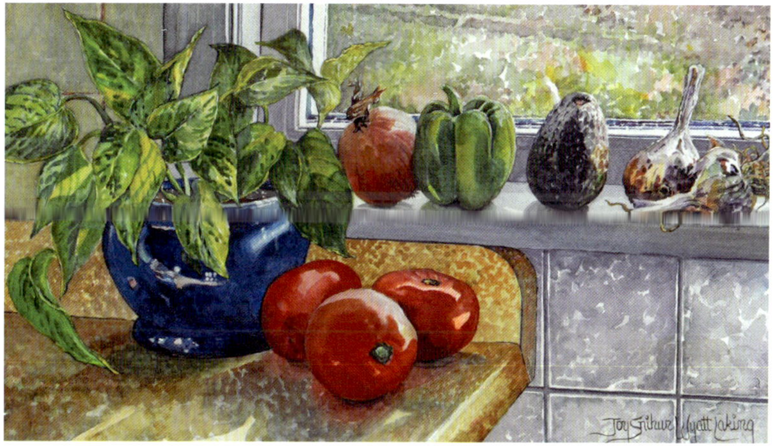

Still Life, Head of St. Margaret's Bay

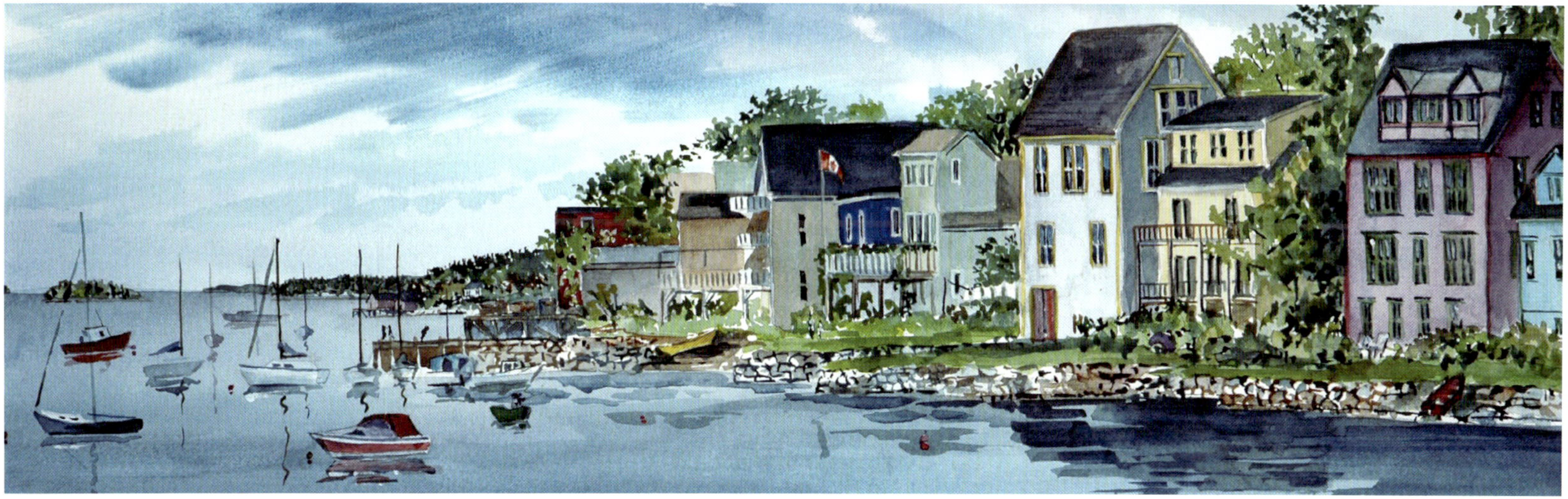

Mahone Bay

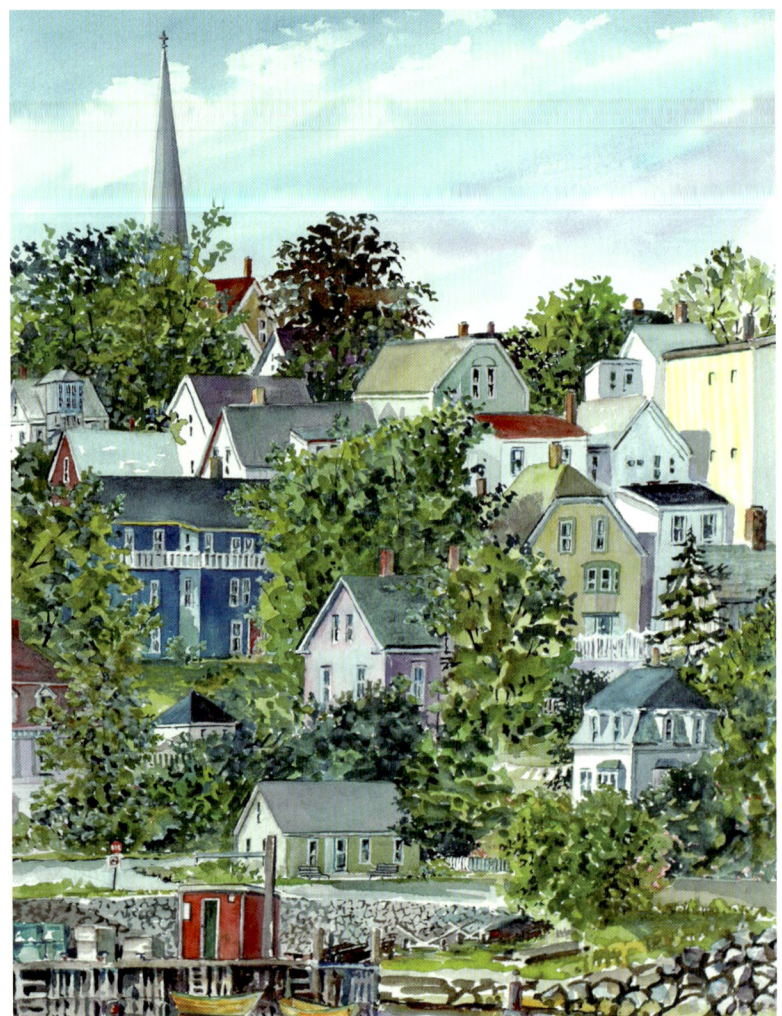

Lunenburg

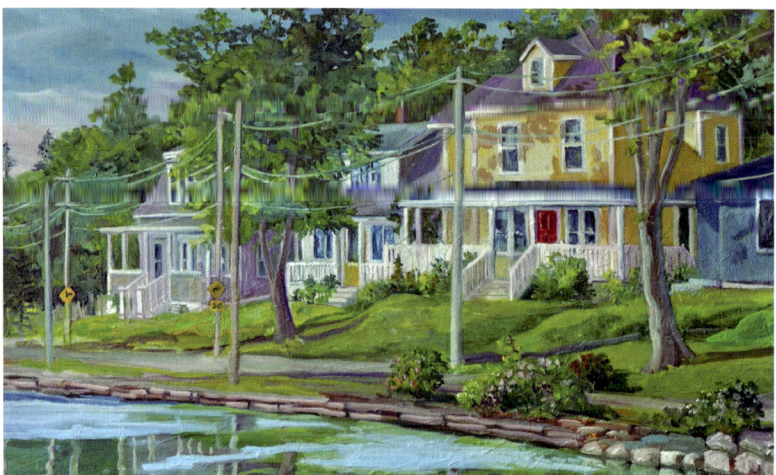

Lunenburg Houses 44.3759 -64.3170

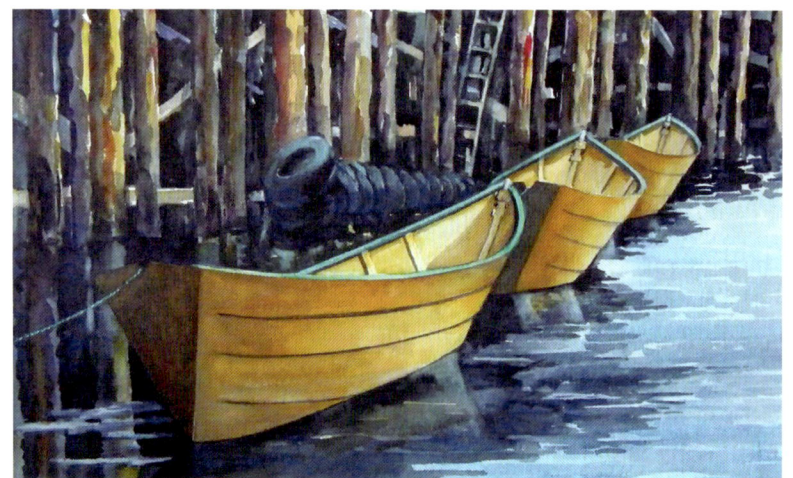

Dories

I met a woman in a big chain store in Dartmouth. "Are you Joy Laking?" she asked. When I nodded, she said that she was my friend on Facebook. I gave her a hug and we chatted for a minute or two.

A year later, I needed a cheap place to stay near Lunenburg. I posted my request on Facebook. Several people suggested places that I could rent, or a relative who might have an empty house available. Then, from the Facebook friend with whom I had briefly spoken a year before came an offer to share her home for a week. It wasn't right in Lunenburg, she apologized. Perhaps it was too far to be considered. When I said that it sounded perfect, she said, "Now I can get excited." She hadn't wanted to get her hopes up.

I went to stay with her and her family. They were in the middle of a family crisis. "You are a welcome diversion," they told me. It rained all seven days I painted in their area. Each day I drove into Lunenburg and painted an oil painting from inside my car. In the evenings, I arrived back to a warm meal, glasses of red wine, and conversation with my new friends. While painting Nova Scotia's beauty, I have met the most beautiful people. As well, my car, Malorie, will never look the same.

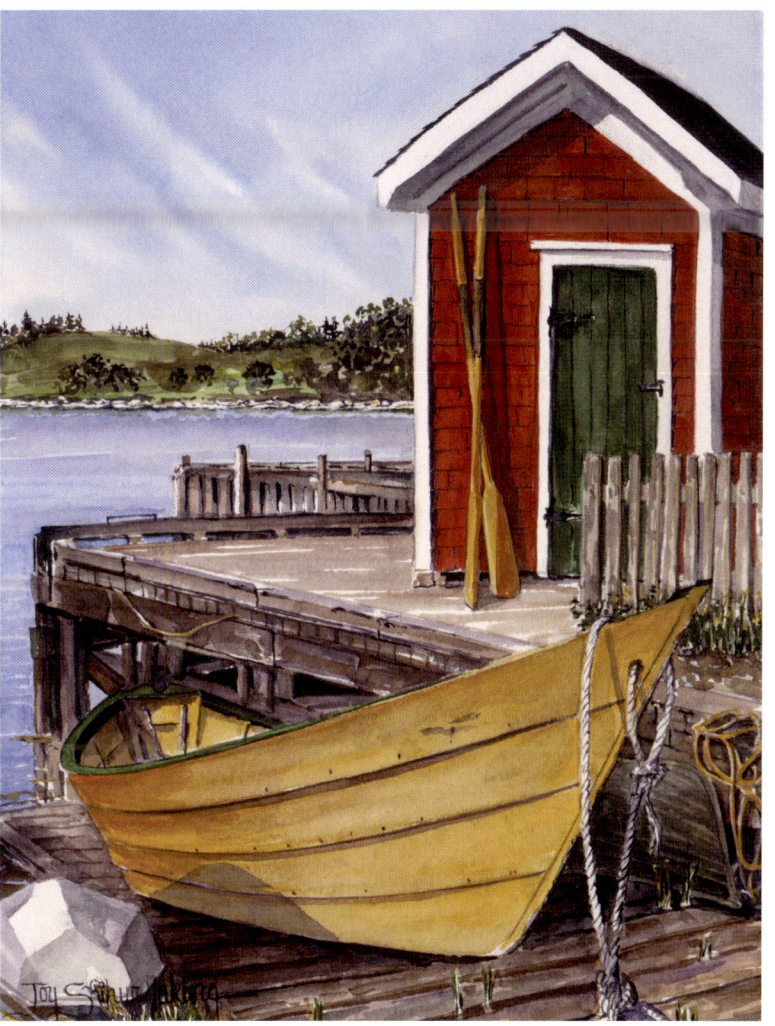

Lunenburg Wharf

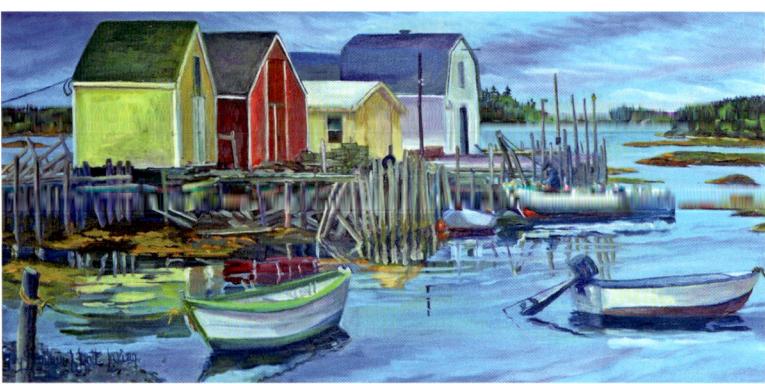

Bringing the Sheep Home from the Islands, Blue Rocks

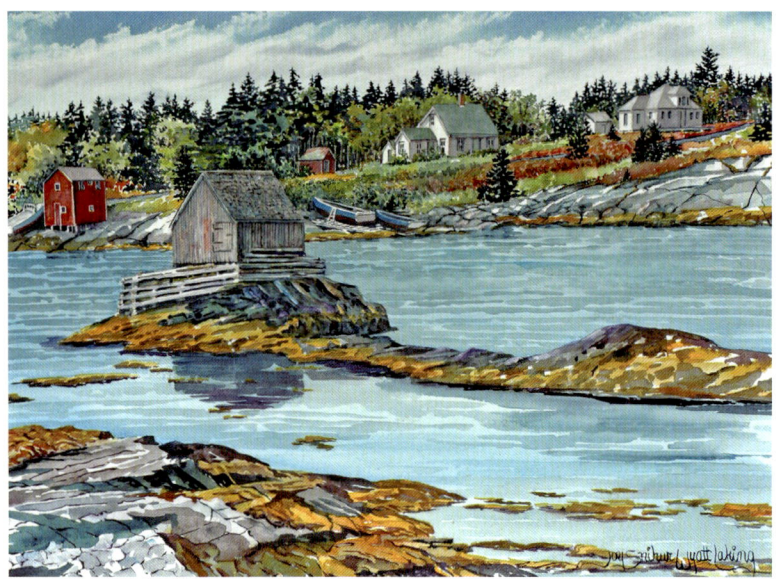

Blue Rocks

Colourful houses and fish sheds
Are plunked higgledy-piggledy
On a tiny rocky island,
Next to a winding gravel road,
Or by storm-battered wharves.
A sprinkling of snow makes all the roofs pristine white
And powders the scruffy brown hillside.
Gone are the lupins, daisies, buttercups,
And Queen Anne's lace.
A serene cove in summer,
In winter, the wharves and rocky shore
Are pummelled and raked by waves and ice.
Boats that have already been hauled out
Sit beside long dead hulls.
For now, a few fishing boats are still moored dockside
To rusting red bollards above solid metal ladders.
These boats look oddly empty and forlorn
With their spring paint job chipped and faded.
Last week, coils of ropes, mountains of netting,
And all the fishing paraphernalia
Were hauled through the open red doors
Of a hundred fish sheds.
Hung in the small upstairs window
Of one particular glowing orange shed
Is a Styrofoam life ring with
Four bright red stripes pointing
North, east, south, and west.
Safety from all directions

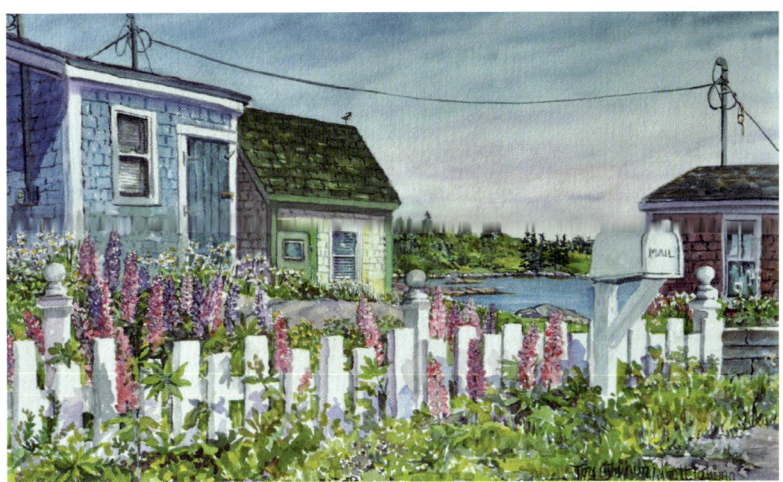

Fish Sheds and Lupins, Blue Rocks

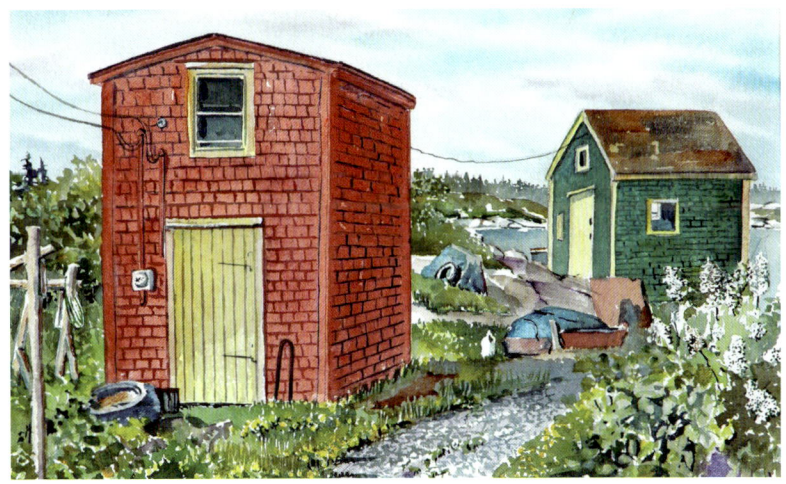

Fish Sheds and Lilacs

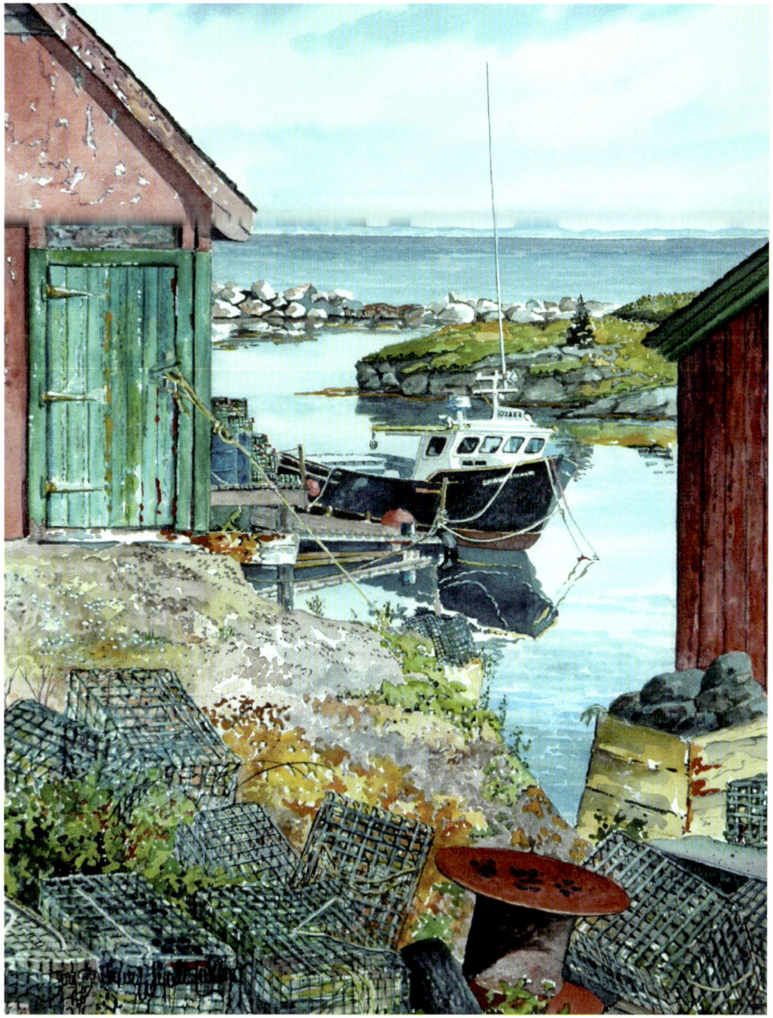

Fish Traps 44.3528 -64.2377

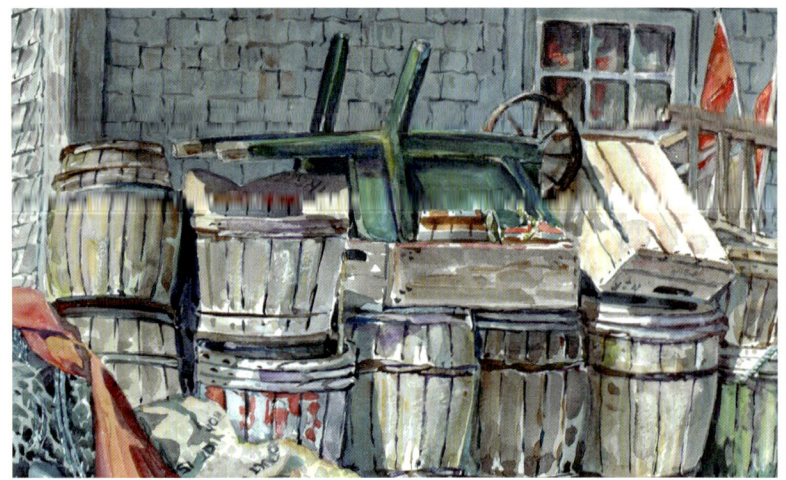

Stonehurst West 44.3637 -64.2108

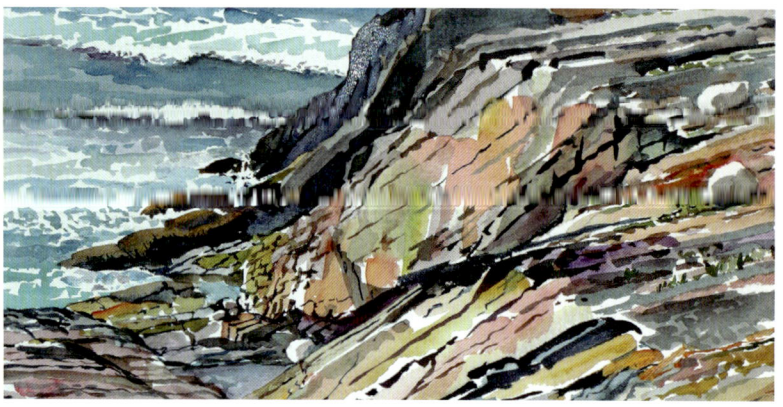

Gaff Point

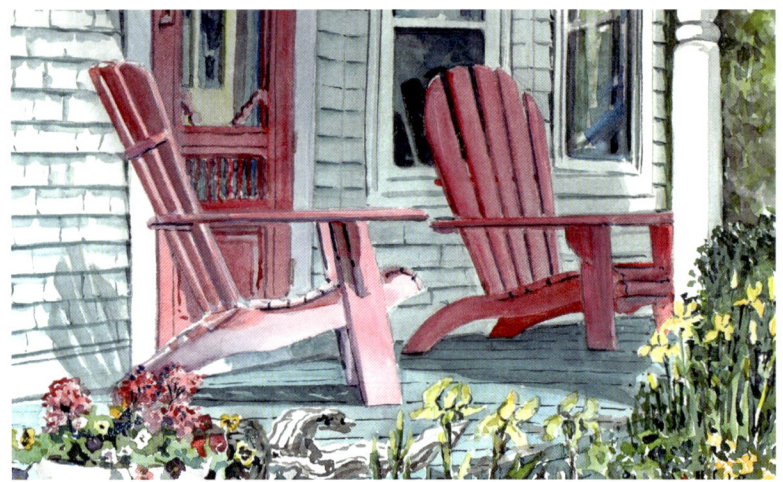

Front Centre

31 One day, years ago, when I was painting down near Blue Rocks near Lunenburg, I found a narrow road that snaked around and over rock and eventually ended at a shed by the salt water. Next to the shed were old wooden boxes and barrels with an old-fashioned wheelbarrow on top. The lighting was perfect and I sat right down and started painting. A half-hour later three huge white trucks pulled in and a small army of people got out. They unloaded some metal barrels and proceeded to paint them pink. Eventually, I couldn't hide my curiosity any longer. I went over and asked the folks just exactly what they were up to. They told me that they were painting up the drums so that they would look like they contained Primrose Oil, an early airplane fuel. This spot was going to be Newfoundland in the Amelia Earhart movie. I resumed painting. Only later did I find out that the random collection of old stuff was also movie props.

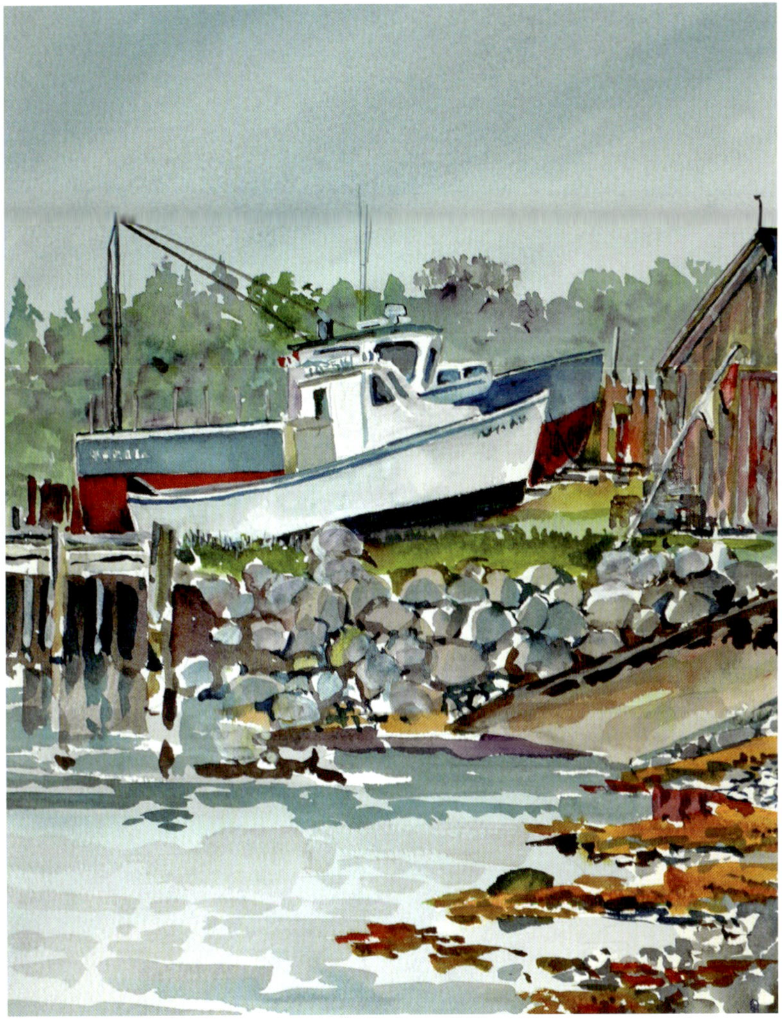

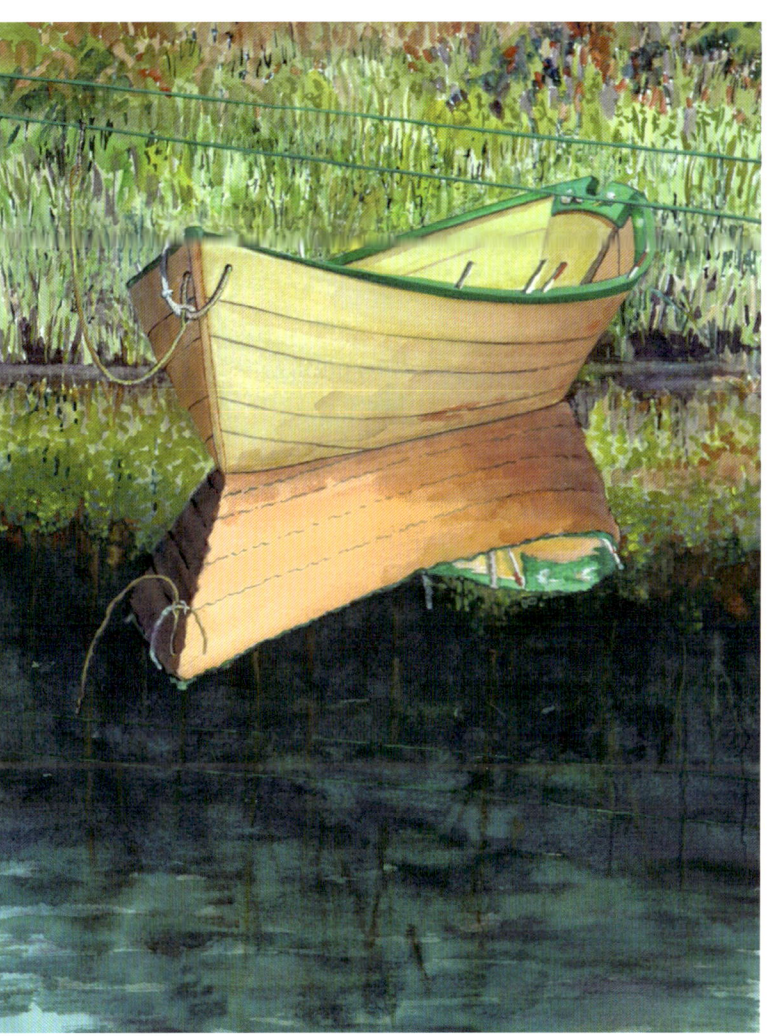

Near the Bayport Wharf

Dory on Mason's Beach Road

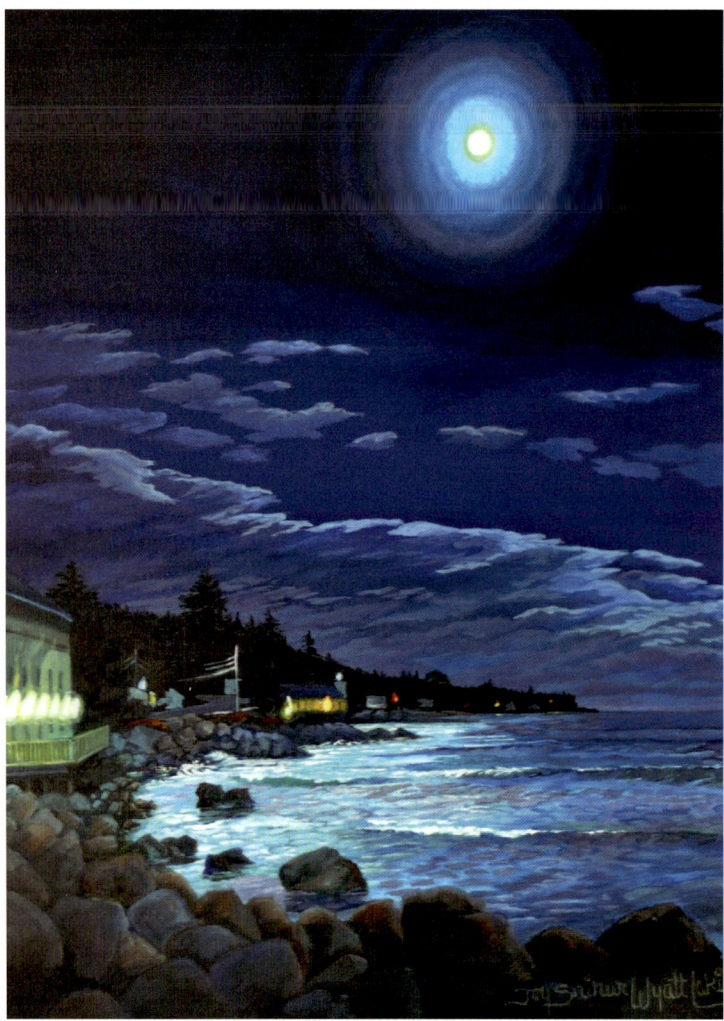

32 I am quite certain that everyone can draw. The problem seems to be in looking. I proved this to my painting classes years ago by getting them to bring a photo of themselves and then turning it bottom side up and drawing it. Because we have never seen our own face upside down, everyone was forced to really look at the angles and shapes to do the drawing. At the end we turned the drawings upright and the likenesses astonished everyone. Really seeing is a wonderful skill that everyone can enjoy. Suddenly there is an appreciation for how branches are attached to a tree, or the shape of the trillium leaves before they unfurl, and everyday there are beautiful surprises. An exercise that will open this ability to you, is to do three little five minute drawings every day for a month. These can be done absolutely anywhere because this is all about the process of really looking.

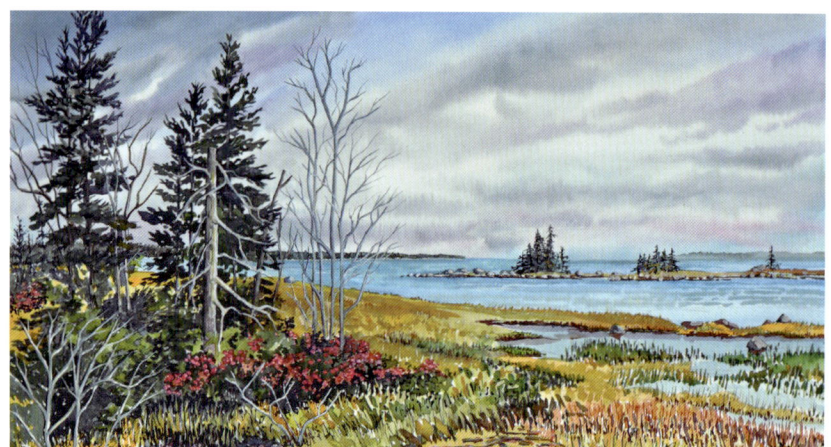

Full Moon from the Quarterdeck, Summerville 45.4061 -63.7136

Port Medway

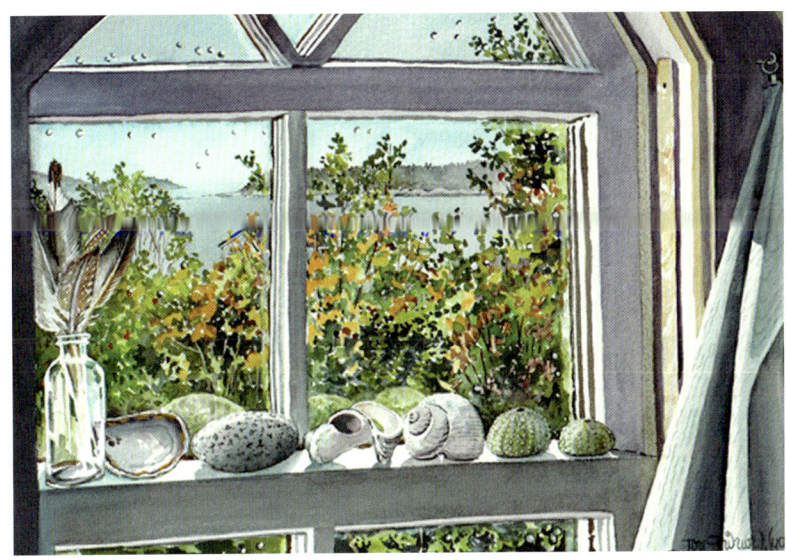

Brigitte's Window

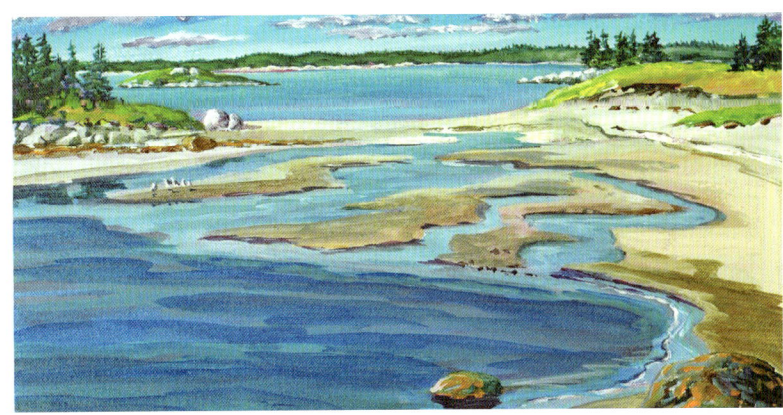

Carter's Beach

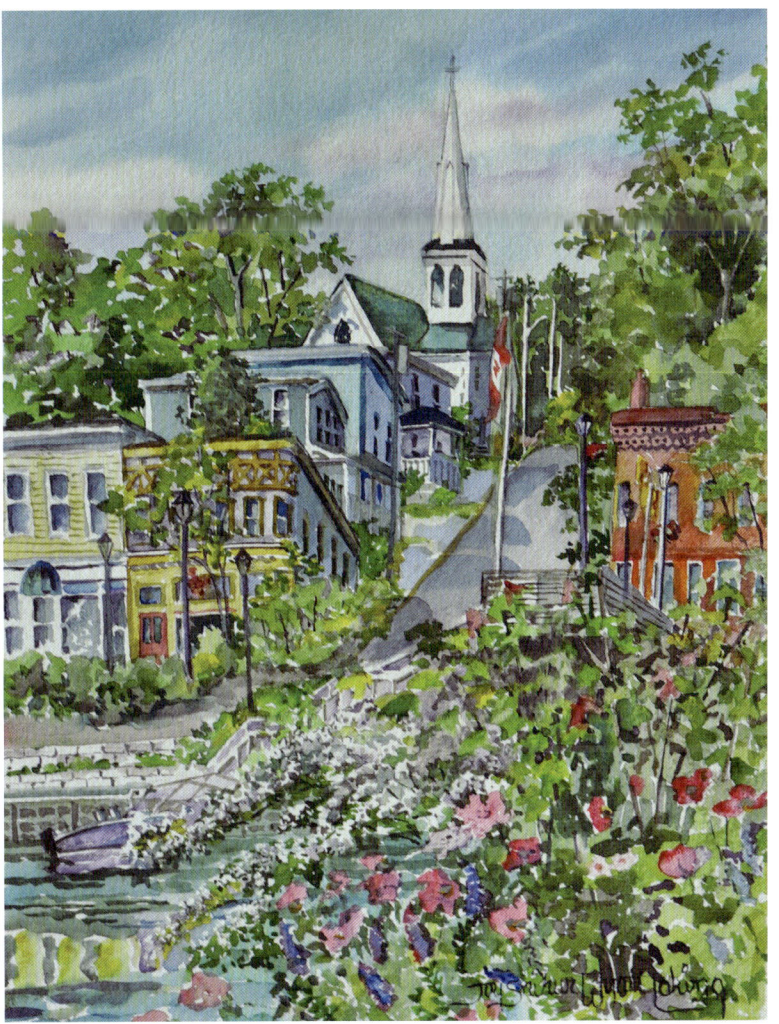

Bridgewater

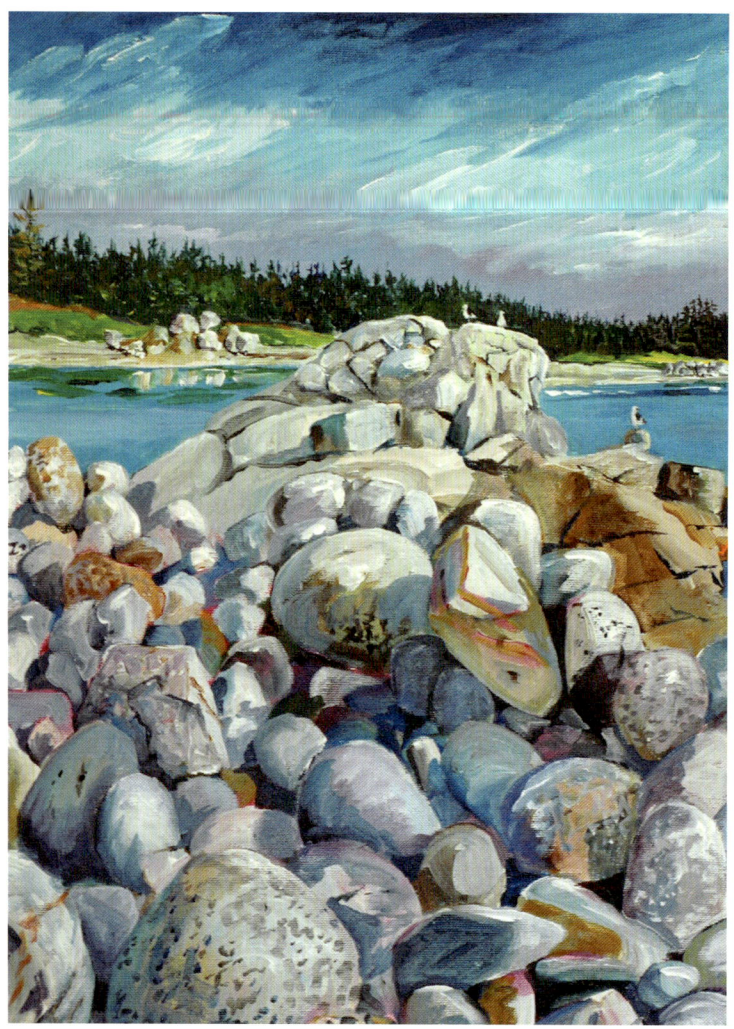

Beach at Port Joli

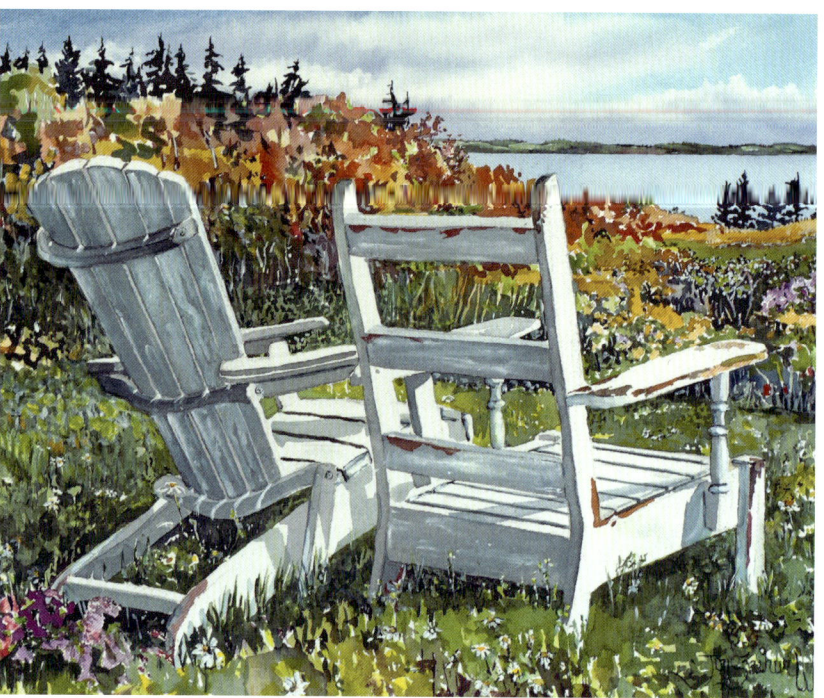

Chairs at Port Joli

33 My first solo exhibition in 1982 at Mount Saint Vincent University was all white flowers on white paper. Not painting the whites in watercolour is still something that I find intriguing. When painting white snow, white chairs, or white rocks or surf, I start by painting the negative space around the white object. I paint flowers, bending grasses, and the distant trees around the white chairs. Then when I paint the shadows on the chairs, they suddenly almost magically appear.

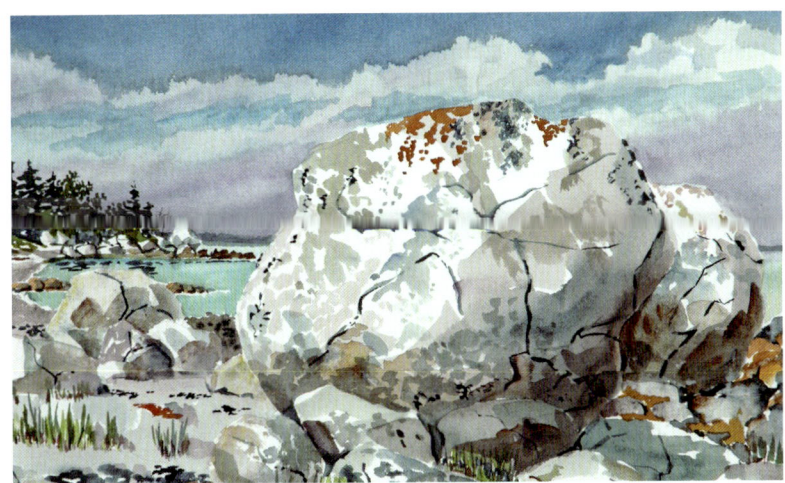
Rock at Port Joli

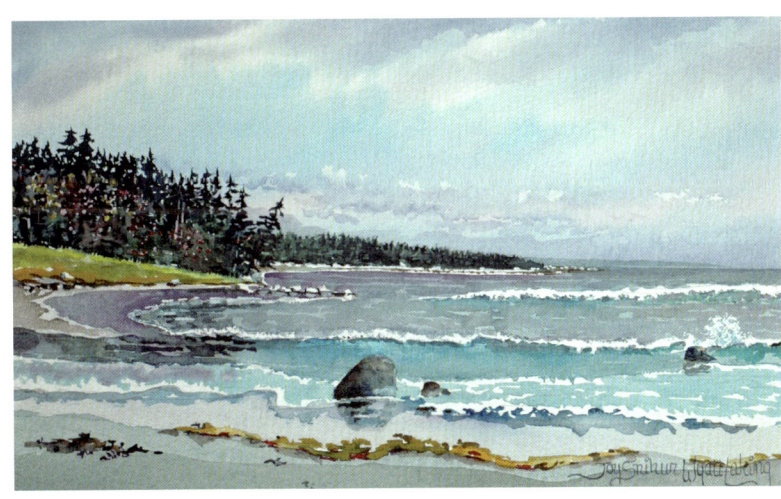
Surf at Port Joli

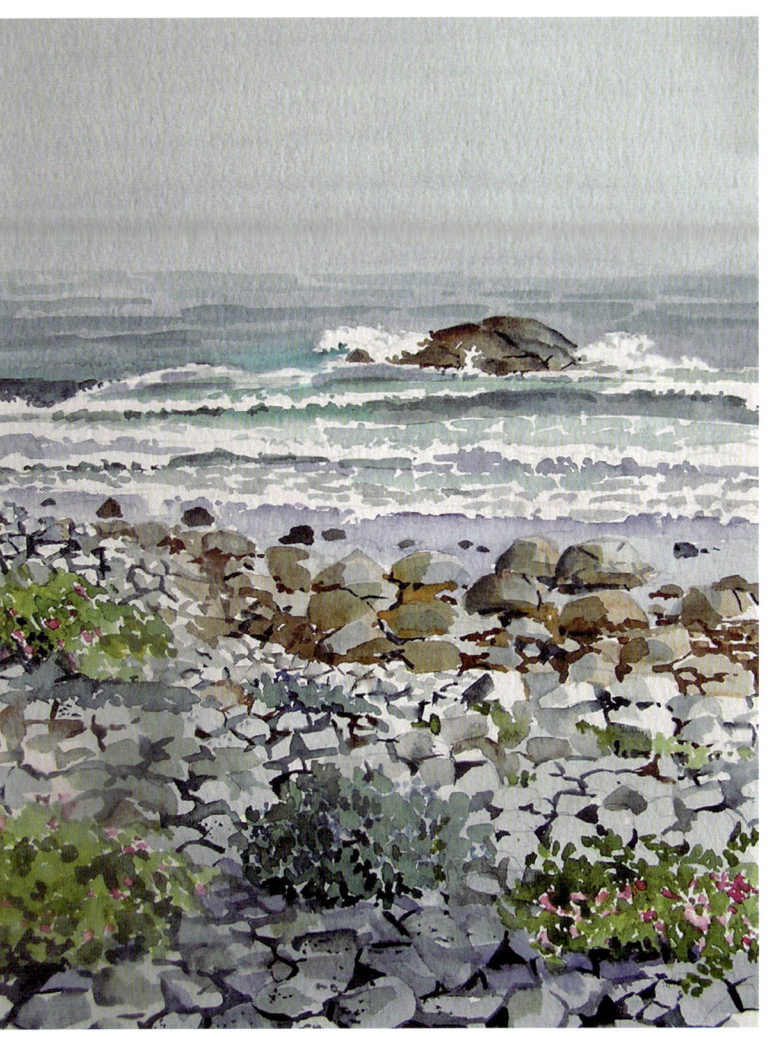
Kejimkujik National Seaside Adjunct 43.4944 -64.5012

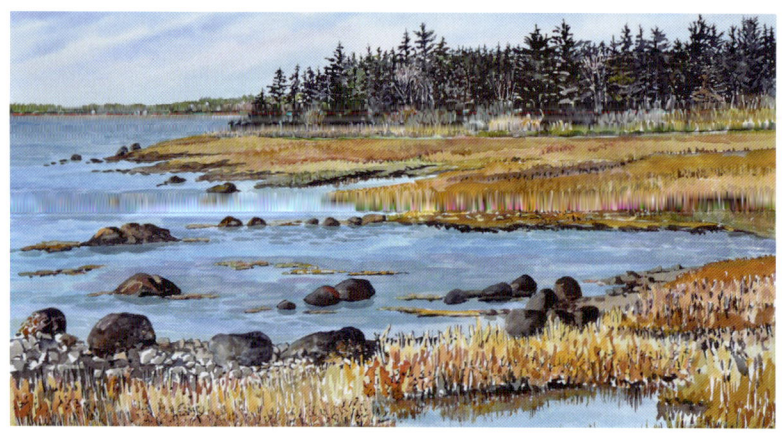

Green Cove

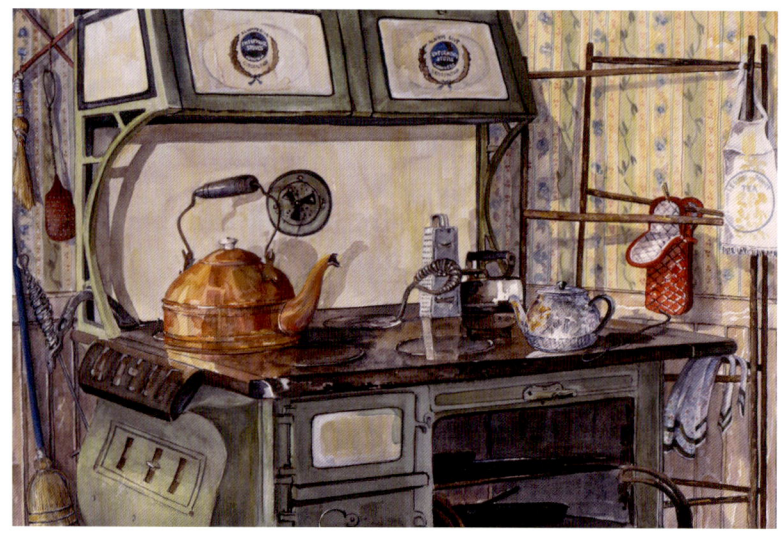

Pauline's Stove

34

Six months ago, the grass grew green and strong.
Yesterday, it was ochre, sienna, and sepia.
A season of tides and biting winds
Have left it flattened or furrowed.
The sky-blue sea meanders in
Through the yellow marsh,
Following old Acadian channels,
Around patches of dark spruce and scruff.
The bases of these marsh islands
Are punctuated with clusters of bright rosehips.

Today it is snowing.
A curtain of white
Obliterates all of the colour.
Even the rosehips are invisible.
A soft gray quiet replaces
The riot of autumn.

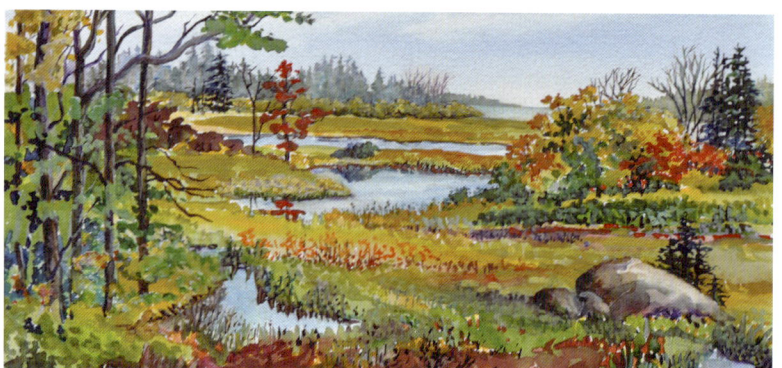

Barrington Passage 43.5498 -65.6062

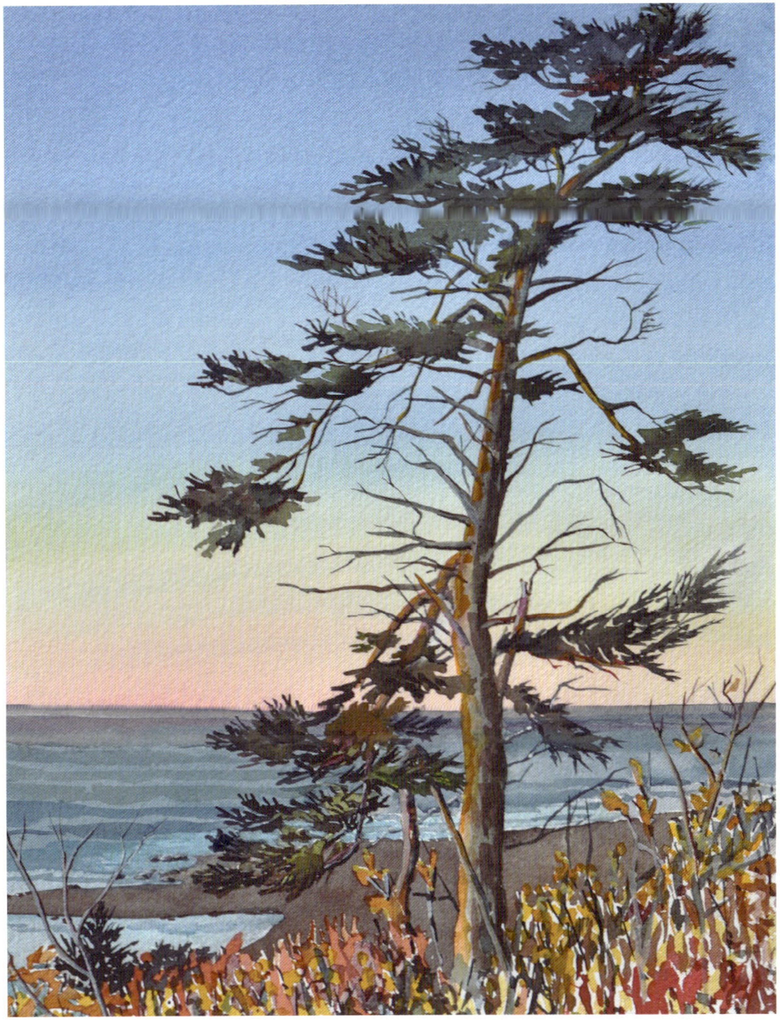

Pine at Sunset

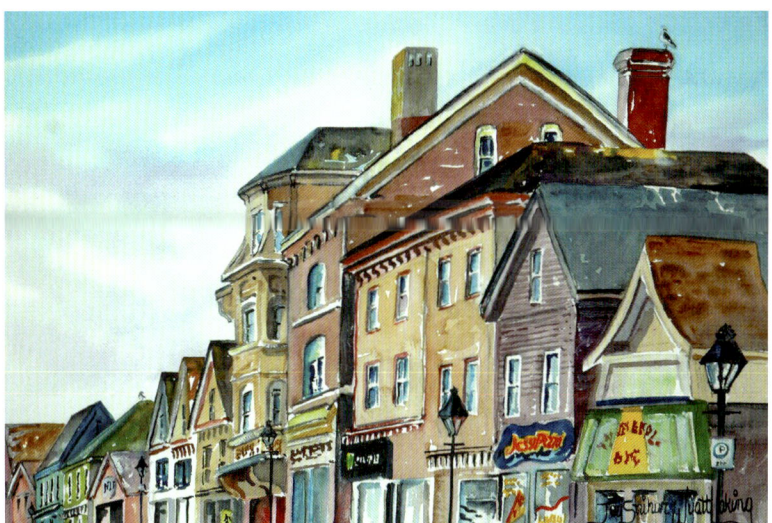
Yarmouth

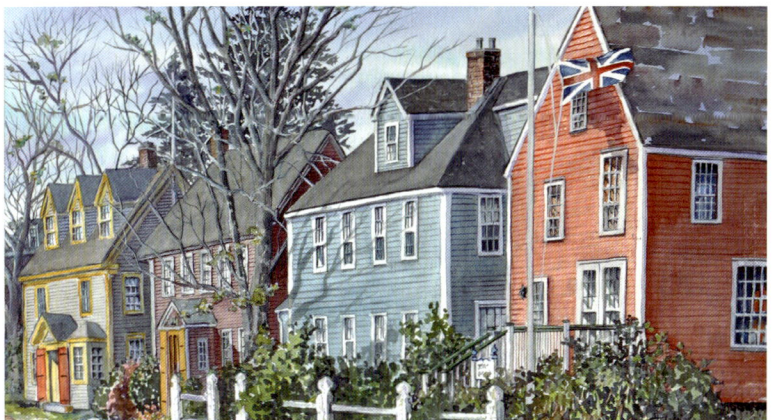
Shelburne

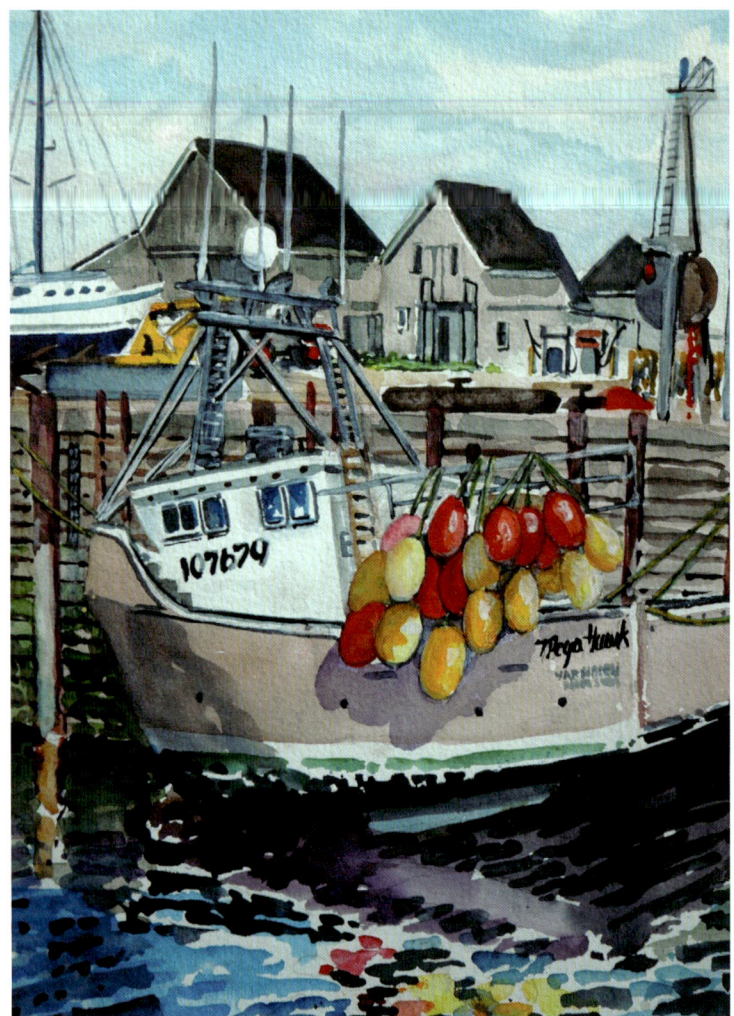

Boats at Meteghan

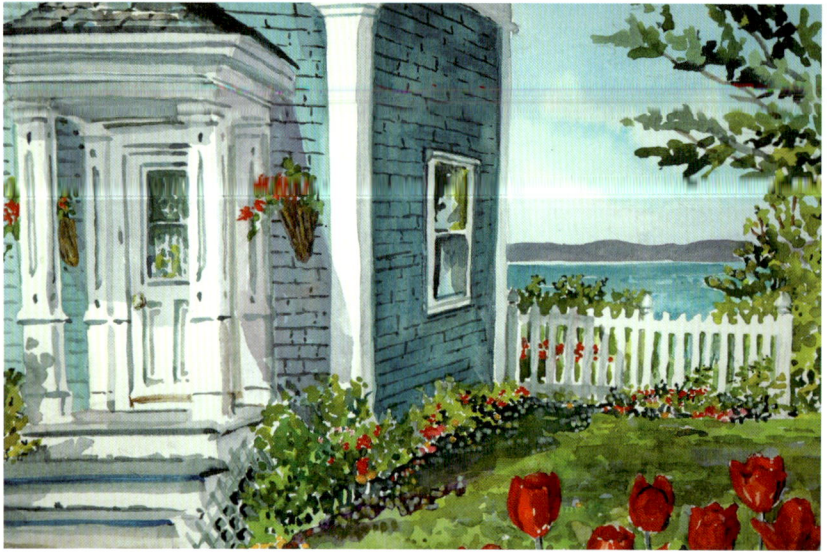

Comeauville

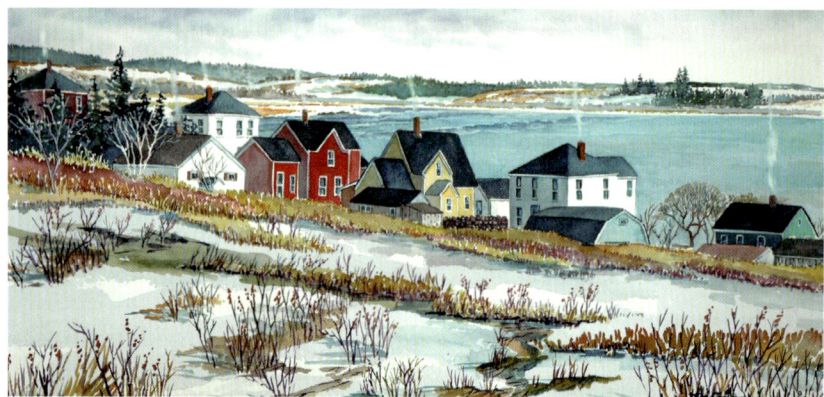

Winter, Cape Saint Mary's

35

When I moved to Portaupique in 1975, I became interested in the people who had lived here in earlier times, such as the Mi'kmaq and the Acadians. They had also loved this land. I collected marsh greens on the marsh, dug tubers under the areas of wild Jerusalem artichoke, and was very interested in the Acadian dyke, including a foundation and well on our property. I read about the Acadian tradition of serving rappie pie on Christmas Eve. I didn't know any Acadians but I had a recipe and I gave it a try. I remember squeezing and squeezing all those grated potatoes to destarch them. Little did I know that most Acadians now buy frozen destarched potatoes when they make rappie pie, which they call râpure.

Years later, I was selling my calendars at a craft show in Halifax and met Denise Comeau, an Acadian artist from Comeauville who had a booth near mine. I think my story of trying to make rappie pie endeared me to her and she invited me to her house to taste "real râpure." Since that time, we have been friends and have enjoyed several painting trips together.
(Denise's website: www.denisecomeau.com)

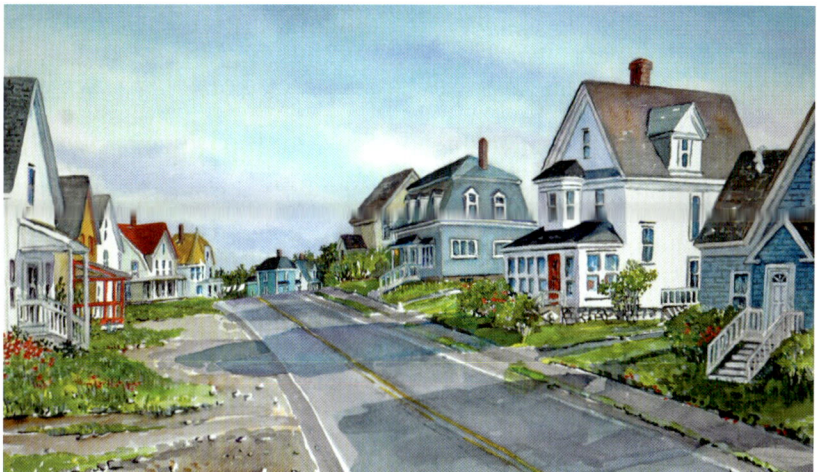

Meteghan

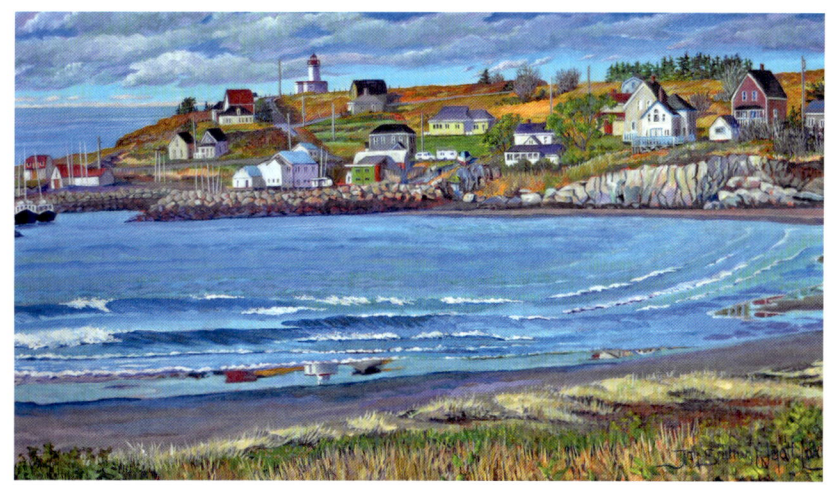

Cape Saint Mary's 43.9709 -66.1571

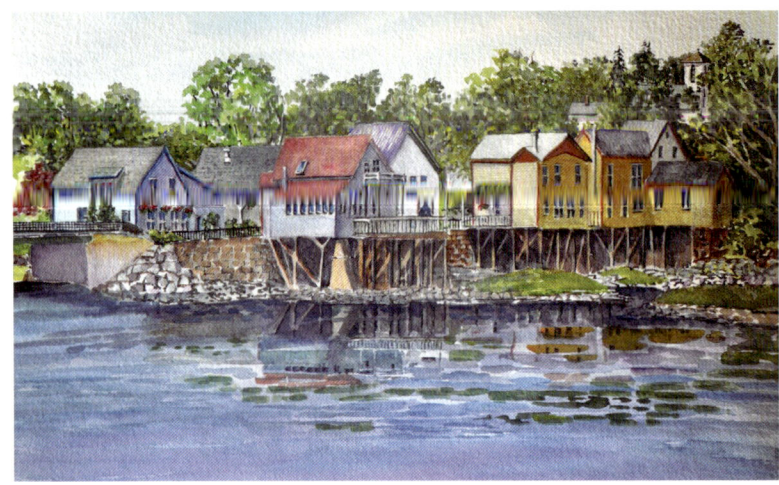

Bear River

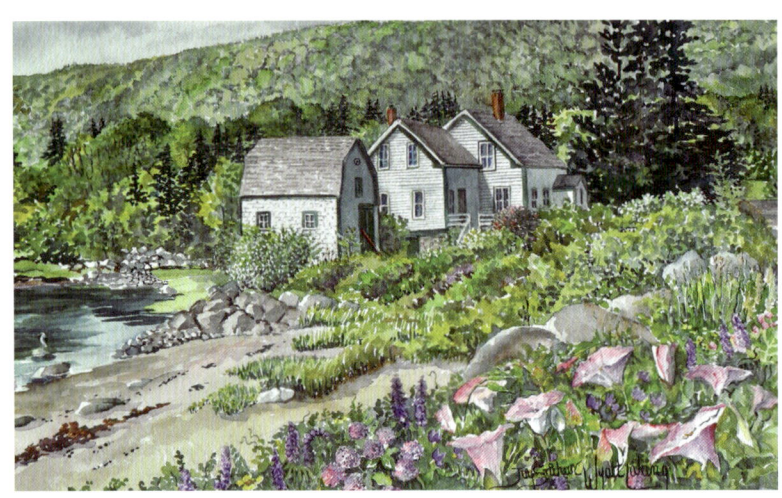

Port Royal 44.7117 -65.6227

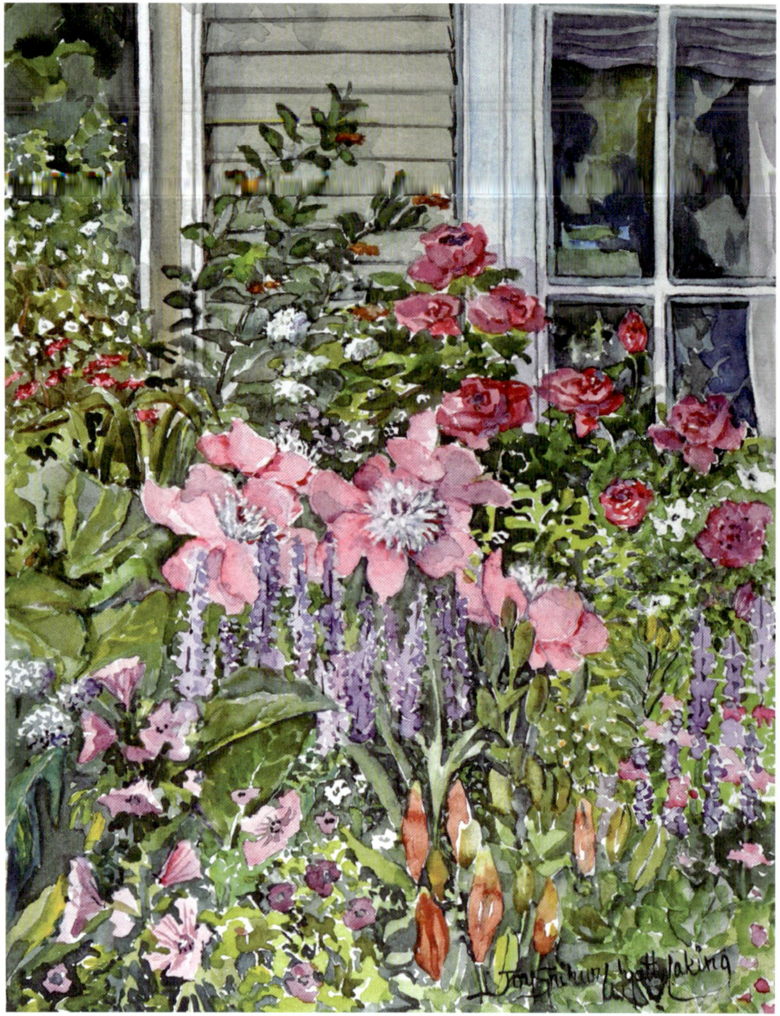

Annapolis Royal Garden

36 A couple of years ago, I sat in a blueberry field for several days, painting and eating blueberries. I did a large vertical painting that caught the ripened berries much larger than they really were from a close-up, on-the-ground perspective. In the background, the hills rolled back in the distance as a traditional landscape. Since then I have been playing with similar ideas in lots of paintings. Most recently I did the wildflowers at Sandy Cove and at Port Royal as dominating featured foregrounds. I haven't been painting flowers as often as I did thirty years ago, but now I am noticing them again and am enjoying painting them in both oils and watercolours.

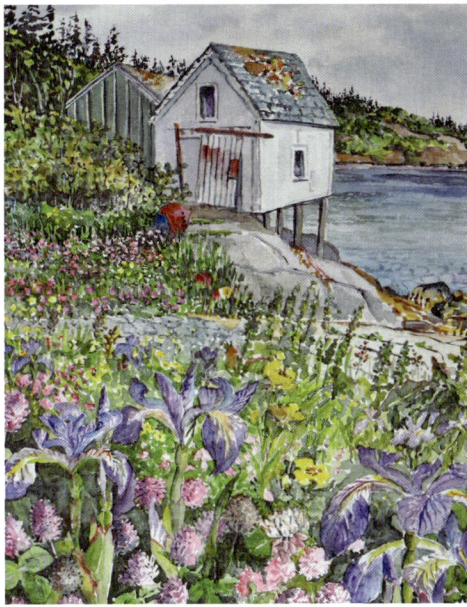

Sandy Cove

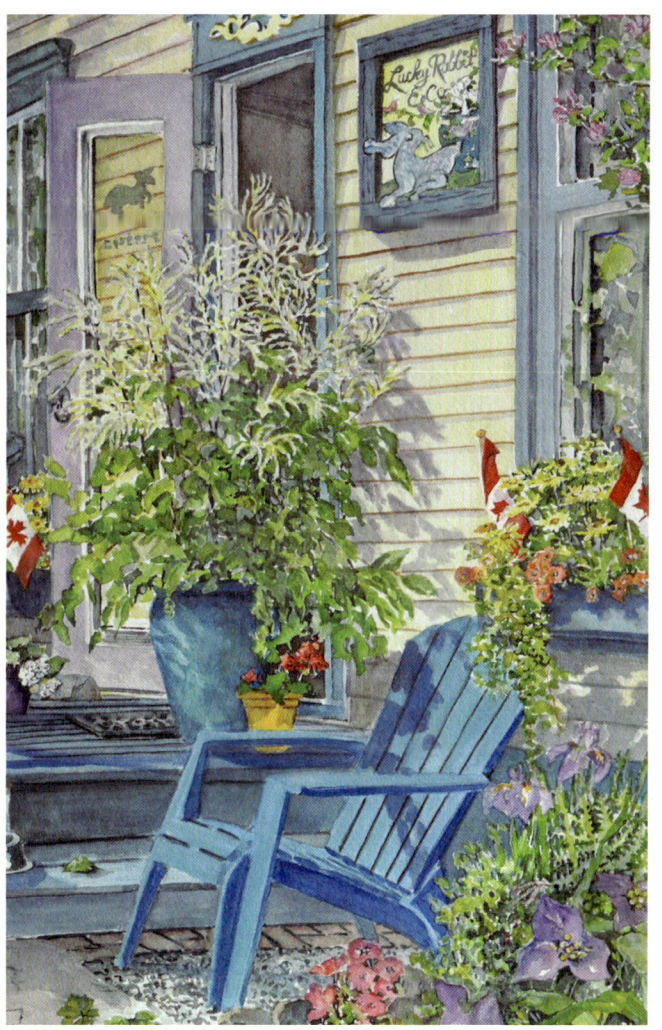

Lucky Rabbit

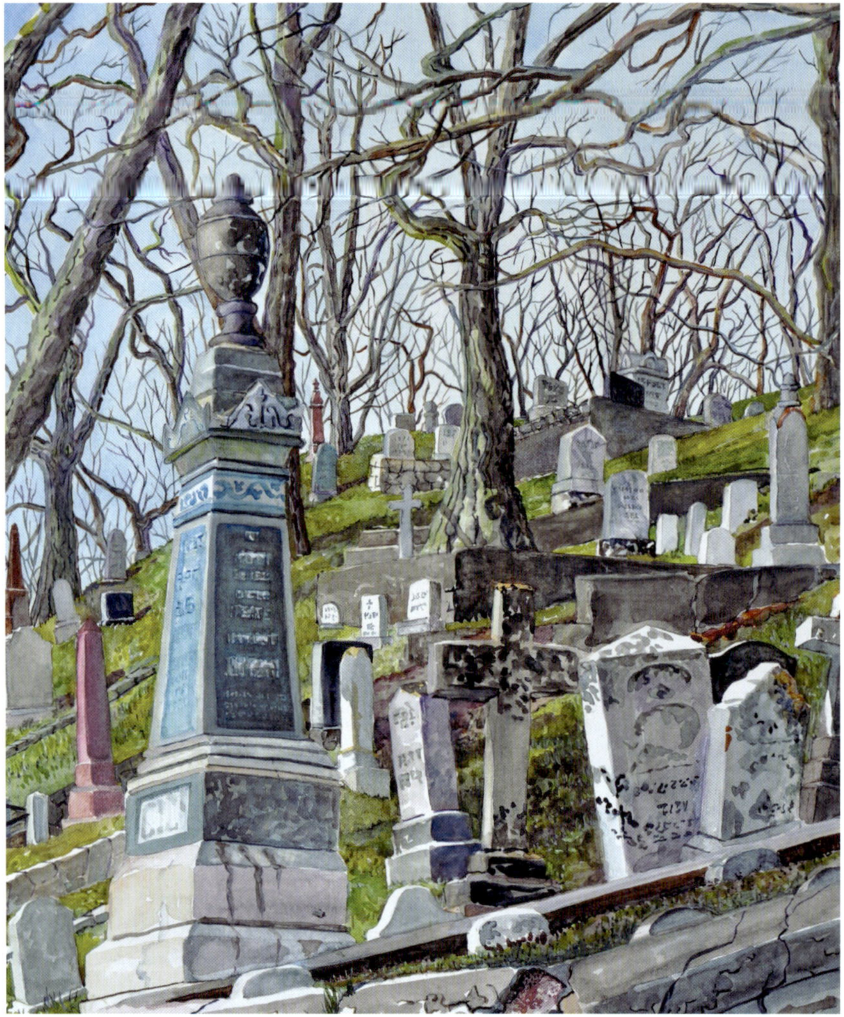

Headstones and English Oaks in Kentville 45.0772 -64.4858

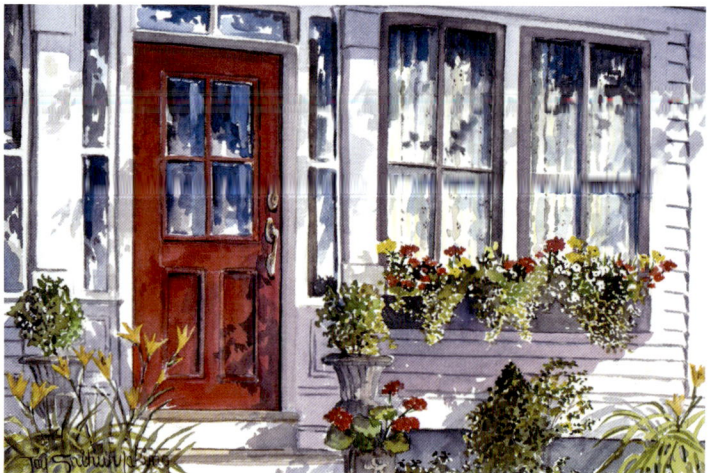

Red Door in Wolfville

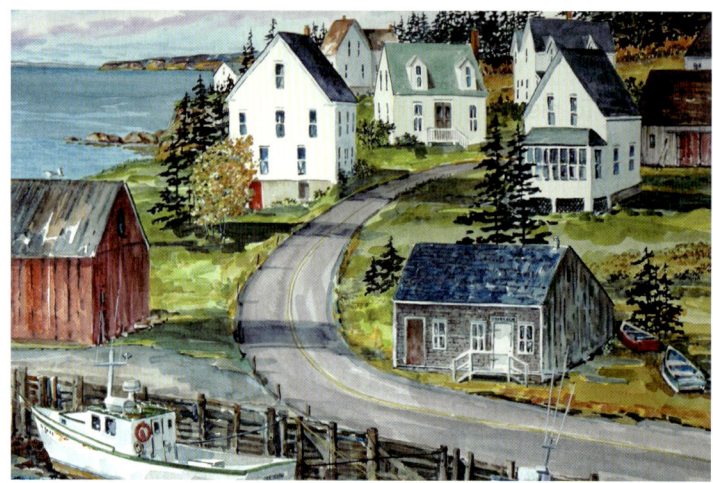

Halls Harbour

Cape Island boats, large and small,
Rest on the mud.
Skewed left and right,
Balanced on keels, propellers, props,
The boats are tethered to the wharf
But they aren't going anywhere.
Gradually the shadows shorten and
The tide flows in over the mauve mud flats.
A pulsing of waves
Continually rolls the gravel.
Suddenly, surprisingly,
The boats are all upright and floating.
Alongside, a lone seal pops his head up.
Trucks arrive on the wharf
Loaded with traps
And all the fishing paraphernalia.
A man scrabbles down a ladder
To his boat.
Another man on the wharf
Throws off the ropes
Before descending the ladder.
Dakota and *Boys* starts her engines
And heads out of the cove.
Raucous seagulls
Swoop and circle overhead,
Snatching any scraps of bait
That are thrown overboard.
The dramatic tides of the Bay of Fundy
Underpin everything.

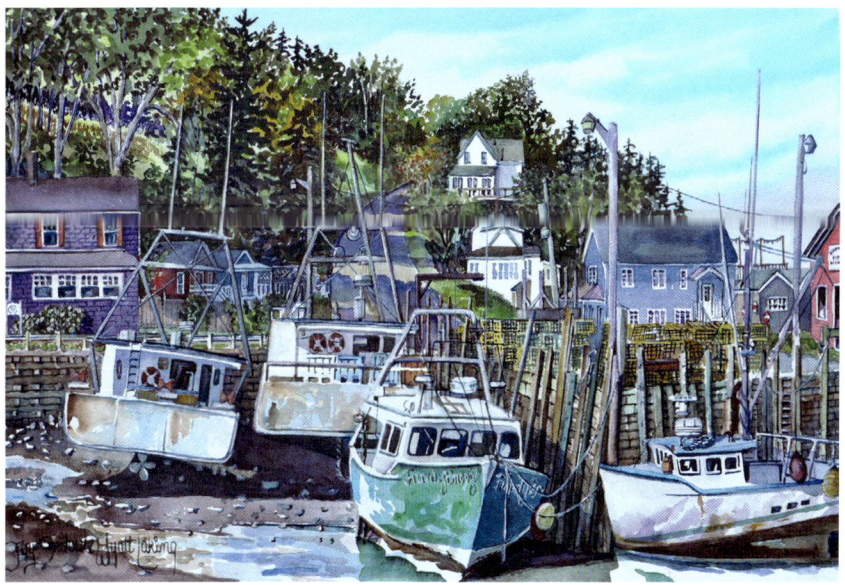

Harbourville

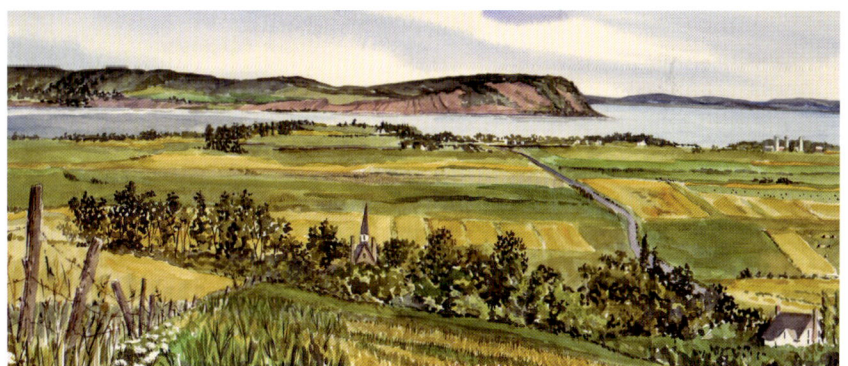

From the Look Off

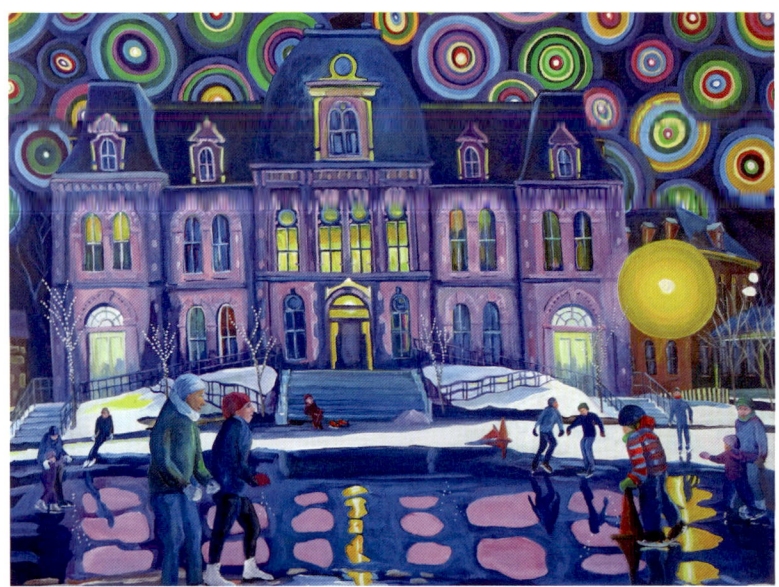

Starry Night at the Library

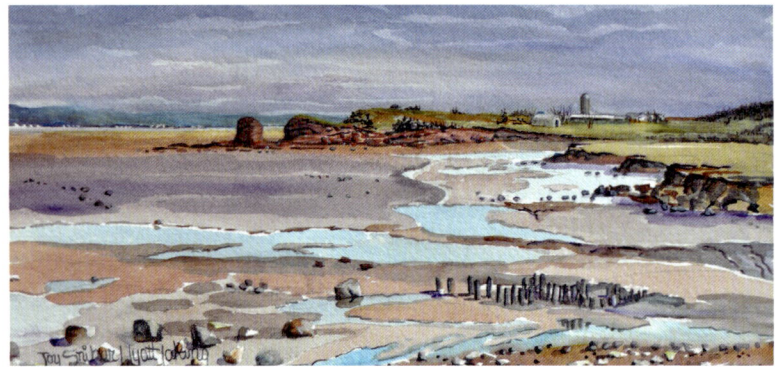

Burntcoat Head 45.4021 -63.6710

 38

A derelict old brick normal college
Has been transformed into
A magnificent community place
Our new library.
Its arched windows, rooftop dormers,
Domed main entrance, embellished façade
Are all restored to glory.
No longer just a place for books
And hushed voices,
Now, the library welcomes everyone.

In winter,
Skaters glide around the rink in front of the library.
Children clutch pylons or parents' hands
And feel like Olympic ice dancers.
In summer,
Families sit and chat in the outdoor public space.
Occasionally, sound systems and signs
Fill the ramped and stepped entryway.
Crowds rally or protest.
On Saturdays,
The community market crowd from next door
Spill across the area.

Inside the library, book are still borrowed,
Clubs, activities, meetings,
Book launches and art exhibitions take place.
Our library is building community.

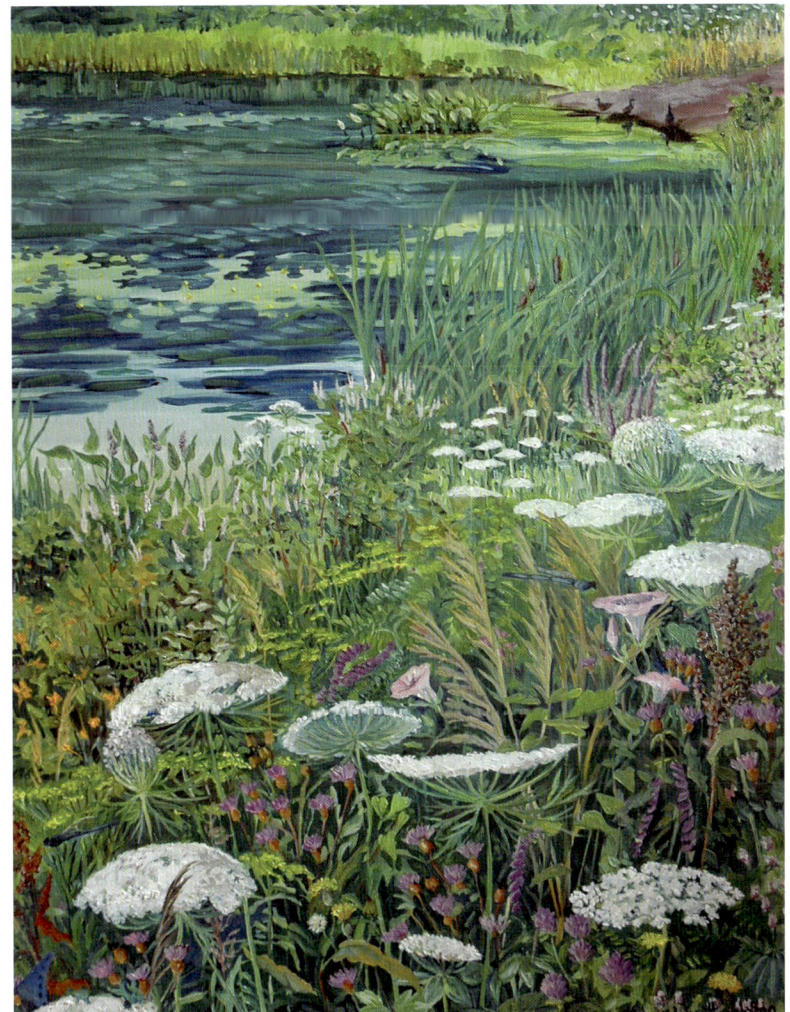

Shortt's Lake

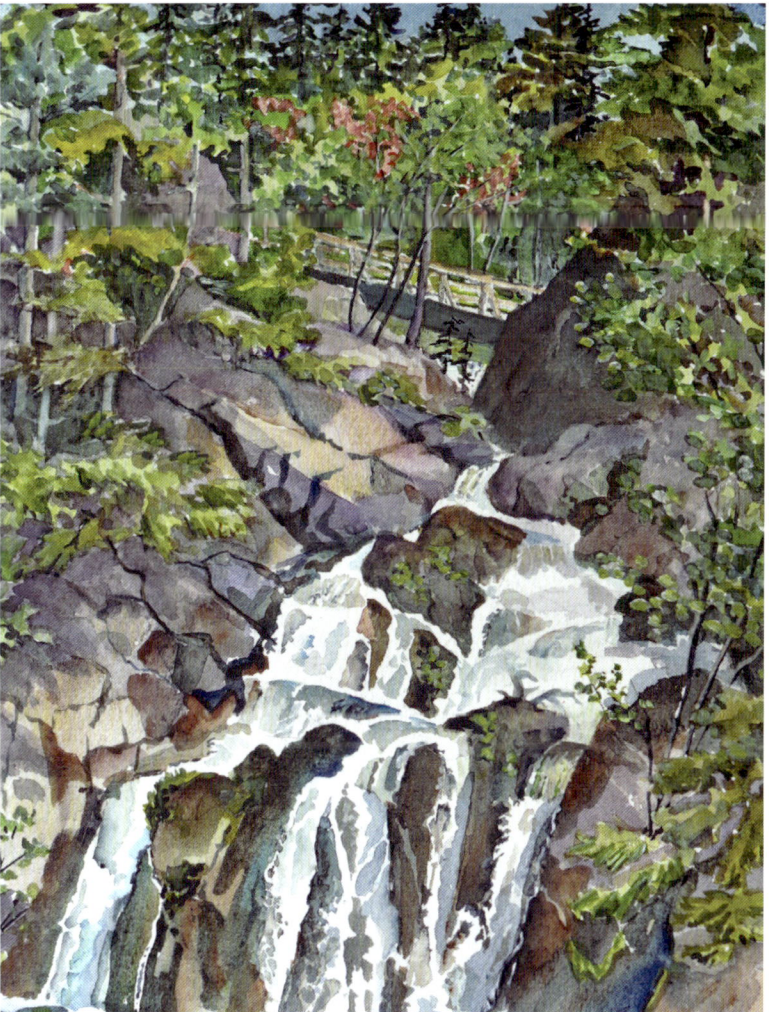

Falls in Victoria Park, Truro

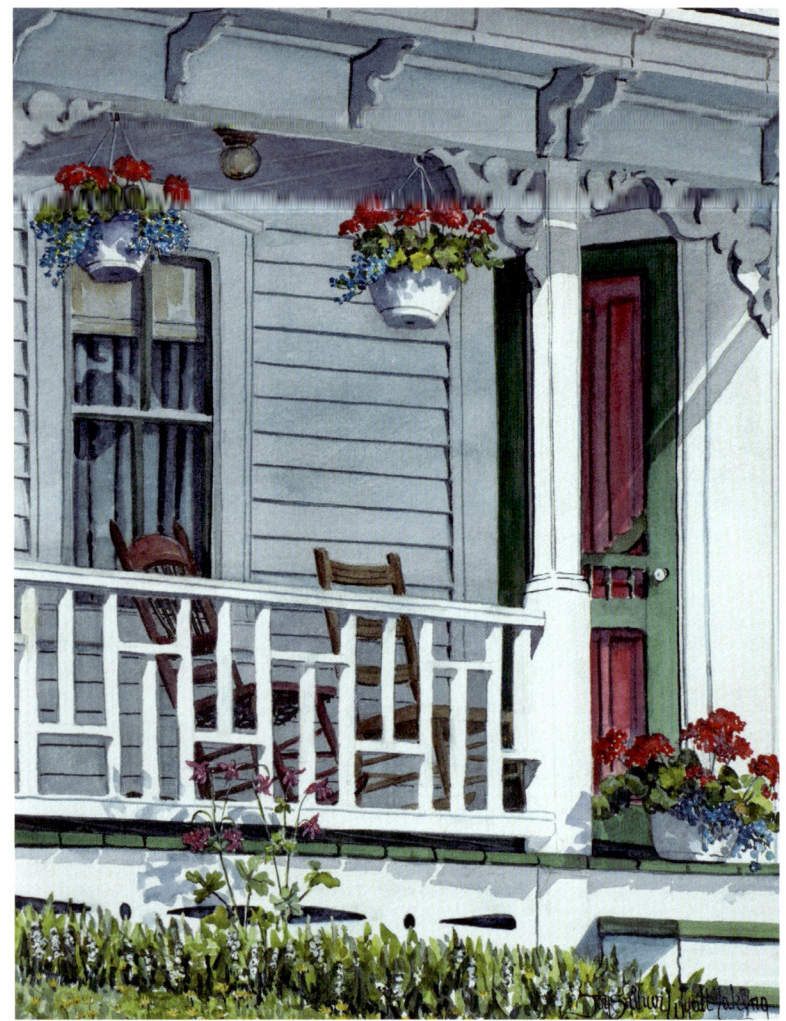

Donald's Porch, Great Village

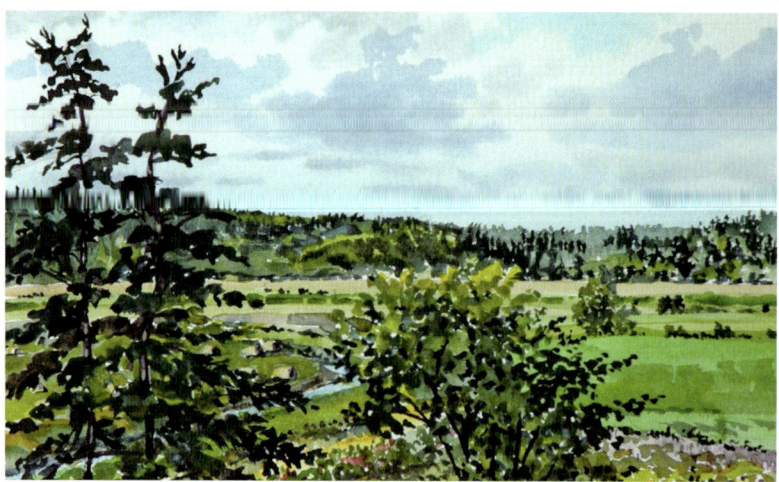

By the Aboiteau in Great Village

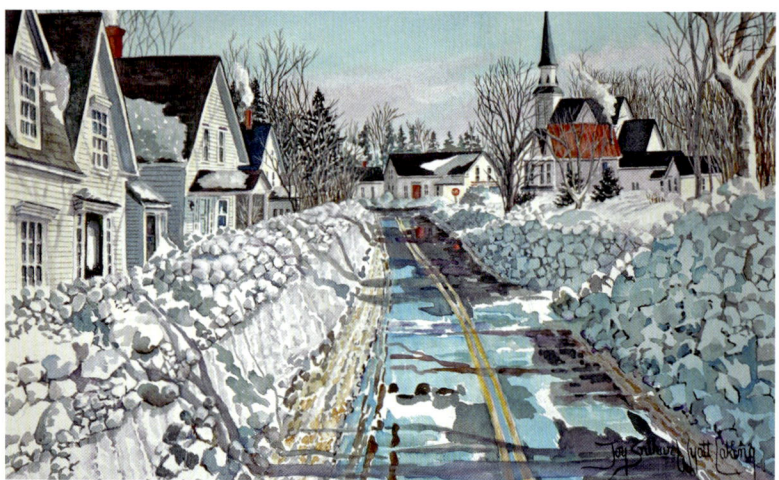

Winter in Great Village 45.2504 -63.3602

Two of these paintings are the same view with completely different feelings. *Great Village* was done as a watercolour on location. When I was painting this, Meredith Layton looked out the shop window and said, "Robert, why do the Mahons have their garbage out today? It isn't Thursday." Then she exclaimed, "Robert, that isn't the garbage. It's Joy." The ideas for studio paintings usually come from on-location paintings. It's an image that I can't stop thinking about. *Starry Night in Great Village* was a winter night after I'd just returned from Africa. The idea was so powerful I drove home for my camera and returned to take photos. I played with the colours and shapes in oil paint in the studio until it was just what I wanted.

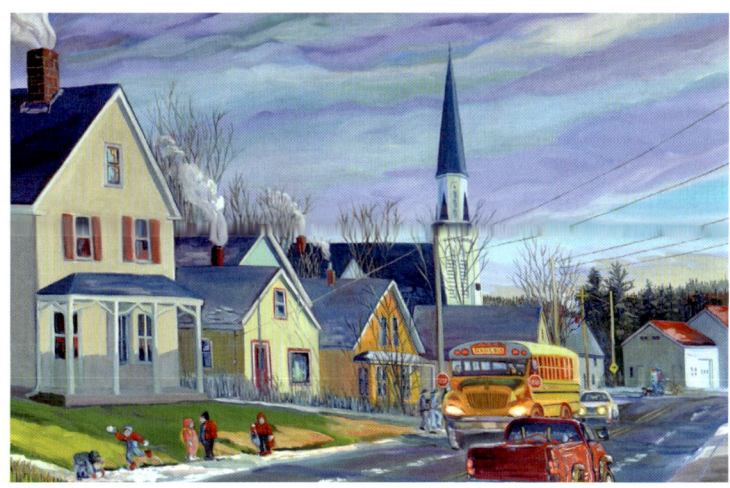

Waiting for the School Buses, Great Village

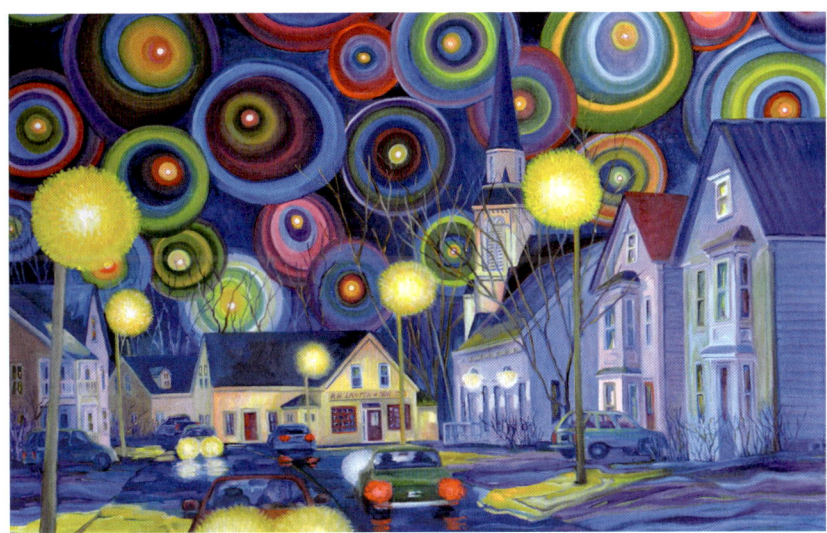

Starry Night in the Village

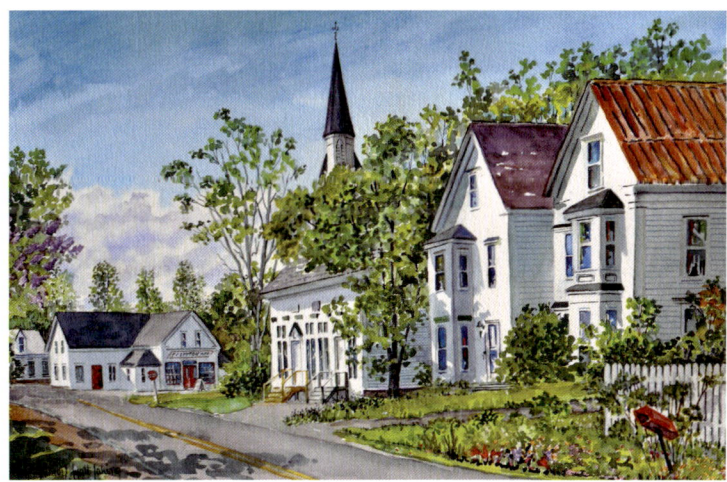

Great Village

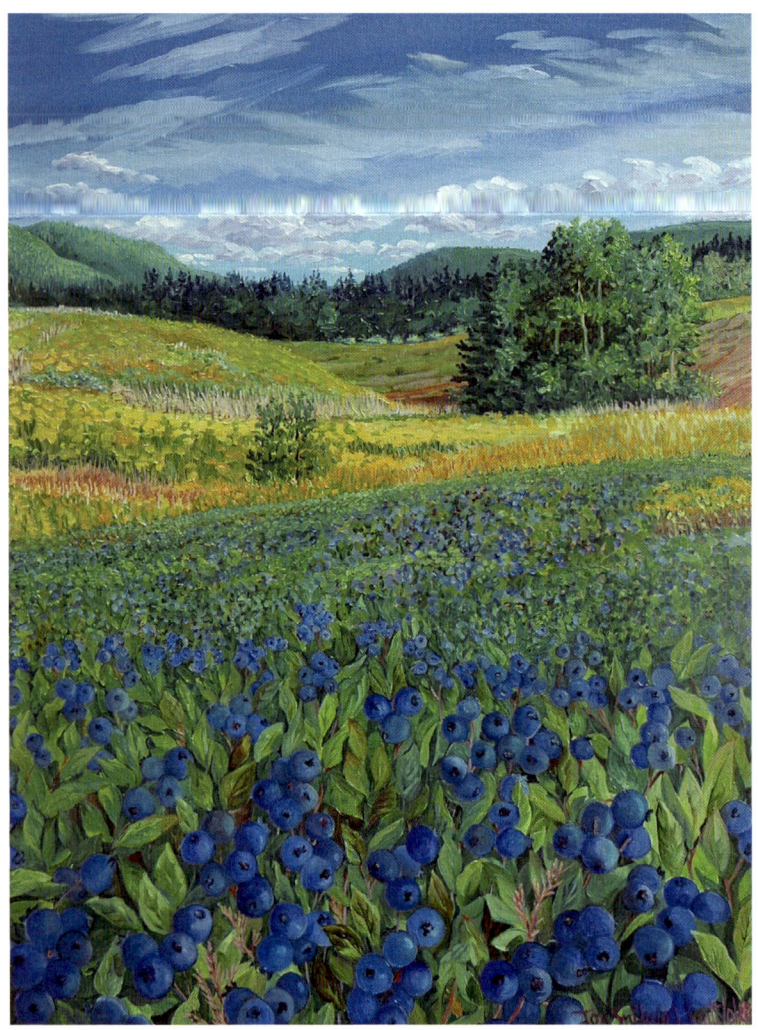

Blueberries on Portaupique Mountain 45.4322 -63.7120

40 The red and green rockers on the white porch or the two white Muskoka chairs are my insurance policy against the times when nothing seems to call to me to paint or when I feel too fragile to sit out in public wearing that required cloak of confidence. These chairs represent more than safety. They are close to home and they exude friendship, acceptance, coffee, cookies, and laughter because they are owned by a wonderful friend and photographer, Laurie Gunn. Highland Village doesn't have the usual stomach-clenching moment of "Can I do this?" because I have painted here so many times in sweltering heat, or bundled in my coat and scarf in the freezing cold. (Facebook: Laurie Gunn Photography)

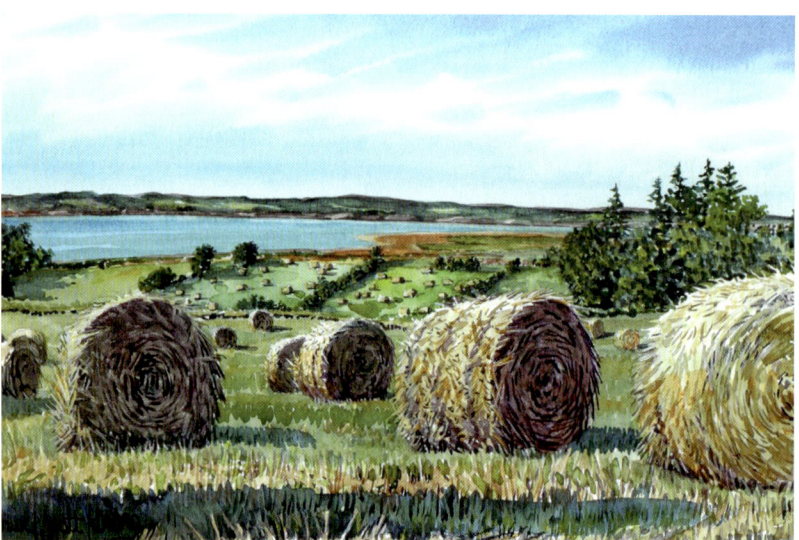

Hay Bales in Highland Village

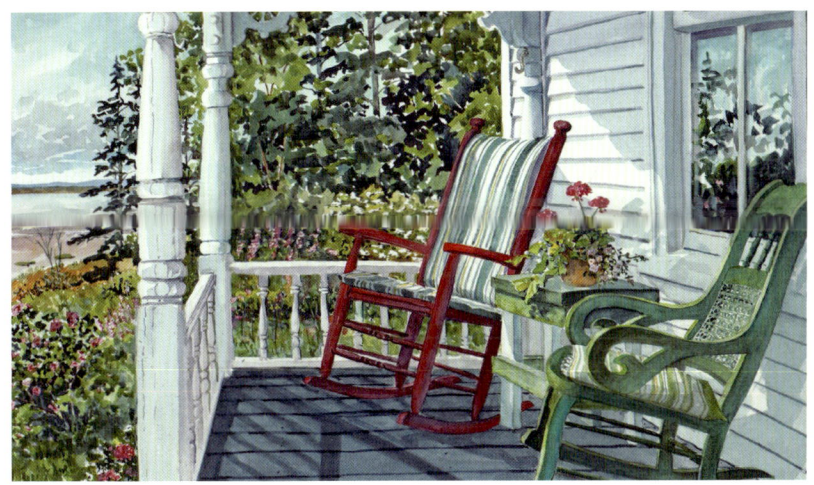

Joan's Chairs, Highland Village

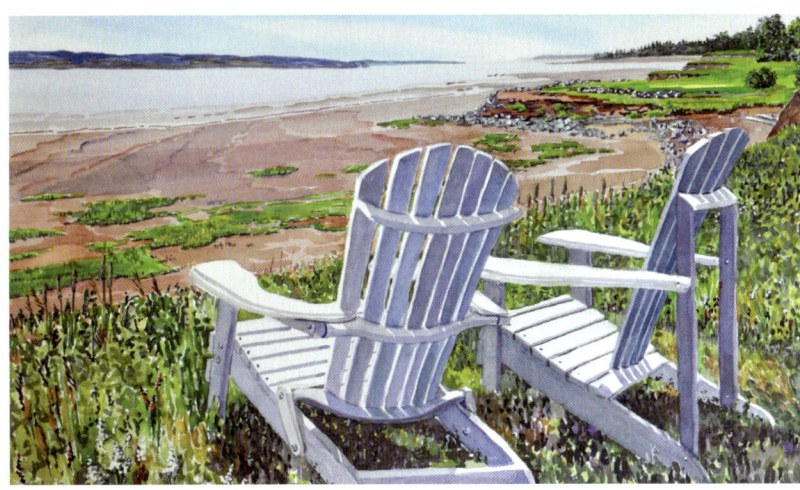

Laurie's Chairs, Highland Village

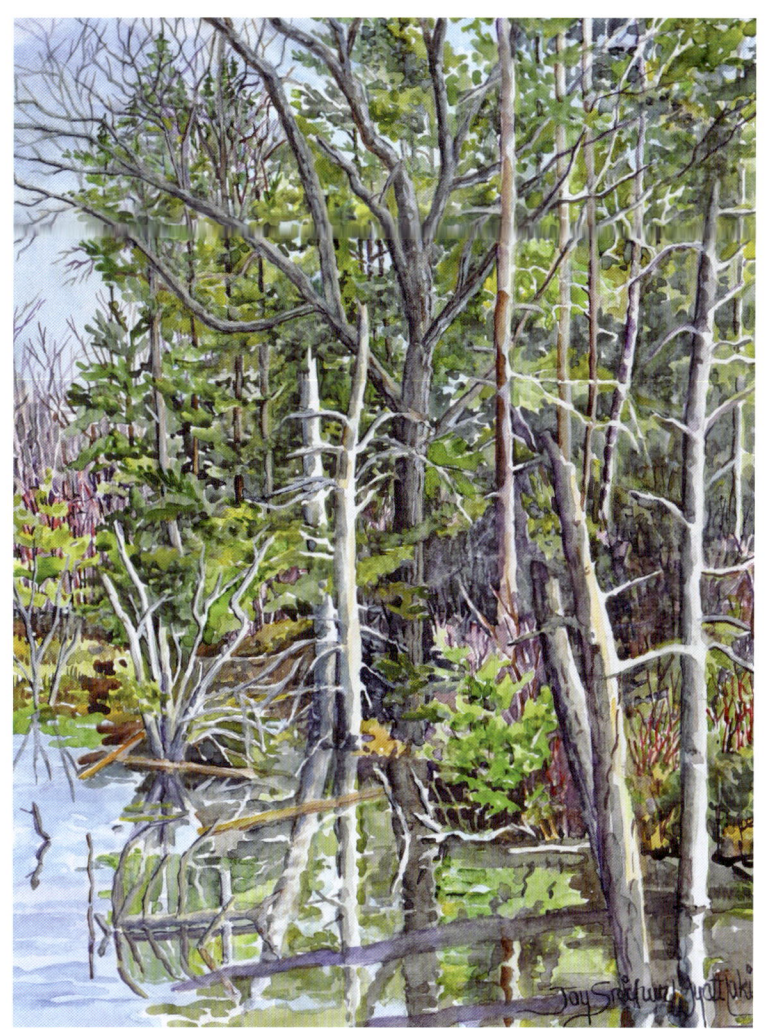

Spring Swamp, Mines Bass River Road

The Painted Province 91

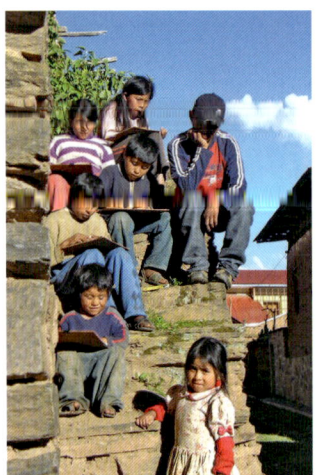

PAINTING
INTERNATIONALLY

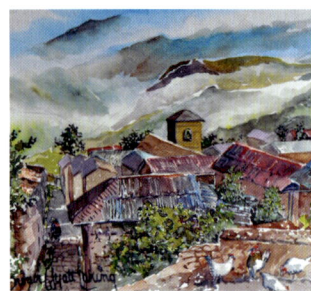

Aucapata, Bolivia

41 Painting in other countries keeps me inspired to look at Nova Scotia with fresh eyes. Jim and I have visited many other countries for a month or two or three and I have painted in all of them. We take advantage of any opportunities we come across and we always return home with lots of stories and great memories.

One of our favourite countries is Bolivia. With the on-the-ground support of the Ivar Mendez International Foundation, we spent a month a couple of times in the very remote community of Aucapata. I taught art at three schools, as well as free after-school and Saturday classes. When we were going to Cosnipata school, our contact, Ernesto, said it was a gentle twenty-minute walk. We never made it in less than an hour with Jim carrying all my supplies and me huffing and puffing uphill. Then Ernesto said I could teach in Charja, a school that was an hour's walk. I knew that was out of the question (the altitude was very high). He told me they would get me a donkey! I wasn't sure that was doable either.

Eventually, Ernesto got us a ride in a truck from the gold mine at the bottom of the mountain. The only catch was we had to arrive at the school two hours early at 8:30. When the lone teacher, who lived in the school, saw that we were there, he immediately blew his whistle and started school. He apologized that he only got six kids for flag-raising!

During one of my after-school classes, I was doing baker's clay sculptures with a big bunch of kids in the street outside our house. Suddenly pigs rushed over and started gobbling down the flour and salt sculptures. I rushed some of the sculptures inside. The next day, because of the altitude and moisture, all the sculptures were flat white pancakes. Never a dull moment when you're open to new adventures.

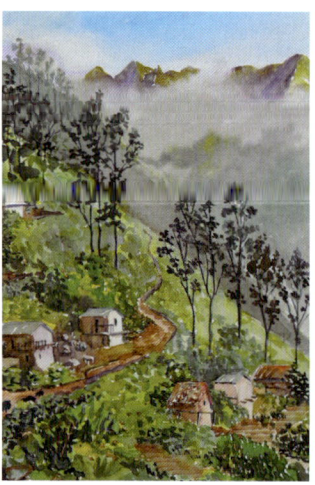

Charja, Bolivia

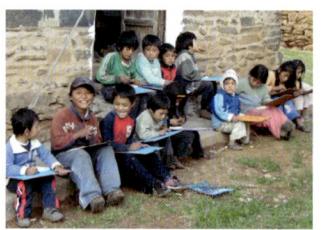

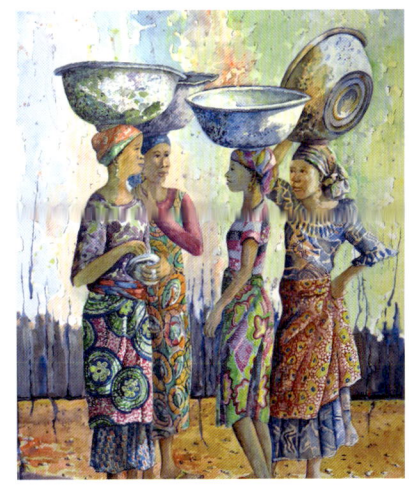

Ghana

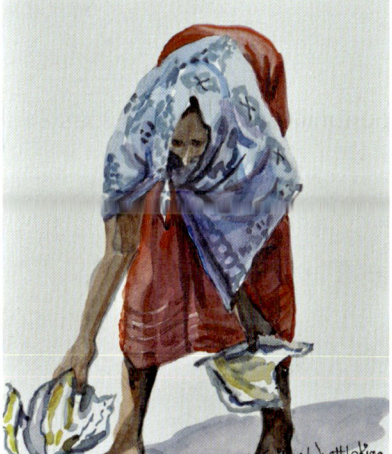

Sri Lanka

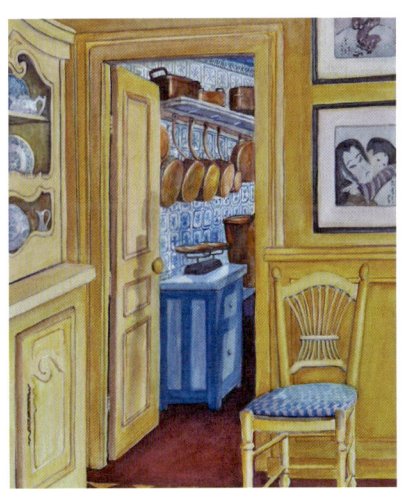

France

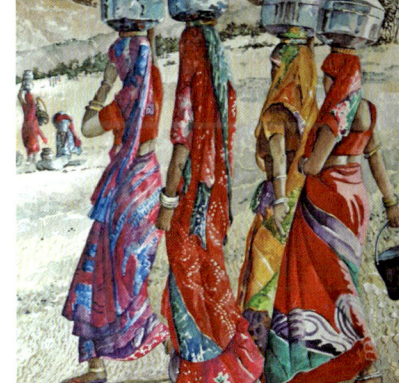

India

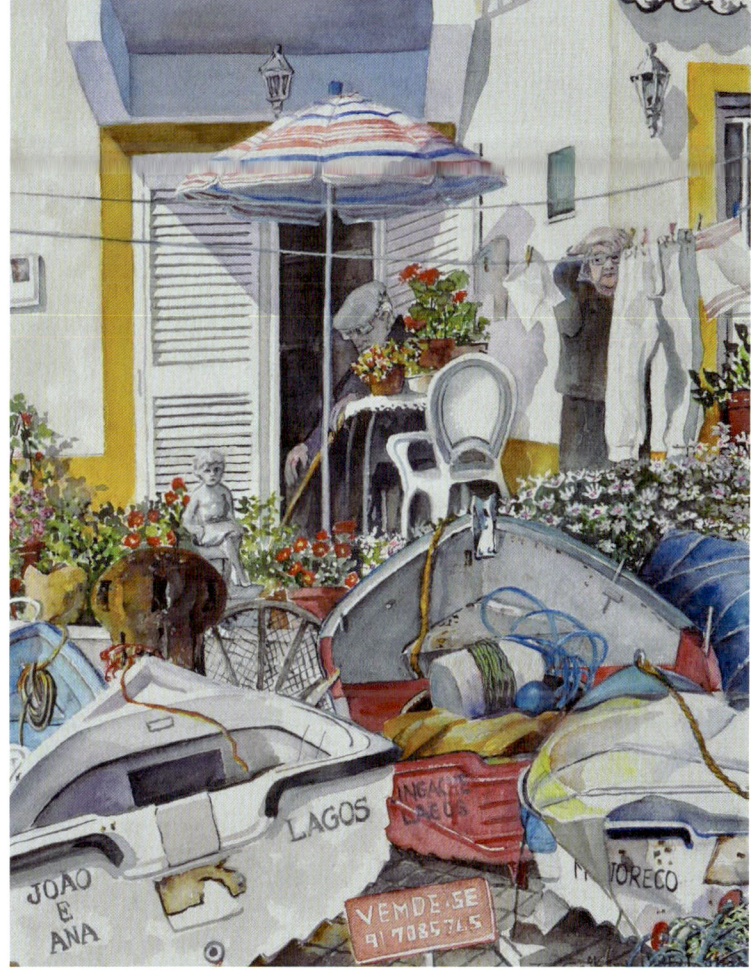

Portugal

The Painted Province

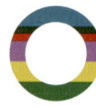

SELF PORTRAIT

This self-portrait was painted about twelve years ago. It is me in my favourite spot (our marsh) with a piece of driftwood/paintbrush in my hand. In my hair are my three kids when they were little and then twenty years older. Also in my hair is my wonderful husband Jim with me and our puppy Marsh. On the lower left are a few of my friends that I love, both those I made as an adult and those I've known since school. In the centre is my childhood family: me with my mom and dad and little brother and sister. On the lower right, I am between my very special grandparents, who were so important in my life. On my neck is an image of me naked, vulnerable, in agony. When I put this in, it was to represent my traumatic first marriage and later health challenges due to a blocked carotid artery. When I look at this self-portrait now, I think of how this entire painting still represents me. I can't forget the challenges that affect us all right now, but I also have to savour the joy of my friends, my family, my home, and my love of painting.

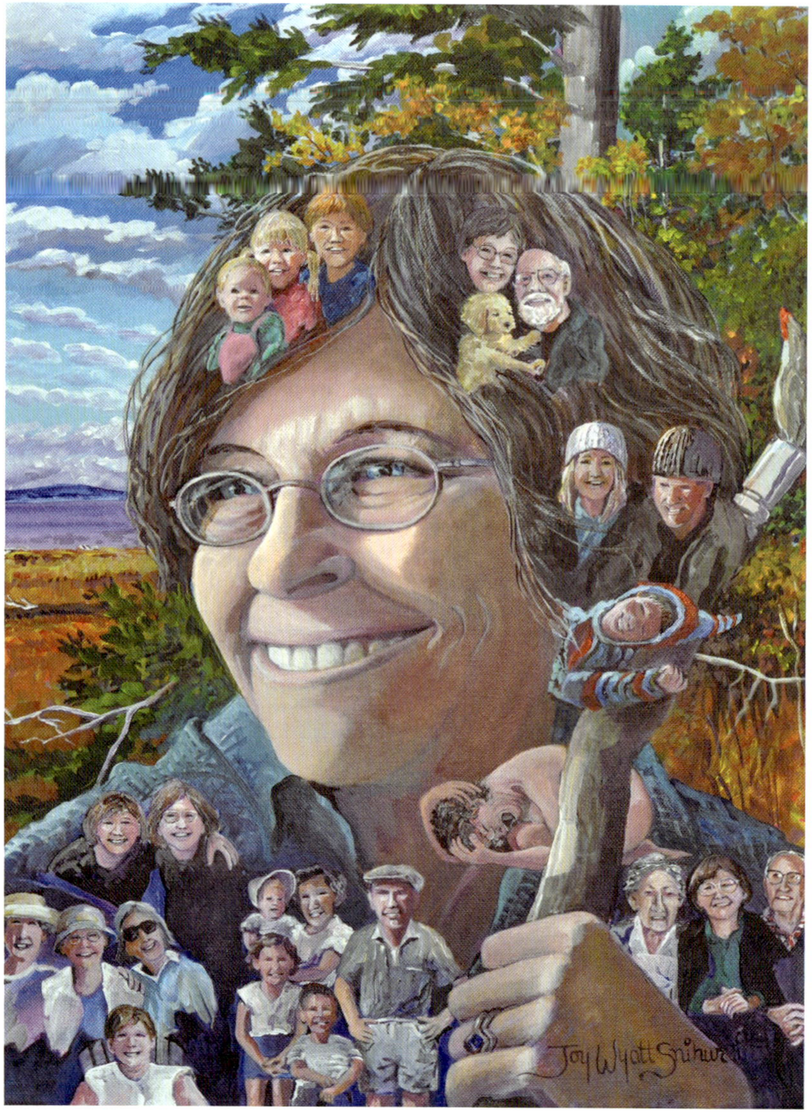

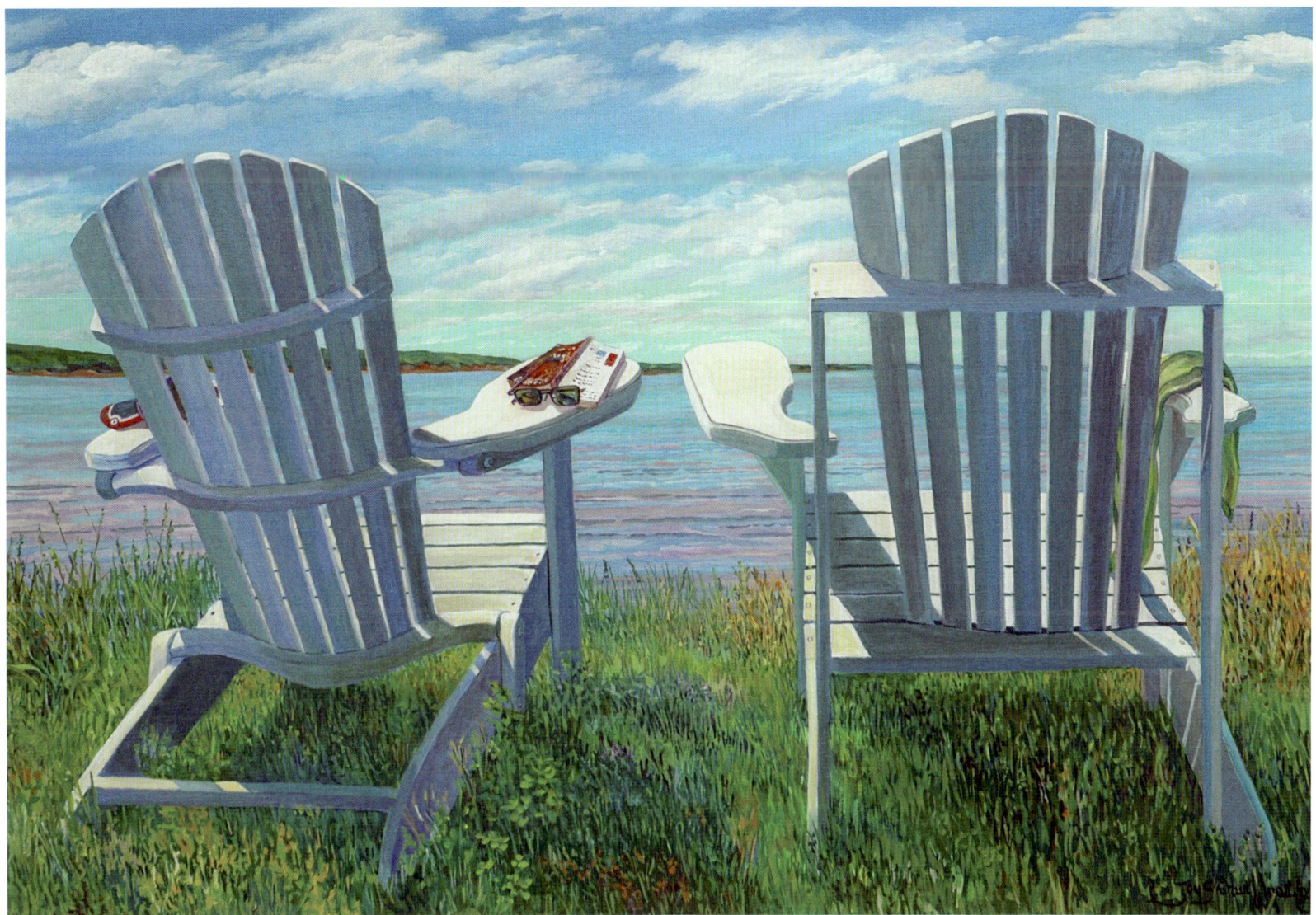